THE LOVECRAFT ANNUAL

Edited by S. T. Joshi   No. 3 (2009)

Contents

I0005837

Abbreviations used in the text and notes:

AT	*The Ancient Track* (Night Shade Books, 2001)
CE	*Collected Essays* (Hippocampus Press, 2004–06; 5 vols.)
D	*Dagon and Other Macabre Tales* (Arkham House, 1986)
DH	*The Dunwich Horror and Others* (Arkham House, 1984)
HM	*The Horror in the Museum and Other Revisions* (Arkham House, 1989)
LL	*Lovecraft's Library: A Catalogue* (Hippocampus Press, 2002)
MM	*At the Mountains of Madness and Other Novels* (Arkham House, 1985)
MW	*Miscellaneous Writings* (Arkham House, 1995)
SL	*Selected Letters* (Arkham House, 1965–76; 5 vols.)

Published by Hippocampus Press, P.O. Box 641, New York, NY 10156
http://www.hippocampuspress.com

Cover illustration by Allen Koszowski. Hippocampus Press logo designed by Anastasia Damianakos. Cover design by Barbara Briggs Silbert.

Lovecraft Annual is published once a year, in Fall. Articles and letters should be sent to the editor, S. T. Joshi, c/o Hippocampus Press, and must be accompanied by a self-addressed stamped envelope if return is desired. All reviews are assigned. Literary rights for articles and reviews will reside with *Lovecraft Annual* for one year after publication, whereupon they will revert to their respective authors. Payment is in contributor's copies.

ISSN 1935-6102
ISBN13: 978-0-9824296-2-4

Lovecraft and the Ray-Gun

T. R. Livesey

We had devised two weapons to fight it; a large and specially fitted Crookes tube operated by powerful storage batteries and provided with peculiar screens and reflectors, in case it proved intangible and opposable only by vigorously destructive ether radiations, and a pair of military flame-throwers of the sort used in the world-war, in case it proved partly material and susceptible of mechanical destruction. ("The Shunned House," *MM* 253)

I threw on the current of the Crookes tube apparatus, and focussed toward that scene of immortal blasphemousness the strongest ether radiations which man's art can arouse from the spaces and fluids of Nature. ("The Shunned House," *MM* 258)

Technological devices are found throughout Lovecraft's fiction: the telepathy apparatus in "Beyond the Wall of Sleep"; the portable telephone outfit in "The Statement of Randolph Carter"; the sensory machine in "From Beyond"; the brain capsules in "The Whisperer in Darkness," and the mysterious mind transfer device in "The Shadow out of Time." Usually, the nature and purpose of the device is either obvious or described in the course of the story. In "The Shunned House," however, Lovecraft's narrator employs "a large Crookes tube" as a weapon, offering only a cryptic explanation of what he hopes to accomplish with it. To appreciate Lovecraft's intent on this detail, an investigation of the Crookes tube is necessary.

The Crookes tube, designed by British scientist Sir William Crookes (1832–1919), is a primitive version of a cathode ray tube (CRT) which—until the advent of LCD displays—were found ubiquitously in television sets and oscilloscopes. What became known as the Crookes tube was adapted from early designs by British physicist William Crookes and others in the latter part of the nineteenth century to investigate the relationships between matter and electricity. The basic design of the device is a sealed tube mostly evacuated of air, containing two metallic plates on either end. When a high potential is placed between the plates, microscopic particles called cathode rays are drawn from the negative potential plate to the other, causing the glass struck by the rays to glow. Crookes developed many variates of tubes to investigate the properties of these rays. The "Maltese Cross" variety (shown below) contained a metallic cross-shaped shield that cast a shadow on the glass behind it, demonstrating that the rays traveled in straight lines and could be blocked by material objects. Other versions demonstrated that the rays could be deflected by electric and magnetic fields, and they carried enough momentum to push a small paddle wheel back and forth through the tube. Other experiments showed that the rays could penetrate only a few inches through open air. Eventually, the rays were determined to be negatively charged components of atoms, now known as electrons.

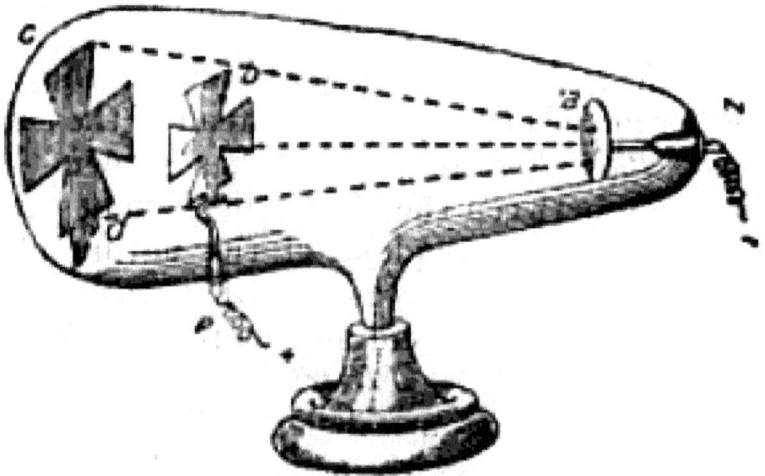

From "Cathode Rays" by Hugh Chisolm, *Encyclopædia Britannica*, 11th ed. (Oxford: At the University Press, 1910), Vol. 6, p. 413

In 1895, Wilhelm Röntgen discovered that a Crookes tube sealed in cardboard at a very high potential caused a screen several feet away painted with barium platinocyanide to glow. These rays were very different from the cathode rays: they were not affected by electric or magnetic fields; they could penetrate material objects with ease, and—as far as he could tell—they exhibited no diffraction as would be expected if they were a form of light.[1] Astonishingly, he discovered that the rays could penetrate the human body and record images of a living human skeleton. In many parts of Europe these mysterious rays are still called Röntgen rays after their discoverer, but in the United States they are referred to by the name Röntgen originally gave them: X-rays. (From "The Röntgen Ray and Its Relation to Physics: A Topical Discussion," *Transactions of the American Institute of Electrical Engineers* 13 (1896): 887.)

After Röntgen announced his discovery, countless scientists, engineers and amateurs immediately began experimenting with these new rays. New tubes were designed to optimize their power. In the image below, the cathode is concave-shaped to direct the cathode rays to a platinum plate tipped at 45°, from which powerful X-rays radiated out the bottom of the tube.

The "vigorously destructive ether radiations" described by Lovecraft were almost certainly meant to mean X-rays. Lovecraft's use of X-ray technology, however, is somewhat confused. Large tubes are capable of conducting more current, but don't necessarily increase power (Kaye 31). In general, the power of the X-ray apparatus is determined by the electric potential applied across the tube, and its design and construction. While battery-operated units existed (Kevles 42), their power could hardly compete with units driven by an engine powered dynamo or driven directly from a mu-

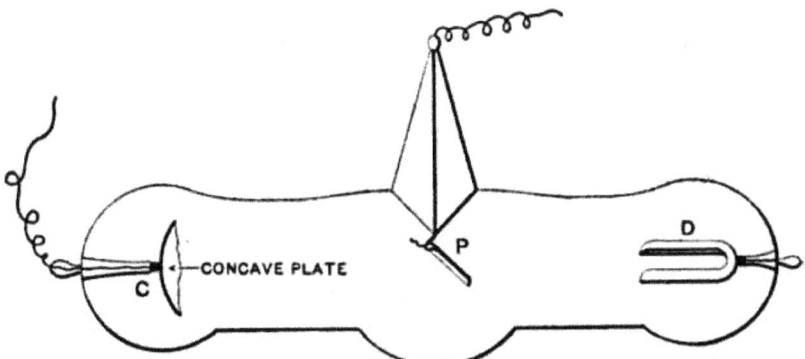

CONCAVE PLATE

C

P

D

GLASS X RAY TUBE

nicipal power grid. In 1913, William Coolidge introduced a new type of tube which used a hot filament cathode in a tube brought to a very high vacuum. The Coolidge tube produced far sharper images with less exposure time. While the old gas Crookes tube X-ray machines were still in use throughout the 1920s (Kevles 75–76), one of these relics driven by batteries could hardly be said to generate the "strongest ether radiations which man's art can arouse."

It is remarkable that Lovecraft would use X-rays as a weapon, since in the year "The Shunned House" was written—1924—there was still considerable controversy as to any harmfulness of X-rays. Concerned doctors recorded cases of strange burns associated with X-ray equipment almost immediately. In cases of technicians and doctors constructing and using the equipment, injuries were nothing short of horrific. In 1904, Clarence Dally—Thomas Edison's chief X-ray tube glass blower—became the first person to die from radiation exposure. Dally began to suffer from rashes on his hands, slight burns and hair loss by 1902. Over the next few years, he developed oozing ulcers and tumors, and suffered from constant pain. Eventually, all his fingers, then both hands, and finally both arms were amputated in a futile effort to save his life. Amputated and gloved hands became common among X-ray technicians (Kevles 47–48). Other pioneers in the field suffered similar fates. Elizabeth Fleischmann, a self-taught expert in radiographs of bone injuries, was hired by the Army during the Spanish-American War; by 1904, she developed open ulcers on both hands, had one arm amputated and finally died in 1905 of radiation poisoning (Kevles 48). Dr. Charles Allen Porter delivered a paper in 1908 to the American Roentgen Ray Society[2] documenting more than fifty cases of radiation poisoning (Caufield 13). In 1936, Dr. Percy Brown published *American Martyrs to Science through the Roentgen Ray*, a collection of twelve biographies of X-ray pioneers who died of complications of radiation sickness. Brown himself died of the same disease in 1950.

---

2. The German umlaut is typically transliterated into English by inserting an *e* after the vowel possessing the umlaut (Knapp 108).

Yet the public—and most of the profession—were not alarmed. Burns were attributed to the electrical and chemical components of the equipment. Others argued that X-rays were a natural component of sunlight, and the burns were just a different kind of sun-

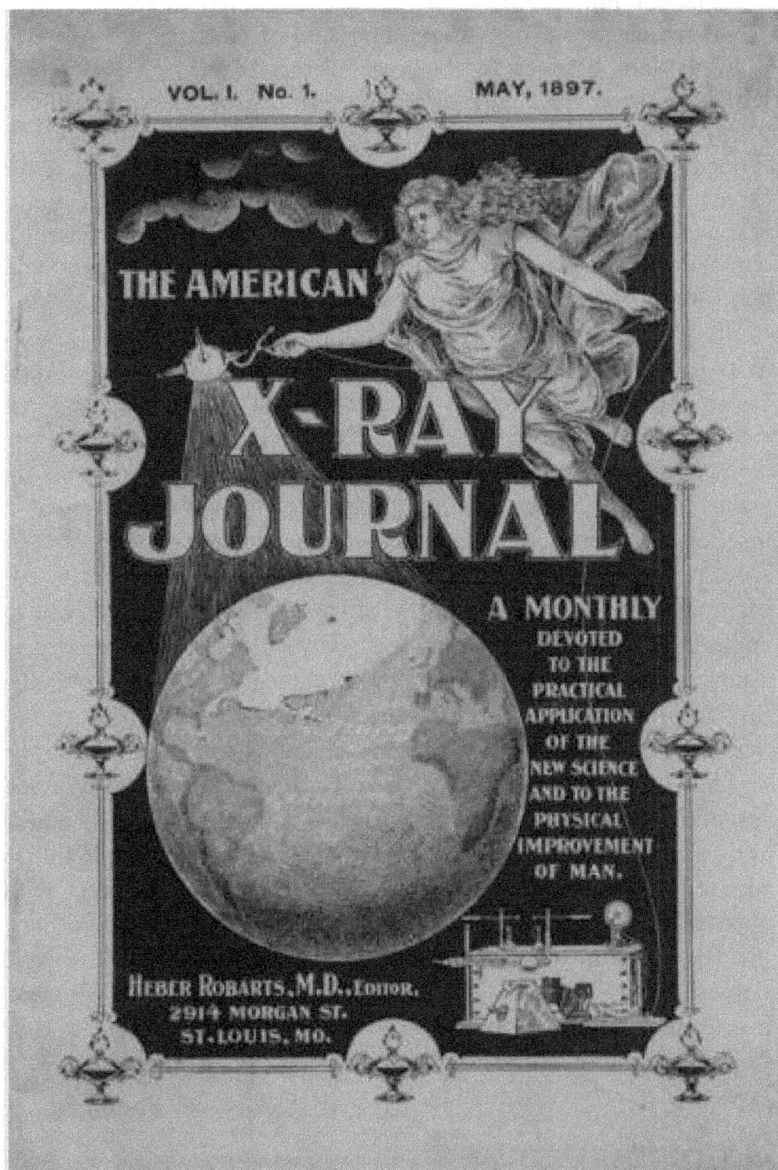

burn. There was also evidence that X-ray exposure cured acne and could be a possible rejuvenation treatment for the skin. The proven value of X-ray technology and the zeal to develop new techniques and procedures with it blinded many doctors and researchers. Suggestions for minimizing exposure were ignored as too expensive, cumbersome, and unnecessary. The lack of concern over exposure is amply demonstrated by the cover of the *American X-Ray Journal*, which featured the figure of Science irradiating the world with an X-ray tube. Children routinely X-rayed their own feet via the "Foot-o-Scope" found in almost every shoe store until 1960, and affluent partygoers enjoyed glowing cocktails laced with radium (Kevles 70, 80). Experimental proof that X-rays caused intercellular damage was not available until 1927 (Kevles 89). Whatever the danger, the public was woefully ignorant.

In "Some Strange New England Mortuary Practices: Lovecraft Was Right," Faye Ringel Hazel has identified an ironclad link between the vampiric basis of Lovecraft's "The Shunned House" with superstitious beliefs of New England, in which deceased victims of consumption spread the disease by feeding on the living from their grave. The cycle was broken only when heart of the vampire was disinterred and burnt. It is therefore somewhat strange that Lovecraft would employ X-rays to combat the intangible entity in the basement of the Shunned House: he offers no explanation of how rays apparently harmless to corporeal entities might prove effective against non-corporeal ones. When, in the course of the story, these rays are immediately found to be ineffective, the reader has to wonder why Lovecraft included the X-ray diversion in the first place. Perhaps Lovecraft was struck by similarities between the symptoms of consumption and X-ray exposure: weight loss, sore eyes (Kevles 47), pale skin (Kevles 49), and a wasting away of the body. While victims of consumption grow thin and weak, X-ray sufferers wither away piece by piece.[3] That Lovecraft's narrator never even bothers to use the flamethrower represents another curiosity. Presumably, the flamethrower would be the ideal weapon to burn out the entity's heart. Instead, acid—not fire—is the preferred weapon, a theme Lovecraft would reuse shortly in *The Case of Charles Dexter Ward*. Lovecraft may have gotten ancient superstitious beliefs of New Eng-

3. Edison described Dally as dying "by inches" (Kevles 48).

landers right, but his attempt at including modern elements in the story are are half-hearted and poorly developed.

Works Cited

Caufield, Catherine. *Multiple Exposures: Chronicles of the Radiation Age*. Chicago: University of Chicago Press, 1990.

Hazel, Faye Ringel. "Some Strange New England Mortuary Practices: Lovecraft Was Right." *Lovecraft Studies* No. 29 (Fall 1993): 13–18.

Kaye, G. W. C. *X-Rays: An Introduction to the Study of Röntgen Rays*. London: Longmans, Green, 1914.

Kevles, Bettyann. *Naked to the Bone: Medical Imaging in the Twentieth Century*. New York: Basic Books, 1997.

Knapp, Robbin D. *German English Words: A Popular Dictionary of German Words Used in English*. N.p.: Lulu.com, 2005.

Briefly Noted

Lovecraft's collected original fiction has now been published in a convenient and inexpensive edition, *H. P. Lovecraft: The Fiction* (Barnes & Noble, 2008). The volume includes all original tales by Lovecraft as well as the ghostwritten story "Under the Pyramids" and the collaboration "Through the Gates of the Silver Key." Unfortunately, although the texts are those established by S. T. Joshi, the volume contains a distressing number of typographical errors; these have now been identified, and they will be corrected in future printings. For the time being, therefore, scholars are urged to continue citing the Arkham House editions—*The Dunwich Horror and Others* (1984), *At the Mountains of Madness and Other Novels* (1985), *Dagon and Other Macabre Tales* (1986), and *Miscellaneous Writings* (1995)—as these remain the most accurate texts. Joshi's three Penguin editions—*The Call of Cthulhu and Other Weird Stories* (1999), *The Thing on the Doorstep and Other Weird Stories* (2001), and *The Dreams in the Witch House and Other Weird Stories* (2004)—contain their share of errors also, although many of these have been corrected. A leatherbound edition of the Barnes & Noble edition is planned, and there is also talk of a volume of selected essays.

What Is "the Unnamable"?
H. P. Lovecraft and the Problem of Evil

James Goho

"The Unnamable" is not customarily considered one of H. P. Lovecraft's classic stories. Peter Cannon (1989) calls it "stagey and static" (41–42). S. T. Joshi says it is "a very slight tale" (*Subtler Magick* 99), although he thinks it can be read as a theory on the aesthetics of supernatural horror fiction. Two recent studies suggest the story has more merit.

Massimo Berruti sees Lovecraft connecting thoughts on the limits of language with ideas on writing supernatural fiction in the story. Lovecraft's use of such words as "unnamable," "unmentionable," "unnamed," and "nameless" reflect his concern with the perimeters within which language works; and thus the limits of rationality. The conflict between rationality and the supernatural can be resolved "by the way of the 'unnamable'" (2), which is, in a sense, the writing of supernatural fiction. This imaginative activity unbinds language and defies the limits of rationality. Lovecraft achieves this by deploying key words to signal where our language fails and our epistemology ends. In the story, reason is not so much argued away (which seems contradictory anyway) but dramatized away.

James Kneale sees the story as exemplifying Lovecraft's fiction as it explores the "paradox of representing entities, things and places that are beyond representation" (106). "The Unnamable" specifically attempts to resolve the problem of naming and knowing what is outside of normal experience. But as language is the tool we are trapped in, it illuminates the indeterminacy in using it to represent things or spaces of an undetermined nature. For Kneale, the textual geography of the story performs a key role in illustrating this indeterminacy and the problems of expressing the "unnamable." The graveyard is a threshold between the known and unknown, and it is the pivotal ground in the plot. Kneale argues that Lovecraft represents thresholds (that is, change) as threats and that is why monsters arise from them; and, moreover, they represent the essential reactionary aspect of Lovecraft's fiction as a struggle against change.

Of course cemeteries in Lovecraft are at the edge of reality, serving as gateways to horror, opening up tunnels from the past; they are places to surface the unknown as Lévy has argued, or as landscapes to reveal evil. But it is not a threshold; it is "a cavernous rift" (D 202) in the settled experience of things that this story is getting at. Here the setting is a clue to readers that Lovecraft is engaged in an archaeology of horror fiction. He is mining below the surface of appearances to reveal an artistic response to a metaphysics of chaos. We are "upon the riven tomb by the deserted house" (D 202) to see what is always before us but ignored, to face the problem of evil.

John P. Langan calls Lovecraft's use of such words as "unnamable" and "nameless" as part of his "approximate language" that is essential to his fictional works. Langan focuses on "nameless" which refers to the failure of language to account for something, the nameless is "a blank spot" (27). Our failure to comprehend the truly alien is mirrored by the language in the stories failing to describe the other. According to Langan, Lovecraft writes a "fiction about the attempt to construct knowledge, often crucial knowledge, through language, an attempt that is hindered, often fatally, by lack of adequate linguistic and therefore representational resources" (41). Lovecraft's work is about the failure to attain meaning and, in a sense, the failure of any epistemology. Donald R. Burleson also focuses on "nameless" in his deconstruction of "The Nameless City." The word "nameless"[1] is also found across Lovecraft's work. For

---

1. Rhys Hughes treats such language in a sardonic manner in "A Languid Elagabalus of the Tombs." This phrase is from Lovecraft's "Herbert West—Reanimator" (D 155). The story verges on a parody of "The Unnamable." In the story Mr. Delves says: "Definition is the foe of horror!" (197). Delves goes through the synonyms of the word and views namelessness as "the key to the bloody lock on the wormy door which led to the slimly dungeon of total horror" (199). In part, the story is about Delves's search for and eventual discovery of a room of nameless and hidden text books of unspeakable horror. Delves solves the problem of namelessness by writing titles and text for what turn out to be college

Burleson, "nameless" is a contradictory word both naming and denying that it names. My intent is to focus on "the unnamable."

In a way both Berruti and Kneale , along with Langan, see the story as confronting epistemological questions and the use of terminology like "the unnamable" speaks to the limits of human knowledge. This also articulates an anxiety about the impotence of language generally and more particularly the impotence of fiction writing to tell us anything meaningful.[2]

In a letter to Clark Ashton Smith in November 1931, H. P. Lovecraft says he is experimenting with an idea for a new story ("The Shadow over Innsmouth") by "writing it out in different manners, one after the other, in an effort to determine the mood and tempo best suited to the theme" (SL 3.435). In the same spirit, this article is a sort of series of field experiments towards understanding what the unnamable means. That is, I will explore "The Unnamable" from several angles, in a broad sense similar to mixed methods in qualitative research in order to comprehend the meanings. As a beginning hypothesis, I think the story and the language deployed in the telling of the story, as well as in others, are really all about metaphysical issues in the end. Indeed, a reading of "The Unnamable" is an introduction to the overall fiction of the unnamable in the Lovecraft canon.

Metaphysics is the philosophical enterprise to make sense of the world. It is a search for the fundamental principles of the world. At its core, metaphysics attempts to answer the questions: what is? As well, a core activity is to clarify the ideas or language that we use in our efforts to understand the world and our place in it. In this article, it is particularly the challenge to make sense of a world where there is evil. The fictions of Lovecraft seem to be saying the only metaphysics that makes sense is one founded on dread and the horror of existence. Is the unnamable then shorthand for a metaphysics

---

unused ledgers. It is a fun story and is a form of homage to Lovecraft in the Rhys Hughes style.

2. The unnamable could be interpreted as a confrontation with the "Real": a notion of Lacan, and used by Eric Savoy in his discussion of the American Gothic. The "Real" is meant to characterize all those things or experiences that are beyond our current knowledge, beyond our current science, beyond representation that yet haunt us and keep demanding attention.

of dread and nothingness, a philosophy of death and negation—the only way to make sense of our blood-stained time? We live in an absurd universe that is not congruent with Hegel's dictum, "when we look at the world rationally, the world looks rationally back" (quoted in Neiman 313). There is really only irrational silence. The lack of intelligibility of the world is not a failure of epistemology but a failure of any first principles. Everything is fabrication; we have our being in a matrix of falsehoods. The visceral power of Lovecraft's works arises from the way he uses language to illuminate that there are no truths, nothing is as it seems; everything rests on the quicksand of metaphysical incomprehension, and, to flash-light the fear we all experience when such an unintelligible world is revealed. That is because the core of this unintelligibility is, to use an old turn of phrase, the evil in creation.

There are several contrasting and intersecting themes at work in the story—the revivification of the past and its chaos overwhelming the present, the limits of science and the illusion of certainty, the instability of language at its core, and the anarchy with no meaningful metaphysics.

Un-definition

To begin, what does it mean to say something is unnamable? Surely, not that something is simply unnamed, without a name yet, such as K2. Nor that the name is waiting to be discovered, or the name is hidden, or secret or forbidden to be told. In *The Golden Bough*, Frazer illustrates the powerful taboos surrounding names and concomitant need to conceal them. "Taboos are applied not only to acts and objects but also to words, and to none more than to names" (187), in many societies. This ban is especially held for the names of sacred kings and priests. Sometimes individuals have two names, one of which is kept secret as the knowledge of a name may give power to another, who may bring harm. That is so because in "primitive thought, the name of a person is not merely an appellation but denotes what he is to the world outside of himself" (219). In a more imaginative and poetic manner, Robert Graves also explores the power of names and the ancient tradition of secret or unknown names and the danger of revealing names in *The White Goddess*. Graves traces the history of the holy unspeakable name of God. In the Jewish tradition, the name of God is sacred and not to be articulated; the Tetragrammaton is the name for the Hebrew symbols which only represent God's name. The hidden or unspeakable name of God is directly related to the essential unknowable nature of God in religious and philosophical contexts. For example, Benedict de Spinoza argues that the ultimate nature of God is unknowable, although for Spinoza the terms God, Nature, and Substance are equivalent. Spinoza was criticized for atheism, even though he was born into a Jewish family that fled to Amsterdam from the Inquisition. He argues that God, or Nature or Substance, is that without which nothing could be, and hence is necessary, and the scope of existence is unknowable.

However, the mystical nature of hidden names or secret names is not what is going on in the story. In the fiction of Lovecraft many narrators are unnamed, suggesting hidden identities for readers or perhaps the unreliability of the narrators as witnesses to the events of the stories or the need for a cover because of their knowledge. It is also true that the past casts a shadow over the story. And to be sure the past is an element in an aesthetics of dread. Horror art calls up what is buried away, reveals what is hidden, unearths, as the New York police detective Thomas F. Malone finds in "The Horror at Red Hook," "secrets more terrible than any of the sins" (D 248). But the story is not centered on name hiding or name fear, or on the mysteries of religion. This is not to say that these human traditions have nothing to tell us as they speak to the fact that naming (let us say to our and the world's identity) is caught up within the web of language.

Lovecraft uses the word "unnamable" in several stories. In some it is paired with "unnamed"; this may seem redundant, but the two words do differ in meaning and perhaps together emphasize the impossibility of rational explanation in the presence of the unknown, of the other, of evil, as will be explored in this article. I searched a selection of the stories of Lovecraft and found the word used in several. As a first approximation toward understanding this terminology, in the following stories, the word is used to indicate the absence of descriptive power: "The Colour out of Space": "breath from regions unnamed and unnamable" (DH 67); "The Lurking Fear": "throngs of natives shrieked and whined of the unnamable horror" (D 181) and "forests of monstrous over-nourished oaks with serpent roots twisting and sucking unnamable juices" (*D* 199); "The Rats in the Walls": "peopled by unnamable fancies"(*DH* 44); "The Dunwich Horror": "deeds of almost unnamable violence and perversity"(*DH* 157); "The Crawling Chaos" (with Winifred V. Jackson): "a curse unnamed and unnamable lowering over all" (*HM* 12); "Through the Gates of the Silver Key" (with E. Hoffmann Price): "*HE WHO will guide the rash one beyond all the worlds into the Abyss of unnamable devourers*" (*MM* 431); *At the Mountains of Madness*: "the responsibility for unnamable and perhaps immeasurable evils" (*MM* 40); "The Shadow over Innsmouth": "unnamable abysses of blackness and alienage" (*DH* 366); and one of two instances from *The Case of Charles Dexter Ward*: "A stench unnamable now rose up from below" (*MM* 206), and one of two from "The Hound": "held certain unknown and unnamable drawings"(*D* 172).

Another reference in *The Case of Charles Dexter Ward* is more complex, I believe, and adds to a deeper appreciation of the nuances Lovecraft is trying to articulate with such words. The sentence reads:

> It is hard to explain just how a single sight of a tangible object with measurable dimensions could so shake and change a man; and we may only say that there is about certain outlines and entities a power of symbolism and suggestion which acts frightfully on a sensitive thinker's perspective and whispers terrible hints of obscure cosmic relationships and unnamable realities behind the protective illusions of common vision. (*MM* 207)

Although used as an adjective, the complete thought contextualizes the phrase within a perspective of metaphysical incomprehension. A second use in "The Hound": "I shall seek with my revolver the oblivion which is my only refuge from the unnamed and unnamable" (*D* 178) is as a noun. In "The Hound" the unnamable seems to be really shorthand for the experience of true dread, the sickness unto death as elucidated by Søren Kierkegaard. It is also interesting to note that the term was used in stories as early as 1922 and as late as 1932–33, in well-regarded tales and those less well-regarded, and in sole-authorships and collaborations. It was embedded in Lovecraft's lexicon.

"The Unnamable" opens with two friends, Randolph Carter[3] and Joel Manton, "speculating about the unnamable" (*D* 201). They are in a graveyard, literally reposing on the past, with the vast hosts of the dead stacked underneath them, at the frontier of life and death, textually digging up the primitive as a form of confronting the unknown or confronting fear or revivifying evil. Interestingly, the miasma arising from the ancient burying ground seems to have a gradual intoxicating effect on the characters and on the language as the story progresses.

The protagonists are part of a tradition of two males on an adventure in American literature, a common theme in mainstream literature and in Lovecraft, who distorts and reframes the theme.[4] But here, this adventure is not in unspoiled nature but in the land of the dead, while arguing about spooks in the dark night. The plot of the story is, in one sense, an urban legend meant to scare Manton into the argument of Carter; and it works. When describing the bones and skull he found in the aged house, Carter felt "a real shiver run through Manton, who had moved very near"[5] (*D* 206).

Theirs is a debate in isolation and desolation. It is almost as if they inhabit two solitudes early in the story as they debate. And the landscape is one of death. This is because horror fiction is outside of conventionality, in the personal space of its protagonists and its landscapes of experience. Carter and Manton argue as night creeps

---

3. This experience of Randolph Carter is summarized in "The Silver Key." "[H]e went back to Arkham, the terrible witch-haunted old town of his forefathers in New England, and had experiences in the dark, amidst the hoary willows and tottering gambrel roofs, which made him seal forever certain pages in the diary of a wild-minded ancestor" (*MM* 413).

4. Based on the work of Fiedler, Cannon (1990) briefly explores this theme in Lovecraft.

5. One could suppose the story is a nightmare or a warning of the dangers of two men out together at night, of the consequences of homoeroticism. What really happened on that tomb or on that farmer's field? Was the attack of the beast due to Manton's moving closer to Carter at night, perhaps embracing? Does the beast represent the outrage of society at this flirtation between two men? And if what happens in the text of the story is mere foreplay, was it rough sex off-stage that left them a mile away, both beaten up? Was it an act *inter Christianos non nominandum*?

over them. In the story, Carter tries to convince Manton that the unnamable is genuine:

> since spirit, in order to cause all the manifestations attributed to it, cannot be limited by any of the laws of matter, why is it extravagant to imagine psychically living dead things in shapes—or absences of shapes—which must for human spectators be utterly and appallingly "unnamable"? "Common sense" in reflecting on these subjects, I assured my friend with some warmth, is merely a stupid absence of imagination and mental flexibility. (*D* 202)

They continue their debate in "utter blackness" seemingly under the surveillance "of a tottering, deserted seventeenth-century house" (*D* 202). The story is stylized, in part, as notes on an academic debate. Lovecraft deploys a traditional scholarly point-counterpoint argument style at first, but this is transformed into a duel between the "objectification" of the common sense view and the mythology of horror fiction, manifested through an increasingly baroque language. Early in the story, Carter says:

> sensitive students shudder at the Puritan age in Massachusetts. So little is known of what went on beneath the surface—so little, yet such a ghastly festering as it bubbles up putrescently in occasional ghoulish glimpses. [. . .] And inside that rusted iron straitjacket lurked gibbering hideousness, perversion, and diabolism. Here, truly, was the apotheosis of The Unnamable." (*D* 203)

Later, Carter exclaims:

> if the psychic emanations of human creatures be grotesque distortions, what coherent representation could express or portray so gibbous and infamous a nebulosity as the specter of a malign, chaotic perversion, itself a morbid blasphemy against nature? Moulded by the dead brain of a hybrid nightmare, would not such a vaporous terror constitute in all loathsome truth the exquisitely, the shriekingly unnamable? (*D* 205)

Always, Manton argues as an idealized rationalist, actually as a religious logical positivist. Carter deploys several strategies, including references to Cotton Mather's writing, to a diary of an ancestor and to his own fiction writing, nearly like citations in a scholarly article; and he also uses his own direct experience with the "bones up under the eaves" (*D* 205) of the house. This strategy blurs the distinctions between journalistic or realistic writing and fiction writing. It acts to disrupt or breach the boundary dividing "reporting" from "speculating" on the universe within which we live and have our being.

In story itself, the word "unnamable" is used nine times. Carter uses it four times, three as a noun, while Manton, when they are arguing uses it as an adjective; but at the end, he uses it as a noun; "the unnamable" is reified, objectified, and Manton has been converted; he is now a believer.

Lovecraft is not alone is using such words or phrases. Of the *Narrative of Arthur Gordon Pym of Nantucket*, Poe says it is "a story of disaster the most unspeakable" (30). It is like violating a terrible taboo, as horror fiction is generally considered to be outside of literary writing in the U.S. Poe used the phrase "Tekeli-li!" as a neologism to express unknown horror. Lovecraft followed suit in the *At the Mountains of Madness*[6] a sort of cover of the *Narrative*. In *Heart of Darkness*, Conrad uses similar language as Marlow confronts the horror of darkness at the edge of the unknown, embodied in Kurtz's indulgence in "unspeakable rites" (123) and in Kurtz's "vast grave of unspeakable secrets" (139). In "Mr. Jones," Edith Wharton writes of the 'unspeakable horror" (195) expressed by the eyes of the dead housekeeper, killed by the ghost of Mr. Jones. We are at the boundary of expression and are limited by our language. This has a long history, in *Oedipus Rex*, when Oedipus is led in, his eye-sockets flowing with blood; Sophocles has the chorus speak but also say that they cannot speak:

---

6. Lovecraft takes the use of the neologism to its awful logical conclusion. It is "that eldritch, mocking cry—*'Tekeli-li! Tekeli-li!'*" of the "demoniac shoggoths—given life, thought, and plastic organ patterns solely by the Old Ones, and having no language save that which the dot groups expressed—*had likewise no voice save the imitated accents of their bygone masters*" (*MM* 101). This is the cry that haunted the narrator and Danforth on their searches for the source of the horror in the Antarctic. And when Danforth is witness to the ultimate abomination, his "shrieks were confined to the repetition of a single, mad word of all too obvious source: *'Tekeli-li! Tekeli-li!'*" (*MM* 106). Danforth becomes inarticulate.

What madness came upon you, what daemon
Leaped on your life with heavier
Punishment than a mortal man can bear?
No: I cannot even
Look at you, poor ruined one.
And I would speak, question, ponder,
If I were able. No.
You make me shudder. (70–71)

The language of the unnamable is not simply misrepresentation. It is the confrontation with the irrational. And irrational impulses arise in us as we experience the world. Poe in the "Imp of the Perverse" writes about standing at the edge of an abyss and as we stare down we grow sick but do not run away and by "slow degrees our sickness and dizziness and horror become merged in a cloud of unnamable feeling." That feeling takes shape as "the idea of what would be our sensations during the sweeping precipitancy of a fall from such a height" (282). This is the urge to death at the critical moment in the experience of the absurdity of the human condition. A similar image is to be found in Lovecraft, Søren Kierkegaard, and Albert Camus.

At least part of the point seems to be that whatever the unnamable is, it is not possible to describe it or place it in a category familiar to human experience. The unnamable cannot be denoted or you cannot link a signifier to such an un-signified. Knowing, in part, is denoting, naming things.[7] In a sense it is grasping the world through categories of language. Ludwig Wittgenstein promulgates: "The limits of my language mean the limits of my world" (68). But the unnamable is outside of experience. It is unknown; at least it is not known in the traditional ways of knowing. Carroll argues that the real issue of horror is to "disclose, and manifest that which is . . . unknown and unknowable" (127).

In a way, whatever the thing, experience or event is, it is not part of our understanding of the world. It is inexpressible, indefinable, infandous (used in "The Dreams in the Witch House"): "Unwholesome recollections of things in the *Necronomicon* and the

---

7. Very young children frequently ask "what's the name of it" about things. It is a way of making the world familiar and known.

Black Book welled up, and he found himself swaying to infandous rhythms said to pertain to the blackest ceremonies of the Sabbat and to have an origin outside the time and space we comprehend" (*MM* 290). "Infandous" is an archaic term defined as "unspeakable," and according to Roger Salomon horror literature's essential aim is to "remind us of the unspeakable" (15).

But using synonyms is not really helpful in moving our understanding forward about "the unnamable" as used by Lovecraft. In the story one of the keys is that the unnamable is used as a noun not an adjective, it is, in a sense, not a descriptive but the thing, or un-thing, its un-self. Not to name a person, animal, place, thing, or abstract idea, but to unname. Moreover, using the definitive article usually means a noun is a special sort of noun, which normally refers to a shared knowledge or something unique. In the story Lovecraft is illustrating writing fiction so perhaps the unnamable is a way of stating the monster in the Gothic and horror tradition is always a textual fabrication, as it must be, but also that all of our ways of knowing the world are fabrications because the world is hideous at its core. And this core is mostly kept at a distance by a "slender gulf that is mercifully fixed between . . . [us] and the Outer World" (Blackwood, *John Silence* 31).

A Forest as Symbol

The story[8] is a fictional exposition on the writing of horror fiction. It is a fictionalized *In Defence of Dagon*, where Lovecraft argues that weird fiction is imaginative literature, akin to realism in psychology and emotion but different in confronting the unknown and different in evoking fear. In "Notes on Writing Weird Fiction," Lovecraft says his stories "emphasise the element of horror because fear is our deepest and strongest emotion. . . . It is hard to create a convincing picture of shattered natural law or cosmic alienage or 'outsideness' without laying stress on the emotion of fear" (*CE* 2.176). In "Supernatural Horror in Literature," Lovecraft articulates in finer detail this fear when he writes that in an effective weird tale: "A certain atmosphere of breathless and unexplainable dread of outer, un-

---

8. "The Unnamable" is a modernist story in that the how of writing is as important as the what of writing.

known forces must be present" and there should be an expression of "a malign and particular suspension or defeat of those fixed laws of Nature which are our only safeguard against the assaults of chaos and the daemons of unplumbed space" (D 368). The story says that artists (here a writer) speak about the unspeakable, arising from an apprehension of the world different from the common sense view, similar to what Poe writes in "Alone": "I have not seen / as others saw" but am enthralled by "The mystery which binds me still" away from the world of ordinary sight to see things as "Of a demon in my view" (73–74). The story is then a sort of exercise (perhaps a primer) in writing horror fiction and the act of writing is art critiquing the accepted norms of understanding, representing or apprehending the world. Horror writing, at its best, opens a fissure in our customary and comfortable living, to expose fear, to illuminate dread; and to give voice to the repressed, the hidden, and the locked away.

It is a space where few venture directly in their art. Roberto Calasso says that Kafka delimited his work to a "zone of the nameable" (3) because the world was turning back into a primeval forest, full of power, dangers and apparitions. A world of "absolute atrocity"[9] (115), as Fielder writes—a world where mass death is nearly commonplace. Kafka, particularly in *The Castle*, describes the human experience within walls, within a perimeter of confusion, away from the dark forest—perhaps the forest where the raven, "in the

---

9. The early twentieth century was a time of mass charges to death, the terror of mustard gas, endless artillery bombardments, horror in the trenches, ever more armaments, and piles of the dead. This turned out to be only a prelude to the killing fields history of the later twentieth century. There are so many that any listing cannot be defended. The Holocaust is beyond thought; in Auschwitz alone, more than one million Jews died in gas chambers, by forced labor, by starvation, and by torture; overall six million were killed by the Nazi regime. Then there are the Armenian massacres, the Gulag, the Ukraine famine, the Khmer Rouge regime of terror in Cambodia, more recently Rwanda and Darfur. Of course, mass societal murders and the deliberate distortions of history are nothing new; Denevan and Wright speak to the effects of the European invasions into North and South America killing millions of American Indians. Waller states that in 1500 the aggregate indigenous American population was 15 million, while in 1890 it had been reduced 98% to about 250,000.

shadow of the silent night, doth shake contagion from her sable wings" (Marlowe 241). It is "the dismal wood" (*Beowulf* 99) of contagion. Lovecraft goes far into this "antediluvian forest darkness" (*D* 190), forest of fear, "nighted woods" (*DH* 137). This journey into the "primal wood" (*AT* 60), is not just literal as "Forests may fall, but not the dusk they shield" (*AT* 60). It is the force of this nightfall that Lovecraft illustrates.

In *The Great God Pan*, Arthur Machen expresses it this way: "Such forces cannot be named, cannot be spoken, cannot be imagined except under a veil and a symbol, a symbol to the most of us appearing a quaint, poetic fancy, to some a foolish tale" (44). The heart of this is the fear of the vast nothingness all around us, yet which we want to unveil and when we do, it tears apart our perceptions and may drive us mad as happens to many of Lovecraft's heroes.

The fiction of the unnamable is a trip into this dusk, a dusk of dread—for authentic apprehension of a cosmos of indifference at best, but also a cosmos with malevolence toward humankind—a cosmos of terror, dread, and hideousness. The opening arguments in the story start with a remark by Carter on "the giant willow in the centre of the cemetery, whose trunk had nearly engulfed an ancient, illegible slab" (*D* 200) and whose roots fed on the dead. Manton mocks this remark, and the debate is on.

Horror literature, at its apex, is at the nexus of the metaphysical paradox regarding humans' quest for meaning in a "world of atrocity" and only finding displacement and the feebleness of any and all principles of comprehension constructed by us about the world. And the forest is both a metaphor of the experience of otherness and descriptive of an actual experience of an individual in a real woods, away from the battlements of home. Both uses suggest uncharted territory, a place where it only makes sense to say, "Here there be dragons."

In his best fiction, Lovecraft evokes that feeling of being in the woods alone, as related by Steve Duffy, away from civilization, where panic grips one, where there are only dark spaces, where the evil breathes. It is where you may be "caught by the goblin touch of the willows" (Blackwood, "The Damned" 156). And this space is located geographically and psychologically, as when the Nurse in Robinson

Jeffers's adaptation of *Medea*, dreads the "where . . . evil stalks in the forest of her dark mind" (11). Later in the play evil is sighted "through the dark wood . . . at the end of the tangled forest" (28).

Carter and Manton argue in the dark, on a tomb, watched over by a tree and in the shade of a crumbling vestige of civilization, the deserted seventeenth-century house—a house that appears early in the story and returns later as a portent of the appearance of the unnamable. The house models in a way the emptiness of the arguments of science and religion and the monsters in our heads. There are things in our minds that we do not know. In Lovecraft, houses are almost always dangerous. Houses are desecrated, unholy, desolate, full of old festering sin and death. It is place not for comfort or protection but for defilement. Here it is vacant of human life—it is the past that we think is dead but sinister things persist. Homes are not safe from the woods. A house is a symbol of past, of the forgotten past, of the loss of memory and impossibility of burying the monstrous, even in our heads. It also represents the intellect of humans, an intellect that in the end is empty, excepting the monstrous deeds of our ancestors. And the beasts infect every floor from basement to attic, representing the depravity in all spheres of the mind. Everything is in chaos, in disorder. Our reason produces monsters as dramatized in the movie *The Forbidden Planet*.

The Eternal Return of the Past

The story illustrates a longing for the past, perhaps a longing for death, perhaps for a dead lover. Yet it also seems to say that such an act only results in guilt and shame as the protagonists must be punished. This story, along with others in the Lovecraft canon, connects us to "face to face with the ancient world of terror and devotion" (297) as expressed by Albert Camus in "On the Future of Tragedy." Revenants of the past come through the fissure because "beneath the ruins of old powers is really a 'deathly chaos'" (Hogle 5). A chaos where it makes no sense to name and where there are no identities. This is a worldview world reviled by science—yet a world that we still inhabit. It is a dangerous world as the heroes of the story discover, a world of terror and revulsion and contagion: the closer we get to it the more likely we are to be infected, especially morally.

As Carter remarks of the "unmentionable nourishment which

the colossal roots [of the willow] must be sucking in from the char-
nel earth" (*D* 200) in the cemetery, so the roots of horror are nour-
ished by a nostalgia for the haunted past, the archaic and atavistic
that continue to trouble us. There is a mood of longing for the past
by Carter, perhaps best expressed in "The Silver Key," where he
knows "he must go into the past and merge himself with old things"
(*MM* 414–15). The ancient lore is not dead yet; it still hints at the
malignant powers surrounding us and shut away in our attics but
yet alive and ready to feast on our fears. In Lovecraft, the monsters
harken back to the pagan gods of myth who, as Karen Armstrong
writes, brought pain, sorrow, and death. In *At the Mountains of
Madness*, upon the discovery of Old Ones found in the ice, the scientist Lake notes: "Important discovery. . . . found monstrous barrel-
shaped fossil of wholly unknown nature . . . Arrangement reminds
one of certain monsters of primal myth, especially fabled Elder
Things in Necronomicon"[10] (*MM* 20). These fossils return to life
and bring death to those who un-iced them. So the return of the
past, the primitive, is code for unexplainable evil.

During the argument, Carter delves into the psychic underworld
to drag out of the past facts that science and religion now shun. He is
a journalist of the haunting, indeed the possession, of the present by
the past. The past is populated by the dead and is an arena of dread.
It is where everything is corrupted and vestigial—a locale of unspeakable acts in the darkness of memory. For Lovecraft, "The past is
real. It is *all there is*" (*SL* 3.31). This is not a salutary past, as it holds a
"shocking and primordial tradition" with "ceremonies older than
mankind" (*D* 249). Part of the aesthetic expressed in the story is an
aesthetic of passivity in the rapture of the past, and it is also an aesthetic of a heroic struggle to express the monstrous fear and darkness
that envelopes us from the past and elsewhere. Out of the vast camps
of loneliness, destruction, and atrocity that define our world, part of
the character of Carter tries to express the consuming howl of an-
guish of past generations along with the awful power of that howl to
capture us and hold us fast. Through the adoration of the past his
"soul has become a ruin" (Poe, "MS. Found in a Bottle" 119).

---

10. The fictional text here cites another fictional text as if literary work is
similar to scientific work and this part of Lake's field notes will be in the
literature review.

Science and Art

Writing a story is not a science, it is "to relate events without analysing causes" (*D* 4). There is no formula for art in fiction, although there are formulaic writers and formulaic stories, which are entertainments and divert attention from the imperative to express the unnamable.

Science and progress are not unequivocal; the unnamable "undermines ordered notions of civilized humanity and rational progress" (Botting 279). The common sense of order is not completed and assured. In fact, horror is everywhere and horror fiction, at its best, is meant to bare these facts which are concealed. The language used in this hopeless endeavor must necessarily be twisted and bizarre. Lévy noted that the "unintelligible is necessary hideous" (88). The unnamable is, in a sense, a "psychic intervention" as described by E. R. Dodds when consciousness is disturbed and jolted out of normality, as Agamemnon was by "Erinys who walks in darkness" (6). It is a force that impels behavior and actions and comes from outside conventional human experience. In a sense, it is the inevitable intrusion of the irrational in our experience. This is the world within which we live, a world of fear and trembling that we often ignore or shun. This necessitates inverting the norms of the aesthetics of beauty. As with Albert Camus, Lovecraft might say, "Beauty is unbearable, drives us to despair, offering us for a minute the glimpse of an eternity that we should like to stretch out over the whole time" (*Notebooks 1935–1942* 10). Lovecraft says that "My reason for writing stories is to give myself the satisfaction of visualising . . . impressions of wonder, beauty and adventurous expectancy" (*CE* 2.175). And fear sometimes becomes ". . . so mixed with wonder and alluring grotesqueness, that it was almost a pleasant sensation" (*D* 195). In the end the beautiful is awful. Camus admits that "At the heart of all beauty lies something inhuman, and these hills, the softness of the sky, the outline of these trees at this very minute lose the illusory meaning with which we had clothed them, henceforth more remote than a lost paradise . . . that denseness and that strangeness of the world is absurd" ("Myth of Sisyphus" 11). To write horror fiction is to display that strangeness, which is often hideous.

The story interrogates science and religion (although religion virtually only in passing) on their claims as the true ways of knowledge.

Lovecraft compares and contrasts art and science as ways of understanding the world. Supposedly, science is the exemplar of truth with
its rigorous methodology, instrumentality, and defined language,
while writing (and art generally) is "lowly" (D 200).[11] The tale speaks
to the limits and distortions of scientific knowledge but also about
the dangers of artistically venturing into the unknown, of venturing
to the frontier of the unknown, that is, of being conscious of the
world of dread—of awakening the destructive force that erodes our
normalized awareness, and that leads to self-destruction as a normalized response, which is what happens to many of Lovecraft's heroes.

Moreover, in doing this Lovecraft illuminates the horror of
modern times and elucidates "a poetics of annihilation and nullity"
(Salomon 124). It is an aesthetics of dread that embraces hideousness, for beauty is not rapture but agony, and an aesthetic that, in
the end, embraces evil as a necessary fact of human existence in an
absurd world.

The story plays off a theme of Edgar Allan Poe, expressed most
concisely in the poem, "Sonnet—To Science." In this poem, Poe
does not so much mock science but describes its usefulness and its
limits. It has demolished the old gods, any gods really, and cleansed
the mind of the folly of silly "summer dreams" in the arms of loving
gods. Science helps us grow up but it is not the truth as it "alterest
all things with . . . peering eyes" (58). It misrepresents. Poe contrasts
the magic of his words and his imaginary worlds with the barren,
"dull realities" of the world of science. A true artist casts aside any
interest in the findings of science and, as Wilbur suggests, constructs
"visionary gropings towards imaginary realms" (9). Poe accepts and
glories in the fact that the artist has been driven deep into the past
or to "some happier star" (9).

Lovecraft did not dismiss science but expressed sentiments simi-

---

11. Counter to this, consider that in "The Call of Cthulhu" the strange
dreams do not inform average people, or scientific men, but "It was from
the artists and poets that the pertinent answers came" (DH 131). And more
tellingly, later archaeologists cannot "form the least notion" of the "linguistic kinship" (DH 134) of the characters on the base of the strange figure
found by Legrasse. In "The Colour out of Space" scientists can make no
sense of the wasteland. These speak to the failure of rationality in the face
of the unknown.

lar about the power of aesthetics. Indeed, perhaps his fiction en-
shrines a counter-myth to the narrow view of logico-empiricism
about the world and our experience in it. His use of language exemplifies this—especially in his evocative descriptions of the unknown where the language itself seems to come alive as bizarre and
ugly. The story challenges the stance that science is the only truth
about the human experience of nature. Imaginative literature is a
way of knowing or describing the world, scientific inquiry is another. Aesthetics is as significant and as meaningful as scientific
methodology.[12] This story is about the dangerous fissures between
the rational and the irrational and the role of art in moving us
through into the perilous wilderness beyond. It is not just that scientific explanation is not the only way of apprehending the world,
there is also artistic imagination; but it is that any authentic apprehension of the world necessarily is full of dread.

In "Facts concerning the late Arthur Jermyn and His Family"
Lovecraft paints a violent perspective:

> Life is a hideous thing, and from the background behind what we
> know of it peer daemoniacal hints of truth which make it
> sometimes a thousandfold more hideous. Science, already
> oppressive with its shocking revelations, will perhaps be the
> ultimate exterminator of our human species—if separate species
> we be—for its reserve of unguessed horrors could never be borne
> by mortal brains if loosed upon the world. If we knew what we are,
> we should do as Sir Arthur Jermyn did; and Arthur Jermyn soaked
> himself in oil and set fire to his clothing one night. (D 73)

---

12. Bruce Aune argues that the way we view and experience the world is
dependent on our conceptual scheme, which is informed and expressed
through our language. But our language is not cast in stone. Science is engaged in fundamental criticisms of our worldview, that is our language
(which it can be argued determines the manner in which we as language-
users characterize the world, indeed, experience the world). In a sense science disrupts our interactions with the outside and changes the way we
control and manipulate the world. It may be argued that literature is doing
something similar. The language employed in *Finnegans Wake*, for example, is radically different from our ordinary discourse and if we were able
to adopt this language, one could give fundamentally different descriptions
of the world legitimately.

Jermyn's suicide is of a particularly gruesome kind.

Camus says "There is but one truly serious philosophical problem, and that is suicide. Judging whether life is or is not worth living amounts to answering the fundamental question of philosophy" ("Myth of Sisyphus" 3). For Camus, an unintelligible world empty of eternal truths or values is still worth enduring even in the face of an awareness of nothingness. "A world which can be explained, even with bad reasons is a familiar world. But, on the other hand, in a universe suddenly divested of illusions and lights, man feels an alien, a stranger" ("Myth of Sisyphus" 5). It is the clear bracing air of awareness of the indifferent universe within which we live. Yet, for Camus, it does not lead to the negation of life but an affirmation of living in revolt while not masking our absurd condition, our world without hope. Matthew Hamilton Bowker argues that "the philosophy of the absurd offers both a grounding for moral and political thinking and an appeal for a unique kind of psychological, moral, and political maturity" (22). This is right, but for Bowker the absurd is psychological experience that demands a morally mature response, and that this is what Camus meant. I think that the absurd for Camus is more than a psychological state; it does demand a moral response, but it is a response to humans' metaphysical condition in the universe. Camus experienced the absurd in a real, visceral manner not in the abstract. The moral response is only real in action not just in words.

The Unreadable

In the story the phrase "illegible slab" (D 200, 205) is used twice to suggest the flip side of the unnamable. That is, a corollary of texts addressing the unnamable is that they should be forbidden, banned, unread. Or they are unreadable, as of the book Poe says "that does not permit itself to be read" ("The Man of the Crowd," *Complete Tales and Poems* 475), which Lovecraft quotes in "The Horror at Red Hook." On a deeper level it may be that true horror cuts off language, obliterates thinking, and ends witnessing. The use of phrases like "unnamable," "inexpressible," and "unmentionable" is to signal that there are experiences beyond our human ability to endure, comprehend, perhaps even imagine.

In attempting to understand the relation between Hebrew literature and the *Shaoh*, Gershon Shaked asked, almost despairingly: "What is, therefore, the way writers choose to express the fundamentally indescribable?" (275). Witness writers of the Holocaust like Elie Weisel and Primo Levi lived the true horror of the twentieth century. They faced the real evil and wrote about it. The first version of Weisel's *Night* was written in Yiddish as *Und di Velt Hot Geshvign*, which translates as *And the World Remained Silent. Night* is a book of moral honesty about a time of the complete failure of all values, including the terrible silence that fell across the world about the Nazis and their engineering of the Holocaust.

But perhaps, in times of such personal and community horror, words work to kill memory, as W. G. Sebald argues in *The Natural History of Destruction*. In the face of horror, there is a conspiracy of silence; we are mute, terrified, like stone. Of course, we want to escape with our wits intact. Some events, experiences, things are too disturbing. What is the authenticity of an experience when words fail because of its terror? How can the truly terrible be expressed, even be stored in our heads without madness? Does survival depend on forgetting, as Sebald wonders, or is his argument merely a cover-up or an excuse for silence by perpetrators after so many victims have been brutally silenced? However, Daniel R. Schwarz, writing about Holocaust narratives, says, "Were the victims to remain numb and mute, they would remain *material* without soul as well as participate in an amnesia that protected the culprits" (37). Lovecraft writes of "that chief of torments—inarticulateness" (*D* 166).

The fiction of the unnamable is saying that in art there must be a revealing of the hideous, even when we want to look away. That is why so many of Lovecraft's stories are filled with references to virtually unreadable texts. The silent cosmos is unreadable, yet we are impelled to read. The use of the unnamable expresses the paradox that there are some things and experiences beyond expression but yet which we must talk about. The best in horror fiction goes where to speak is to be in danger, to be with the alien—where to be articulate is to be a stranger—society shunned—to be outside the norms of society away from established ways of getting round the world, away from common sense. Manton in the story represents the commonplace with which the world abounds. Carter speaks about the extremes of otherness—an otherness that sur-

rounds us and comes from inside and outside. The point of his argument is, in part, not to be silenced about that world, which is different from the ordinary world of everyday experience.

Conventional arguments speak from a view of the world which
"behold, without perceiving" (Hardy 262). And Manton's critical argument is: "even the most morbid perversion of Nature need not be
unnamable or scientifically indescribable" (*D* 205). At this point,
Carter does not argue logically; rather his endgame is to unleash
florid language about "monstrous apparitions more frightful than
anything organic could be; apparitions of gigantic bestial forms
sometimes visible and sometimes only tangible, which floated about
on moonless nights and haunted the old house, the crypt behind it,
and the grave where a sapling had sprouted beside an illegible slab"
(*D* 205). And Carter now reveals the nearby house is the locus of
the beast and where he had found the disturbing bones.

Manton's argument is founded on logico-positivism, a school of
philosophical thought modeled after scientific inquiry, or so believed
by its adherents, who wanted to have a philosophy like a science.
For logical positivists, statements are only meaningful if they are
verifiable. Statements are verifiable in two ways. There are empirical
statements, including scientific theories, which are verified by experiment and evidence; and there are analytic truths, statements
which are true or false by definition. But even science is circum-
scribed by our confrontation with the world through the perception
of appearances and our inability to know really what is behind those
appearances, except by conjecture. In a sense we are captives of appearances. Logical positivists thought that the scientific method was
the only way of knowledge and the only true way of apprehending
the world. This was how to make the world intelligible. This is still
true of a core of modern analytical philosophy. This viewpoint is
expressed by Manton, except that he also believes in the word of
God as expressing the truth about the world.

Wittgenstein writes, "What we cannot speak about, we must
pass over in silence" (89). So ends the *Tractatus*. Wittgenstein recognizes here the vast unnamable and urges that we must be silent
even though there is a world beyond our current powers of expression. He is arguing for the inadequacy of language and the irrationality of going beyond it.

Marlowe has Faustus express the power of words to reveal too much, when he says, "Be silent, then, for danger is in words" (157). If we say too much, perhaps the real power of darkness will be unleashed, as happens in "The Unnamable" when Manton's "odd cry" (*D* 206) is answered horribly. This may be the other side of Wittgenstein's admonition. If we venture too far away from ordinary discourse, we will discover things or have experiences that will destroy us. And once experienced we are forever changed. This break between speaking out and keeping quiet is the fissure we must go through to overcome our fear. It is the crack, from an aesthetic perspective, that must be penetrated to achieve the expression of the unnamable, to reveal that which is buried, ignored, shamefaced.

The story relies upon old tales, "spectral legends" (*D* 205), myths to move the action forward; a strategy used by Lovecraft in other stories. Karen Armstrong says that myth "looks into the heart of a great silence" (4). The so-called Cthulhu Mythos reflects the interconnections of several of Lovecraft's stories, which seem to arise from a common font of anxiety or reflect an attempt to speak to a deep despair and unconscious chaos. Myth is a way to persist in the inscrutable, silent world.

The aesthetic imperative to overcome silence is also a task in mainstream literature, as the unnamed hero in Samuel Beckett's *The Unnamable* enters the same space: "I shall have to speak of things of which I cannot speak." He "is obliged to speak. [. . .] never be silent. Never" (291). As readers we are not sure in that novel who or what is speaking and what the narrator is speaking about, and whether to believe anything because all that is said can "be invalidated as uttered, sooner or later" (293). This is the condition of the unnamable. As with the Lovecraft story, there is an attempt to find grounding outside language, to go beyond our normalized experience conditioned by state, religion, family and culture.

But what is beyond our accepted or customary ways of speaking, writing or representing experience? It does not seem to make any sense. Language is our conscious means of understanding the world, even as it reveals and distorts things. Words are the carriers of meaning normally, but in this story words are distorting; in the end, are they empty of significance? But silence is anathema; we must not be like Cotton Mather who did not tell all: "Perhaps he did not know. Or perhaps he knew but did not dare to tell. Others knew, but did not dare to tell" (*D* 204). In *At the Mountains of Madness* the narrator declares, "I am forced into speech because men of science have refused to follow my advice without knowing why" (*MM* 3). But his partner refuses to witness all: "Danforth is closer mouthed than I: for he saw, or thinks he saw, one thing he will not tell even me" (*MM* 33).

The conclusion of "The Unnamable" calls up the other, the disfigured one, the dead one, to evoke expression, or rather, the unnamable itself attempts to speak at the end. Manton is found with "two malignant wounds in the chest and less severe cuts or gougings in the back" (*D* 207). Carter "was covered with welts and contusions of the most bewildering character" (*D* 207). This is the unnamable, itself, attempting to verbalize, leaving a message, but it is illegible, unreadable, illustrating the instability of all texts, of all understanding, of all metaphysics. What we are supposed not to speak about are the most important things, as even Wittgenstein came to believe later in his life.

The Problem of Evil

The traditional problem of evil is how evil can exist in a world created by an all-knowing, all-loving, all-powerful God; simply, how God can allow evil. Even in this world of contingency, how can evil be reconciled with God? Much has been written on this matter; and many have attempted to reconcile a God with evil through arguments about free will or this being the best of all possible worlds. It is an attempt to overcome the problem through reason; others simply rely on faith. The arguments based on reason seem to have been demolished by David Hume, especially in the *Dialogues concerning Natural Religion*, published in 1779, three years after his death. But even in the *Enquiry concerning Human Understanding*, published in 1748, he notes all the hard work we do "to save the honour of the gods; while we must acknowledge the reality of that evil and disorder, with which the world so much abounds" (104). And the real issue is that reason itself seems not only impotent but "in pain" in the face of evil (Neiman 168). Acknowledging the fact of evil, in the precise manner of Hume, results in realizing that we cannot simply explain it away.

For purposes of clarification, let us say that evil as a noun means something like undeserved harm or a wicked or morally wrong act or thing or event or a force that governs and brings about wickedness. For Mary Midgley the problem of evil is a human problem and "wickedness" means "intentionally doing acts that are wrong" (vii). Susan Neiman says the problem of evil is really about the intelligibility of nature. It goes to our ability to understand the cosmos and ourselves. She argues that the fact of evil works to freeze our attempts to make sense of the world, that is, to make sense of our place in the world; yet it is also the key to understanding.

In the grand tradition, philosophy's purpose was to make sense of the world. And Neiman argues that the problem of evil is the driving force of philosophical inquiry. It might be helpful to review Leibniz's distinctions of evil. Natural evil is like a hurricane that causes widespread suffering, destruction, and death. Moral evil is sin against God, according to Leibniz, but from a secular point of view, it is a deed or act or a failure to act that causes undeserved harm. Then there is metaphysical evil, the imperfection of creation that infects everything. Ari Hirvonen argues that the problem of evil must be disconnected from religion: "from the perspective and standpoint of our own time, we have to start again and again to deconstruct evil, to take responsibility for the problem of evil, and to be sensitive to new forms of the phenomena of evil" (48). The terrors of the twentieth and the twenty-first centuries are the driving force for Hirvonen's argument for a secular rethinking of evil, with humans at the center of evil. He says evil must be brought back into law. It is not a theological matter but a human matter for response even in a world of metaphysical chaos.

There are some events so horrible that all would call them evil, such as the Holocaust. Such a hideous thing can only be called evil. How does such an organized, almost industrialized, evil killing for the sake of complete annihilation make any sense? Levy notes Emil Fackenheim's assertion that what else can it be but radical evil when children were thrown into the ovens alive to save money on Zyklon-B gas, and their screams could be heard echoing throughout the death camps. How do we make sense of a human world of such irreducible horror, rationally planned, executed and recorded? Kant writes of a natural propensity to evil, which he calls a radical innate

evil in human nature. He says: "This evil is radical, because it cor-
rupts the grounds of all maxims; it is, moreover, as a natural propensity, inextirpable by human powers, since extirpation could
occur only through good maxims, and can not take place when the
ultimate subjective ground of all maxims is postulated as corrupt"
(108). This means that there is an evil that is a natural predisposi-
tion in humans, and Kant believed that this was brought upon humans by themselves as they are free. The word "radical" signifies
that we are "corrupted" (104) fundamentally and there is a "foul
taint in our race" (109). Although perhaps not the standard interpretation of Kant's notion, this speaks to the contagion or infection
of evil that affects humans and that seemingly is a part of nature.
Does this help us understand how supposedly ordinary people
become torturers and mass murderers, committing heinous crimes,
engaging in hideous cruelty and atrocities? The suffering of the
innocent conforms to no logic.[13] Modern times, indeed, perhaps all
times, have been evil times.

   We are near a disturbing aspect of Lovecraft's work in horror.
Fiedler wrote that literary criticism is "an act of total moral en-
gagement" (xiv). It is obvious that what one tries to say about literature arises from one's own experience in a particular time. And the
truth of what one writes is mirrored by one's personal authenticity
and commitment to understanding the texts one reads. There is
something offensive in many of Lovecraft's stories; not the raw,
grating, baroque style, not the sometimes loose plots and the over-
the-top monsters. It is the elitism, the overt racism, the social reac-
tionary-ism,[14] and a fascination with fascism (especially the linkage

---

13. In *The Brothers Karamazov*, Ivan Karamazov, speaks about the evil of
the suffering of innocent children. No God can be worshipped with the
knowledge of the facts of children suffering horrible fates and brutal
deaths. He knows the evil in the world and rebels and remains unforgiving.
"It is not worth one little tear of that tortured little girl who beat herself
on the breast and prayed to her 'dear, kind Lord' in the stinking privy with
her unexpiated tears. It is not worth it, because her tears remain unexpiated" (286). There is no possible explanation or sense in such suffering.

14. In 1933, Lovecraft in a letter says: "No settled & homogenous nation
ought (a) to admit enough of a decidedly alien race-stock to bring about an
actual alteration in the dominant ethnic composition, or (b) tolerate the
dilution of the culture-stream with emotional or intellectual elements

between anti-democratic political systems and racism) that infects some of the fiction and that is clear in his letters and other writings. The elitism is reflected in even minor comments such as Lovecraft writing that his paternal side is of "unmixed English gentry" (*SL* 1.296).

In "The Shadow out of Time," the political system of the four divisions of the Great Race is described as "a sort of fascistic socialism, with major resources rationally distributed, and power delegated to a small governing board elected by the votes of all able to pass certain educational and psychological tests" (*DH* 399). This is echoed in "Some Repetitions on the Times," where Lovecraft argues that a fascistic, non-democratic government would be best for the U.S. for economic recovery during the 1930s.

There is a fetish for the Nordic and the superiority of a certain class of people.[15] Lovecraft expresses support for the actions of Mussolini (see *SL* 1.208) and even writes favorably about Hitler in a letter dated September 23, 1933, to J. Vernon Shea. In the letter he refers to the "rabble-catering equalitarian columnists of the Jew-York papers" (*SL* 4.247).[16] Adolf Hitler became chancellor on January 30, 1933. The Reichstag building was burned on February

---

alien to the original cultural impulse" (*SL* 4.249). These are the words of a social reactionary. Lovecraft says this logic shows that "Hitler's basic racial theory is *perfectly & irrefutably* sound." Where Hitler's race theory logic led was the Holocaust.

15. In a 1926 letter to Frank Belknap Long, Lovecraft express his admiration for the Nordic and writes: "There are two Jew problems in America today—one national and cultural, and to be met by a firm resistance to all those vitiating ideas which parasitic subject-races engender; and another local and biological—the New York Mongoloid problem, to be met God only knows how, but with force rather than intellect" (*SL* 2.68–69).

16. Lovecraft is not alone as a writer in his racism. Anthony Julius details the anti-Semitism of T. S. Eliot. In *After Strange Gods: A Primer of Modern Heresy*, Eliot writes that a well-formed society must "make any large numbers of free-thinking Jews undesirable" (20). In "Burbank with a Baedeker: Bleistein with a Cigar," Eliot writes: "The rats are underneath the piles / The Jew is underneath the lot" (*Collected Poems* 43). In "Gerontion" he writes: "My house is a decayed house, / And the Jew squats on the window sill, the owner, / Spawned in some estaminet of Antwerp" (39). Like Lovecraft, Eliot has his defenders and apologists.

27, 1933, and on February 28 the German government suspended basic rights. In March the Nazi-controlled Reichstag passed the Enabling Act, which, combined with the suspension of freedoms as a result of the Reichstag fire, made Hitler's government into a dictatorship. In April, Hitler's boycott of Jewish shops was proclaimed. Lovecraft's entire letter (and others) is filled with racial slurs, directed at blacks[17] and Jews mostly, and expressions of support for the actions of Hitler and admiration for the German people in supporting him. Joshi (*Life*) argues that Lovecraft's expressions of support modified over time and that his attitude toward fascism was not of the Nazi type. In a letter to Robert E. Howard in 1936, Lovecraft does say the "the most repellent and exasperating of the great powers are Soviet Russia and Nazi Germany" (*SL* 5.247), although he goes on to say that these countries had many points of superiority. It seems clear that Lovecraft's examples of fascism are governments led by an elite, who are in some sense superior to others, and the state is nationalistic with a strong unity of control and development (with economic and social regimentation) and with individuals subordinated to the state. Although the governmental system of the Old Ones in *At the Mountains of Madness* is called socialism, the culture is founded upon an underclass of slaves.

Lovecraft's racism has been self-documented in his fiction and in his letters. Houellebecq argues that Lovecraft's power arises in part from racism, which can be found in such stories as "The Shadow over Innsmouth," "The Horror at Red Hook," "He," and "Herbert West—Reanimator,"[18] not to mention his letters, which Houelle-

---

17. Lovecraft's invectives against African Americans are sharply contrasted by the efforts of Olivia Howard Dunbar, a writer of ghost stories in the early twentieth century, and her husband, the playwright Ridgeley Torrance, in the support of rights for blacks (see Salmonson). Ridgeley published a collection of plays written specifically for black actors in 1917 and wrote a biography of the black educator John Hope. Dunbar published essays on a range of liberal issues including the education of African Americans.

18. As an example, consider Lovecraft's descriptions in "Herbert West—Reanimator"of Buck Robinson: "He was a loathsome, gorilla-like thing, with abnormally long arms that I could not help calling fore legs, and a face that conjured up thoughts of unspeakable Congo secrets and tom-tom

becq quotes with relish, such as the vile letter to Frank Belknap Long, wherein Lovecraft writes about the inhabitants of New York slums:

> The organic things—Italo-Semitico-Mongoloid—inhabiting that awful cesspool could not by any stretch of the imagination be call'd human. They were monstrous and nebulous adumbrations of the pithecanthropoid and amoebal; vaguely moulded from some stinking viscous slime of earth's corruption, and slithering and oozing in and on the filthy streets or in and out of windows and doorways in a fashion suggestive of nothing but infesting worms or deep-sea unnamabilities. (SL 1.333–34)

Houellebecq goes on to assert that the works of Lovecraft proclaim the "universal presence of evil" (111). Indeed the works insist that "life is itself evil" (113).

Lovecraft throws lit gasoline on the problem of evil. The barrage of calamities, of senseless sorrow, of atrocity, of continuous violence that engulfs humans and is perpetuated by humans is in his stories just a fact and simply that. Predominantly, there is no hidden thing that will survive and prosper; no hope of escape, rather the hidden thing, if there is one, is even more monstrous and destructive. The visceral, raw power of Lovecraft's best work arises from the reader colliding with metaphysical evil—that is, whether the world is truly intelligible, worth living in, surrounded as we are by endless cruelty and atrocity, for that is the core of the problem of evil.

Two Faces of Manton

The action in the graveyard may be understood as an initiation rite of Joel Manton; defilement is necessary to go through the fissure;

---

poundings under an eerie moon. The body must have looked even worse in life—but the world holds many ugly things" (D 146). And yet, although Herbert West believes that his revivifying fluid failed on Robinson, because the fluid came from white specimens, at the end of the episode we learn differently. In The Case of Charles Dexter Ward, here is the description of Joseph Curwen's servants, "a sullen pair of aged Narragansett Indians; the husband dumb and curiously scarred, and the wife of a very repulsive cast of countenance, probably due to a mixture of negro blood" (MM 119).

experiencing the unnamable is to expose oneself to the unholy. Manton, who has been subject to sleep deprivation, incessant inter-rogation, and shock, finally collapses and "actually cried out with a sort of gulping gasp" (D 206), as if waterboarded. Afterwards, Man-ton is changed, he has lost his identity, he becomes someone else. His words are like blasphemies, like chants from a savage time. It is the return of the primitive similar to Malone's contemplations in Red Hook:

> that modern people under lawless conditions tend uncannily to re-peat the darkest instinctive patterns of primitive half-ape savagery in their daily life and ritual observances; and he had often viewed with an anthropologist's shudder the chanting, cursing processions of blear-eyed and pockmarked young men which wound their way along in the dark small hours of morning. [. . .] he seemed to see in them some monstrous thread of secret continuity; some fiendish, cryptical, and ancient pattern utterly beyond and below the sordid mass of facts and habits and haunts. (D 248)

This theme is explored in several stories and is explicit in "The Rats in the Walls," where the civilized American regresses to cannibal-ism. Carter has lured Manton to where "The soul of the beast is omnipresent and triumphant" (D 265).

In the beginning of the story Manton is vigorous and active. At the end he is passive in the face of horror. It is like a paralysis in-duced by Carter. Menaced, Manton submits; he now accepts the propagandistic story line of Carter. The language used by Carter is meant to distort reality, disrupt thinking, and convert. It works. In a way, Manton gives in to the forces of oppression; the terror world wins, and it is as if fascism marches triumphant.

Of the real nature of the final defilement there must be silence or lies; that is why Manton (who now has the mark of the beast or bears the scars of torture or is an unreadable text) ends the story with a story about a bull. The witness here lies to the world as if it is a story that is ineffable, that should not be told. It is like another story made up for reporting to the masses while the truth is buried. Or is this really just false witnessing? Or is all "bull"? That is, bullshit, horror writing is just nonsense. Lovecraft does have a sense of humor.

The unnamable is the instability of any apprehension of the

world, including art rooted in our fears. The unnamable speaks about the "beyondness" (*MM* 29), of certain experiences of "utter remoteness, separation, desolation, and aeon long death" (*MM* 29). It is a confrontation with the abnormal that disrupts our comfort with the everyday accepted ways of ignoring the vastness of the nothingness within which we live. Speaking of the unnamable is an attempt to contextualize the problem of the human response to fact of evil. Part of the context is the absurd experience of the indifferent world, but also it is the reality of humankind's steel savagery of bullets, bombs, and torture, where science and technology are used to engineer malevolence.

Hannah Arendt compares evil to a fungus or an infection that has no intentions but may work according to some unknown law of nature. This is the metaphysics of evil of the unnamable. Metaphysics states what we hold to be self-evident and even possible; it is the foundation of our understanding of the world. It is the fundamental principles of our worldview that are not themselves explained. The metaphysics of "the unnamable" is disorder as the norm; the world is a "blasted heath" (*DH* 54) as described in "The Colour out of Space."

Within this world of dread and despair, there is no salvation in a Lovecraftian universe. We are separate from and meaningless in the universe. Within such an absurd environment, Kierkegaard believes the only overcoming is by a leap to faith founded on belief that only a God makes sense in an awful universe, because we have within us a vision of the truly beautiful and beneficent. Kierkegaard argues that the absurd is that which is contradictory to reason itself, but resignation and belief will deliver an individual to God. For him, this makes faith courageous in a world of uncertainty, a world that is unknowable. Rationality and logic have gaping holes and fail to account for our experience in the world. The leap to faith is over a chasm of uncertainty and the flight is propelled by fear and trembling over the bottomless void.

For Camus, the condition of humans is also absurd; we live in solitude and separation. Our unattainable desire for a communion with and in nature results in the sense of the absurd, which is heightened by our glimpses of beauty. Simply, the absurd is the human condition. There is no religious salvation in Camus, but humans rebel and persist without hope within the danger zone. "The danger ... lies in the subtle instant that precedes the leap. Being able to remain on that dizzying crest—that is integrity and the rest is subterfuge" ("The Myth of Sisyphus" 37). Camus repudiates Kierkegaard's religious leap. The authentic act of humans is to be aware of the absurd and yet not accept a false god and not commit suicide. Camus links this absurd rebellion to creativity and the creative process. For him "art is the activity that exalts and denies simultaneously ... Artistic creation is a demand for unity and a rejection of the world" (*The Rebel* 253).

Samuel Beckett ended *The Unnamable* with: "I can't go on, I'll go on" (414). It is persistence in the face of nothingness, and it is akin to writing your name on the walls of time knowing they will erode and vanish. This seems true of Lovecraft himself, for as Lévy writes he was "a man without hope" (115).

Of course, there is no hope in a Lovecraftian universe. In "The Call of Cthulhu" Thurston says, "I have looked upon all that the universe has to hold of horror, and even the skies of spring and the flowers of summer must ever afterward be poison to me" (*DH* 154). This is the bitter taste of beauty overthrown. Lovecraft's characterization of the danger zone, of being poised on the perilous crest of life, is different from Kierkegaard and Camus. In a number of stories the characters choose death, none seem to choose religion. Moreover, the fiction implies that there is nothing in common human resistance or rebellion, or fellow-feeling or community solidarity. In the fiction of the unnamable, "it is a relief and even a delight to shriek wildly and throw oneself voluntarily along with the hideous vortex of dream-doom into whatever bottomless gulf may yawn" (*D* 195).

The Pit—the Maelstrom—the Ultimate Abomination

At the end of "The Unnamable," Manton exclaims: "It was the pit—the maelstrom—the ultimate abomination. Carter, it was the unnamable!" (*D* 207). Here, Lovecraft pays homage to his master, Poe; the references to the "Pit and the Pendulum" and "The Descent into the Maelström" are clear. But why these two stories? Both of them take their narrators to the brink of death in an abyss. In these stories the narrators initially react to the chaos, within which they find themselves, rationally, by measuring the dungeon and timing the maelström; this is akin to Manton's initial response to Carter speculations. Then they realize they are in an irrational world, but the bedlam appears wonderful; for example, the unnamed narrator sees the descending blade "somewhat in fear, but more in wonder" (*Complete Tales and Poems* 149). Gerard M. Sweeney argues this is the first step toward salvation, but really deliverance is only possible by entering or embracing the horror event. The sailor in "The Descent into the Maelström" throws himself into the water, embracing the chaos, entering the abyss. And the prisoner of "The Pit and the Pendulum" escapes the blade by embracing "the irrationality and absurdity of the dungeon-world, by inviting the rats to his ropes and his lips" (23). It is by recognizing and acknowledging the irrational that one becomes free. But there is a difference between the stories. The pit is a monstrous torture chamber created by humans. The gigantic whirlpool exemplifies the essential irrationality of our experience in nature. The sailor/narrator realizes the futility of any attempt to define it. Sweeney points this out, noting that the sailor concludes his naming of the surrounding islands with: "These are the true names of the places—but why it has been thought necessary to name them at all, is more than either you or I can understand" (179–80). This is the absurdity of naming and reflects the powerlessness of our language in the face of the anarchic and baleful power of the world.

The first word of the final phrase "ultimate abomination" may also arise from Poe. In "The Pit and the Pendulum" the narrator says the pit is "typical of hell, and regarded by rumor as the Ultima Thule of all their [the Spanish Inquisition] punishments" (252). That is, it is final realization or epitome of delivering pain and terror. The phrase is also found in "Dream-Land":

> By a route obscure and lonely,
> Haunted by ill angels only,
> Where an Eidolon, named NIGHT,
> On a black throne reigns upright,
> I have reached these lands but newly
> From an ultimate dim Thule—
> From a wild clime that lieth, sublime,
>   Out of SPACE—out of TIME. (90)

Ultima Thule is thought of as the extreme limit of discovery and sometimes as ultimate ideal or exemplar; Thule was the northern most limit of exploration. Clearly this poem influences Lovecraft as he uses the final words in two important stories; his admiration for Poe runs deep. So, perhaps the final phrase is saying that at the limit of rationality we encounter the abomination.

The word "abomination" is derived from the Latin *abominatus*, past participle of *abominari*, which means to denounce as an ill omen. "Abomination" signifies something that is exceptionally loathsome, hateful, vile, or wicked. It is something that should be avoided; perhaps it is taboo as it spreads pollution or is contagious, and it should not be touched. It is a source of dread. It is evil. In "The Lurking Fear" the narrator, again in a sinister house, upon seeing the shadow of the "death-demon" can only describe it as "but a blasphemous abnormality from hell's nethermost craters; a nameless, shapeless abomination which no mind could fully grasp and no pen even partly describe" (*D* 184).

The three phrases are fossil traces in the Lovecraftian fiction of the unnamable about three types of evil: natural evil, so called by humans for natural events or things, such as a maelstrom, that cause destruction and death; moral evil or human wickedness against humans, such as the pit of inquisitorial cruelty and death; and the overwhelming evil that seems to infect everything in the world we experience; ultimate metaphysical incomprehension.

Lovecraft uses these images in other stories. The pit is best exemplified in *The Case of Charles Dexter Ward*. Dr. Willett explores the "black pit" (*MM* 201) beneath the old bungalow of Joseph Curwen. This is a story of the possessive power of the past; the revivification of the dead, the allure of torture, and the glorification of a deathly chaos. Joseph Curwen rediscovered an ancient process to bring the dead back using their decomposed remains. He then tortured and killed them, perhaps repeatedly. The force of evil is forever. In exploring the vile underground chambers, Dr. Willett witnesses the harrowing outcomes of Curwen's experiments. The dungeon is like a Nazi prison. Surveying a vast open space, Dr. Willett spies "a large carved altar" and turns away from the "dark stains which discoloured the upper surface and had spread down the sides in occasional thin lines" (*MM* 205–6). Flashlighting the distant

wall, he sees it is "perforated by occasional black doorways and in-
dented by a myriad of shallow cells with iron gratings and wrist and
ankle bonds on chains fastened to the stone of the concave rear ma-
sonry" (MM 206). The whole subterranean abyss sounds of wailing,
yelps, and screams, and is filled with "a stench unnamable" (MM
206). Narrow cylindrical cells are sunk deeply down below the slimy
stone floor. Within the shafts, Dr. Willett sees something that could
only be hinted at: "unnamable realities behind the protective illusions of common vision" (MM 207). This is the environment of evil
brought back from the past, built by humans where identity is
erased, and suffering and cruelty are everlasting. Unlike Poe's pit,
there is no real escape for the inmates from Lovecraft's pit.

In "The Dreams in the Witch House," Walter Gilman is sucked
into an abyss of evil. "On the morning of the twenty-ninth Gilman
awaked into a maelstrom of horror" (MM 287). The witch house is
another dangerous house located in Arkham. Gilman's room in the
house has odd dimensions and appears to be off geometrically with its
slanting wall and ceiling. The horror arises from the realization of the
import of the muddy marks in his room as evidence that Gilman's
dream, where he joins the ancient witch Keziah Mason and her rat-
bodied, human-skulled companion Brown Jenkins in kidnapping a
child, is real. Gilman dreams that he stops Keziah from killing the
child but does not save the child from Brown Jenkin. But he does not
escape as the sailor narrator does in Poe's story. Later Gilman is found
dead in his room. Keziah returns from the past and shows the horror
delivered by the "Sheeted Memories of the Past" (Poe, "Dream-Land"
91). There is no salvation from the maelstrom in Lovecraft.

"The Colour out of Space" is a story from the view of yet
another unnamed narrator, a surveyor for a new reservoir, who
finds the "blasted heath," a wasteland. It is a zone of death where a
prosperous farm once existed, run by the Gardner family. The story
is a sinister retelling of the Gawain Grail legend. The sickness of
Nahum Gardner is a reshaping of the sickness of the Fisher King,
and this has spread to the land. It is an area of compete desolation
and nothing lives. The king is now dead and the surveyor is like
Gawain, who Jessie L. Weston says came to "restore the waters"
(19) and bring the land back to life, although in Lovecraft's tale it is
to flood the area. To end the waste of the land in the original

Gawain legend, it is critical to ask the right questions. The surveyor
also asks about the wasteland. He is told that a mysterious presence
or color from the meteorite seemingly had infected the family,
leading to illness, insanity, and horror. The presence spreads across
the property, killing all living things. It is like a "maelstrom of
horror," a natural contagion that comes out of space and may or
may not be a conscious alien. The presence appears to be
unknowable, another manifestation of the unnamable. From the
story it does not seem to have any intentionality; it is like a blind
infection. It is like Arendt's image of evil as a fungus. In this story,
Lovecraft writes a tale that dramatizes this sense of evil—an evil
that sucks all life away.

The real meaning of abomination is expressed in *At the
Mountains of Madness*. This story evokes a vast feeling of existential
despair and loneliness. Reading the story is like experiencing a deep
loss; this mood is pervasive. The survivors of the Miskatonic
expedition are bewildered as they explore the cold desolation, the
odd geography and sense terror everywhere. They are in an alien
landscape beyond the edge of the known world. The story tells of
the brutal slaughter of expedition members by the Old Ones dug
up from the ice,[19] the strange city built by the Old Ones, which has
long been abandoned but is still plagued by monsters, and beyond
the mountains, the ultimate evil that strikes Danforth dumb when
he sees it (that is, becomes fully aware that evil is omnipresent).

Flying into the heart of the Antarctic, upon first sight of the
"jagged line of witchlike cones and pinnacles" (*MM* 28) Dyer says:

> I could not help feeling that they were evil things—mountains of
> madness whose farther slopes looked out over some accursed ulti-
> mate abyss. That seething, half-luminous cloud background held in-
> effable suggestions of a vague, ethereal beyondness far more than
> terrestrially spatial, and gave appalling reminders of the utter re-
> moteness, separateness, desolation, and aeon-long death of this un-
> trodden and unfathomed austral world. (*MM* 29)

Later, beyond the "cube-barnacled peaks" (*MM* 105) Dyer and

---

19. This is the recurrent theme of digging up the past. The past haunts the
now because, as Delmore Schwartz writes in "Personae," "Only the past is
immortal" (65).

Danforth discover a strange stone city of odd volumes and cones and star-shapes, a nightmare city. Interestingly, there is a deliberate blurring of the distinction between made and natural landscapes in the description of the mountains; as, in the end, evil pervades both landscapes. The two explore the alien environment and eventually enter "the black inner world" (*MM* 77). They find the remnants of the exploration party's camp and the bodies of decapitated Old Ones, mutilated by the shoggoths, who once were "ideal slaves to perform the heavy work of the community" (*MM* 62). But these protoplasmic beings eventually revolted against their masters.

Deep in the cavern the pair hears a monstrous shuffling and whistling, and they turn and run away back to their airplane. Danforth apparently sees something that cripples part of his intellect. And this is compounded on the flight out where Danforth has "a single fantastic, demoniac glimpse, among the churning zenith clouds, of what lay back of those other violet westward mountains which the Old Ones had shunned and feared" (*MM* 105). Danforth cannot speak about it, the final picture of evil. The scene represents dread and despair in the face of a world incomprehensible to humans and anathema for humans. The setting for *At the Mountains of Madness* is the Ultima Thule of metaphysical evil.

Innominate

At the end of "The Unnamable" there are only sentence fragments, like verbal shrapnel. These broken phrases, askew words, are akin to incoherent stammers as language is powerless, a mere figment of human egoism; it is incommensurate with our experience of the world. There is cacophony[20] here as not only language but our place in the world is in chaos. Manton's final words seem like a bestial cry after the embrace from the unnamable. It is an expression of moral chaos. What response is meaningful while confronting the fact of evil in the world? In "The Shadow over Innsmouth" it seems that, in the end, the only possible act other than death (and perhaps it is really another form of death) is to join evil, enlist in the army of

---

20. Berruti discusses the cacophony in "The Call of Cthulhu" as a symbol of the chaos of language and more deeply the moral chaos of confronting the alien, or the moral chaos of the problem of evil.

death. That is the only "salvation."

On the other hand, "The Shunned House" gives us a different perspective on the problem, a sense of the moral commitments we have to our fellow humans. It is unusual in the Lovecraft canon in that the protagonist overcomes the monster and seemingly lives on, while fully aware of the "tenacious existence of certain forces of great power and, so far as the human point of view is concerned, exceptional malignancy" (*MM* 251) In the story the explanation for the monster hinges on a sort of scientific rationale (as Manton might give):

> Such a thing was surely not a physical or biochemical impossibility in the light of a newer science which includes the theories of relativity and intra-atomic action. One might easily imagine an alien nucleus of substance or energy, formless or otherwise, kept alive by imperceptible or immaterial subtractions from the life-force or bodily tissue and fluids of other and more palpably living things into which it penetrates and with whose fabric it sometimes completely merges itself. (*MM* 252)

The narrator flees from the terror of the basement, to "where tall buildings seemed to guard me as modern material things guard the world from ancient and unwholesome wonder" (*MM* 259). A reader suspects that the hero does not really believe in the guarding power of the tall buildings but soldiers on anyway. The narrator extirpates the alien thing, the intruder, the monster, as a "duty with every man not an enemy of the world's life, health and sanity" (*MM* 252). One can see Manton in that noble role before he is contaminated by Carter, before he hits the wall of the unnamable, before he is infected by the world of nothingness and alienation, before he fails to witness and try to read the message left on his body. "The Shunned House" is a story of a human trying to live in a world of evil and working to eradicate it, doomed surely, as the story suggests, but still the effort continues. That is because the important thing is a common social purpose, a common moral purpose even in metaphysical chaos.

More congruent with the fiction of the unnamable is "The Shadow over Innsmouth," a story that chronicles the descent into and the embrace of evil. Evil is characterized as coming from the sea and drawing humans back into the sea, as deformed beings, in a deformed world but where they "shall dwell amidst wonder and glory forever" (DH 367); that is, they are converted to the culture of Innsmouth, where "some cryptic, evil movement was afoot on a large scale" (DH 345). It is like an infection spreading across a populace, but a disease gladly embraced by some including the protagonist, who discovers his Innsmouth look and accepts the call of Cthulhu, the call to evil. It is more than an acceptance of the fact of evil; it is an overwhelming loss of ethics, as if a lover forgoes humanity and ethics to carry out the vile orders of the beloved, or the terror orders of a dictator. It is akin to the loss of identity as one joins in the death march of fascism, a return to chaos, an adoration of atrocity.

The fiction of the unnamable expresses this corruption as if it is an infection. It is dangerous, as Sir Thomas Browne writes: ". . . tempt not contagion by proximity, and hazard not thyself in the shadow of corruption" (252).[21]

In the fiction of Lovecraft, there are contradictions, of course. And this is not a weakness but a strength. These works are not trivial entertainments. Lovecraft mined the true vein of horror. The original spring of the Gothic was to question the legitimacy of the sovereignty of state and religion and to reveal the duplicity of societal bonds among classes. It revealed the decadent social edifice for what it really was: built on the bones of the working class, violent in maintaining a rigid social order, and full of horror against the poor, women, and outsiders. The fiction of the unnamable asserts the sovereignty of dread, and the metaphysics of incomprehension within a world of fear and the insoluble problem of evil. It reveals the duplicity of language, science, and the human intellectual enterprise generally. There is a loss of all humanity. In doing so the fiction illuminates the fact of evil in the universe and humankind; it is a place where we lose our identities; we are all captives on a death march. There is a rawness in his stories—a savage, stammering, dis-

---

21. Lovecraft's reaction to New York is expressed as a form of infection of a population "the broad, phantasmal lineaments of the morbid soul of disintegration and decay ... a yellow leering mask with sour, sticky, acid ichors oozing at eyes, ears, nose, and mouth, and abnormally bubbling from monstrous and unbelievable sores at every point" (SL 1.334).

turbingly familiar strangeness. Something awful hits you when you read his words—as if you have stepped into a propeller. Franz Kafka, in a letter to Max Brod, says writing is a "decent toward the dark powers ... [an] unchaining of spirits that are naturally kept bound" (quoted by Calasso 111). More than others, Lovecraft unchains the spirits of dread. At his best you begin to feel those awful, diabolical spirits disgustingly touch you. Sometimes it is as if Lovecraft is retelling something you have tried to forget, forcing you to listen. And ultimate meaning is not the point of the tales; rather, it is the effect. Clear meaning is incompatible with art anyway. For Lovecraft the power or effect is to incite fear, and that is through the dramatization of the metaphysics of evil. Poe saw art as a way to escape from mundane consciousness into a world of beauty and wonder; for Lovecraft the escape leads to more terror.

"The Unnamable" is a foundational story in Lovecraft's canon of work, wrestling with the problem of our place in an unintelligible world. Although the story does not have the sustained brilliance of some stories, it is a sketch of the power of dread and is the start of a journey into the fiction of the unnamable. Even on the surface, it is important as it uses Arkham as a fictional site for the full story, deploys the serial character, Carter, and is Lovecraft's fictional treatise on the poetics of horror writing. But most importantly, it is an early story in the fiction of the unnamable and provides a gateway into the major texts. In short form, it explores the human condition in an irrational world and the metaphysical incomprehension of being in an unreadable world of evil.

Works Cited

Arendt, Hannah. Letter to Gershom Scholem. *Encounter* 23, No. 1 (January 1964): 51–56.

Armstrong, Karen. *A Short History of Myth*. London: Cannongate, 2005.

Aune, Bruce. *Knowledge, Mind, and Nature*. New York: Random House, 1967.

Beckett, Samuel. *The Unnamable*. In *Three Novels* by Samuel Beckett. New York: Grove Press, 1965. 291–414.

Beowulf: A New Verse Translation. Tr. Seamus Heaney. New York: Norton, 2001.

Berruti, Massimo. "The Unnamable in Lovecraft and the Limits of Rationality." Paper presented at Research Seminar, University of Helsinki, 2005. Retrieved February 27, 2009: http://www.helsinki.fi/filosofia/tutkijaseminaari/berrutti.pdf

Botting, Fred. "Aftergothic: Consumption, Machines and Black Holes." In *The Cambridge Companion to Gothic Fiction*, ed. Jerrold E. Hogle. Cambridge: Cambridge University Press, 2002. 277–300.

Blackwood, Algernon. *John Silence—Physician Extraordinary.* Boston: John W. Luce, 1909.

———. "The Damned." In *Tales of the Mysterious and Macabre.* London: Spring Books, 1967.

Bowker, Matthew Hamilton. "Albert Camus and the Political Philosophy of the Absurd." Ph.D. diss.: University of Maryland, College Park, 2008.

Browne, Sir Thomas. "Christian Morals." In *The Voyce of the Worlds: Selected Writings of Sir Thomas Browne.* Ed. Geoffrey Keynes. London: Folio Society, 2007.

Burleson, Donald R. *Lovecraft: Disturbing the Universe.* Lexington: University Press of Kentucky, 1990.

Calasso, Roberto. *K.* New York: Alfred Knopf, 2005.

Camus, Albert. "On the Future of Tragedy." In *Lyrical and Critical Essays.* Tr. Ellen Conroy Kennedy, ed. Philip Thody. New York: Knopf, 1968. 295–310.

———. "The Myth of Sisyphus." In *The Myth of Sisyphus and Other Essays.* Tr. Justin O'Brien. New York: Vintage, 1995. 1–102.

———. *Notebooks 1935–1942.* Tr. Philip Thody. New York: Modern Library. 1965.

———. *The Rebel: An Essay on Man in Revolt.* Tr. A. Bower. New York: Vintage, 1956.

Cannon, Peter. *H. P. Lovecraft.* Boston: Twayne Publishers, 1989.

———. "Lovecraft and Classic American Literature." In *"Sunset Terrace Imagery in Lovecraft" and Other Essays.* West Warwick, RI: Necronomicon Press, 1990.

Carroll, Noel. *The Philosophy of Horror; or, Paradoxes of the Heart.* New York: Routledge, 1990.

Conrad, Joseph. *The Heart of Darkness and Two Other Stories.* London: Folio, 1997.

Denevan, W. M. "The Pristine Myth: The Landscape of the Americas in 1492." *Annals of the Association of American Geographers* 82 (1992): 369–85.

Dodds, Eric R. *The Greeks and the Irrational.* Berkeley: University of California Press, 1951.

Dostoevsky, Fyodor. *The Brothers Karamazov.* New York: Penguin, 1979.

Duffy, Steve. "'They've Got Him! In the Trees!' M.R. James and Sylvan Dread." In *Warnings to the Curious: A Sheaf of Criticism on M. R. James,* ed. S.T. Joshi and Rosemary Pardoe. New York: Hippocampus Press. 2007. 177–83.

Eliot, T. S. *After Strange Gods: A Primer of Modern Heresy.* New York: Harcourt, Brace, 1934.

———. *Collected Poems 1909–1962.* London: Faber & Faber, 1974.

Fiedler, Leslie. *Love and Death in the American Novel.* New York: Criterion, 1960.

Frazer, Sir James George. *The New Golden Bough.* Ed. Theodor H. Gaster. New York: Criterion, 1959.

Graves, Robert. *The White Goddess.* London: Faber & Faber, 1961.

Hardy, Thomas. "To Sincerity." *Collected Poems.* New York: Macmillan, 1926. 262.

Hirvonen, Ari. "The Problem of Evil Revisited." *No Foundations: Journal of Extreme Legal Positivism* (October 2007): 29–51.

Houellebecq, Michel. *H. P. Lovecraft: Against the World, Against Life.* Tr. Dorna Khazeni. San Francisco: Believer, 2005.

Hughes, Rhys. "A Languid Elagabalus of the Tombs." In *Stories From a Lost Anthology.* Leyburn, UK: Tartarus Press, 2002. 184–208.

Hume, David. *An Enquiry concerning Human Understanding: A Critical Edition.* Ed Tom L. Beauchamp. Oxford: Oxford University Press, 2000.

Jeffers, Robinson. *Medea: Freely Adapted from the "Medea" of Euripides.* London: Samuel French, 1976.

Joshi, S. T. *H.P. Lovecraft: A Life.* West Warwick, RI: Necronomicon Press, 1996.

———. *A Subtler Magick: The Writings and Philosophy of H. P. Lovecraft.* 1996. Berkeley Heights: NJ: Wildside Press, 1999.

Julius, Anthony. *T. S. Eliot, Anti-Semitism and Literary Form,* Rev. ed. London: Thames & Hudson, 2003.

Kant, Immanuel. *Religion within the Limits of Reason Alone*. In *Readings on Human Nature*, ed. Peter Loptson. Broadview Press, 1997. 99–113.

Kierkegaard, Søren. *Fear and Trembling and The Sickness unto Death*. Ed. and tr. Walter Lowrie. Garden City, NY: Anchor, 1954.

Kneale, James. "From Beyond: H. P. Lovecraft and the Place of Horror." *Cultural Geographies* 13 (2006): 106–26.

Langan, John P. "Naming the Nameless: Lovecraft's Grammatology." *Lovecraft Studies* No. 41 (Spring 1999): 25–30.

Leibniz, Gottfried Wilhelm. *Theodicy: Essays on the Goodness of God, the Freedom of Man, and the Origin of Evil*. Trans. E. M. Huggard. London: Routledge & Kegan Paul, 1951.

Levy, David B. Review of Bernard J. Bergen. *The Banality of Evil: Hannah Arendt and "The Final Solution."* H-Holocaust, H-Net Reviews. August 1999. Retrieved on January 27, 2009 http://www.h-net.org/reviews/showrev.php?id=3372

Lévy, Maurice. *Lovecraft: A Study in the Fantastic*. Tr. S. T. Joshi. Detroit: Wayne State University Press, 1988.

Machen, Arthur. *The Great God Pan*. In *Tales of Horror and the Supernatural*. New York: Pinnacle, 1983. 1–51.

Marlowe, Christopher. *The Jew of Malta*. In *The Plays and Poems of Christopher Marlowe*. London: George Newnes, 1905. 221–87.

Marlowe, Christopher. *The Tragical History of Doctor Faustus: From the Quarto of 1604*. In *The Plays and Poems of Christopher Marlowe*. London: George Newnes, 1905. 123–63.

Midgley, Mary. *Wickedness: A Philosophical Essay*. London: Routledge Classics, 2001.

Neiman, Susan. *Evil in Modern Thought: An Alternative History of Philosophy*. Princeton, NJ: Princeton University Press, 2002.

Poe, Edgar Allan. *Poe: The Complete Poems*. Ed. Richard Wilbur. New York: Dell, 1959.

———. *The Narrative of Arthur Gordon Pym of Nantucket, and Related Tales*. Ed. J. Gerald Kennedy. Oxford: Oxford University Press, 1998.

———. *The Complete Tales and Poems of Edgar Allan Poe*. New York: Random House, 1975.

Salmonson, Jessica Amanda. "Introduction." In *The Shell of Sense: Collected Ghost Stories of Olivia Howard Dunbar*. Ed Jessica Amanda Salmonson. Uncasville, CT: R. H. Fawcett. 1997. 3–11.

Salomon, Roger, B. *Mazes of the Serpent: An Anatomy of Horror Narrative*. Ithaca, NY: Cornell University Press, 2002.

Savoy, Eric. "The Rise of American Gothic." In *The Cambridge Companion to Gothic Fiction*, ed. Jerrold E. Hogle. Cambridge: Cambridge University Press, 2002. 167–88.

Schwarz, Daniel R. *Imagining the Holocaust*. New York: St. Martin's Press, 1999.

Schwartz, Delmore. *Selected Poems (1938–1958): Summer Knowledge*. New York: New Directions, 1967.

Sebald, W. G. *On the Natural History of Destruction*. Tr. Anthea Bell. New York: Random House, 2003.

Shaked, Gershon. "Afterword." In *Facing the Holocaust: Selected Israeli Fiction*. Ed. Gila Ramras-Rauch and Joseph Michman-Melkman. Philadelphia: Jewish Publication Society, 1985. 273–88.

Sophocles. *Oedipus Rex*. In *The Oedipus Cycle: An English Version*. Tr. Dudley Fitts and Robert Fitzgerald. New York: Houghton Mifflin Harcourt, 2002. 1–81.

Spinoza. *Selections*. Ed. John Wild. New York: Scribners, 1930.

Sweeney, Gerard M. "Beauty and Truth: Poe's 'A Descent into the Maelström.'" *Poe Studies* 6, No. 1 (June 1973): 22–25.

Waller, James. *Becoming Evil: How Ordinary People Commit Genocide and Mass Killing*. Oxford: Oxford University Press, 2002.

Weston, Jessie L. *From the Ritual to Romance*. Mineola, NY: Dover, 1997.

Wharton, Edith. *The Ghost Stories of Edith Wharton*. New York: Scribners, 1973.

Wilbur, Richard. "Introduction." In *Poe: The Complete Poems*. New York: Dell, 1959. 7–40.

Wittgenstein, Ludwig. *Tractatus Logico-Philosophicus*. Tr. D. F. Pears and B. F. McGuiness. London: Routledge Classics, 2001.

Wright, Richard. *Stolen Continents: The Americas through Indian Eyes since 1492*. Boston: Houghton Mifflin, 1992.

Briefly Noted

Italian Lovecraftian activity continues at a commendably vigorous rate. The eighth issue of *Studi Lovecraftiani* (Autumn 2008), edited by Pietro Guarriello and published by Dagon Press, contains original articles by Umberto Sisia, Luca Foffano, translated articles by Rusty Burke and H. P. Lovecraft (a "Viaggio a Salem" [trip to Salem]—a translation of his letter to Frank Belknap Long of 1 May 1923—and a translation of Lovecraft's several discussions of Robert E. Howard in letters), and an extensive section of Lovecraftian news by Guarriello and Andrea Bonazzi. Dagon Press has also issued Lorenzo Mastropierro's brief monograph *Il tema della distanza nei racconti di H. P. Lovecraft* (2008), a condensed version of which appears in this issue (p. 64).

As of this writing, the publication of the collected joint correspondence of H. P. Lovecraft and Robert E. Howard—titled *A Means to Freedom: The Letters of H. P. Lovecraft and Robert E. Howard*—is imminent. The editors, S. T. Joshi, David E. Schultz, and Rusty Burke, have worked for years on the edition, which shall be issued in two large hardcover volumes. An edition of the joint correspondence of Lovecraft and Clark Ashton Smith is now being planned, probably in two volumes. The Hippocampus editions of the letters of Lovecraft and August Derleth (2008), Robert E. Howard, and Clark Ashton Smith constitute the informal beginning of a series of volumes—as many as twenty—over the next decade or so that will gather all Lovecraft's extant letters into annotated editions.

Some Notes on the
Topographical Poetry of H. P. Lovecraft

Phillip A. Ellis

The rare topographical poems of Lovecraft's oeuvre occur over the entire range of his poetic career. The earliest, "Quinsnicket Park," dates from 1913; the latest, "On an Unspoil'd Rural Prospect," dates from 1931. In a sense, then, they span the majority of his years as a mature poet. Yet, although some among the more meritorious have been briefly discussed here and there, as in both S. T. Joshi's biography and in his Lovecraft encyclopaedia, the topographical poems have largely been neglected or, rather, treated alongside the poems on seasonal topics as a broader grouping of Lovecraft's verse. The basic problem, then, is that some account of the poems, their themes, and why they fail and why they succeed is needed. Doing so will help redress the overall critical neglect shown to Lovecraft's poetry in general, and to these poems in particular. For not all the poems are failures. And those that succeed need to be identified and recognised. By looking at the topographical poems, we look, in a sense, at the wider body of verse in microcosm, and we can trace some elements of its success as Lovecraft matured in diction and technique as a poet.

If we look, then, at the poems, with brief remarks, and save a fuller examination for later, we will be able to identify them and to set the boundaries for this essay's discourse. Which ones, then, are the topographical poems? The topographical poems consist of a dozen pieces, on topographical themes, or dominated by strong, insistent motifs. The earliest, "Quinsnicket Park" (1913), is written in heroic couplets, and it demonstrates the basic reasons for the failure of Lovecraft's poems: although the problem is not that the heroic couplets are inherently weak, it is, rather, in Lovecraft's facile handling of this poetic form that the seeds of his failure lie. "New England" (1914) is immediately more successful, even as it is more seasonal than strictly topographical, as it contrasts the seasons through its regional place. "A Mississippi Autumn" (1915) again mixes seasonal verse with topographical. Its reversion to the heroic couplet is a step away from the advances shown in "New England." "On Receiving a Picture of the Marshes at Ipswich" (1917) is again marred by use of heroic couplet. It is also, overall, a slight poem, with few redeeming qualities. "A Garden" (1917) is successful, like "New England," and in part for similar reasons. It is also a more metaphorical poem than most of the others, and, as such, it deserves more attention than it has received.

"On Receiving a Picture of ye Towne of Templeton, in the Colonie of Massachusetts-Bay, with Mount Monadnock, in New-Hampshire, Shewn in the Distance" (1917; hereafter referred to as "Templeton") is a reversion to the style and diction of "On Receiving a Picture of the Marshes at Ipswich." Although longer than the earlier poem, it is in no real way superior to it. "[On Marblehead]" (1923), although also in heroic couplets, reflects some of the changes that had been occurring in Lovecraft's prosody, so that it reads as less stilted, more free than the earlier topographical poems that rely upon the heroic couplet for their form. Lovecraft may have inherited the heroic couplet from the eighteenth century, but he had not, to any real degree, developed until almost too late the insights into that form's abilities and strengths as a poetic measure. "[On a Scene in Rural Rhode Island]" (1923) is similar to "[On Marblehead]" in nature and origin (both are to be found in letters, to Maurice W. Moe and Frank Belknap Long respectively, and both were written within four months of each other). It shares a similar technique and value as the earlier, longer poem.

"Providence" (1924) is a further break from the heroic couplet of the earlier poems; here, it uses the quatrain, and Lovecraft here achieves a strong sense of poignancy in evoking his beloved hometown. It is among the most meritorious of Lovecraft's topographical poems, and for good reason. "[On Newport, Rhode Island]" (1927) is, again, in heroic couplets, but heroic couplets that have a relatively high degree of metrical substitutions, thereby alleviating the meter. Thus it is interesting for metrical reasons, rather than for rea-

sons of diction or subject matter. "The East India Brick Row" (1929)
is probably among the best-known of Lovecraft's topographical poems, as well as being surely his most meritorious one. It is marked
by high technical skill and an utter poignancy that help make it a
pleasure to read. "On an Unspoil'd Rural Prospect" (1931) is in quatrains like both "Providence" and "The East India Brick Row," and, in
some ways, is a step back from the latter poem in terms of diction
and technique. These, then, are the topographical poems, a relatively minute proportion of his overall body of poems, but one that
demonstrates in microcosm the strengths and weaknesses of his poetry in general. Yet they demonstrate themes that, though shared to
some degree by other poems, largely help to distinguish the topographical poems among Lovecraft's wider oeuvre.

There are a number of different, though related, themes in
Lovecraft's poetry. There is, for example, the contrast of an ideal-
ised landscape to the decadent present. We see this in "Quinsnicket
Park," particularly close to the beginning couplet, where we read:

> Amidst decadent sights a spot disclose
> Where ancient woodlands give their blest repose;
> Where clement Time hath spar'd his alt'ring hand,
> And left unchang'd our own ancestral land. (ll. 3–6)

In a "A Mississippi Autumn" we read, in the opening couplet, "The
genial summer hours, so lately flown, / Still haunt the mind, a pre-
cious mem'ry grown" (ll. 1–2). Further, in "Templeton," this contrast
is implied in the questions posed in lines 15–16: "Can with'ring
Change ancestral Shades o'erride, / And aliens live where sturdy
Saxons died?" Finally, in "On an Unspoil'd Rural Prospect" the contrast is implied, as the past is made present, whilst the spoiled present is left unstated yet implicit.

In contrast, "The East India Brick Row" is concerned with the
preservation of the past, as opposed to its threatened destruction. In
this way, it is similar to "On an Unspoil'd Rural Prospect," with the
latter poem's emphasis upon the unspoiled nature of the rural setting. Yet it is a polemical poem, an exhortation to preserve the past,
rather than acting, like the others above, as a lyrical evocation of it.
In this way, it could be said that this poem is both the successor and
culmination of Lovecraft's earlier political verse.

Another theme is the escape from reality to an idealised past. "Quinsnicket Park" demonstrates this: "Away, Reality! and let us roam / Quinsnicket's realm—Imagination's home" (ll. 29–30). It is significantly related to the previous theme, particularly in "Quinsnicket Park." We see this in the following lines: "Bewitching distance! by thy aid alone / The sordid town to splendour thus hath grown" (ll. 37–38). This theme also occurs elsewhere, specifically in "Old Christmas," one of Lovecraft's seasonal poems, and a splendid evocation of the past.

"[On Marblehead]" alters this theme, so that it forms either a subset of or alternative to it. This theme is the survival of the idealised past into the present. In doing so, Lovecraft at last begins to capture the importance that the colonial past has, in topographical terms, to his sense of aesthetics. For this is taken up in "Providence," where Lovecraft evokes his hometown in poignant, skilfully written quatrains. For the most part, it is the enumeration in sentence fragments of the mysteries and marvels of Providence that enrapture the poet.

Another theme is the idealisation of the rural present. Rather than remain content to idealise the past, as he does in a number of poems on political themes, which fall outside of the scope of this essay, Lovecraft approaches the present in the same basic terms and degree of idealisation. "On an Unspoil'd Rural Prospect" is one that does this, especially in conjunction with the references to mythology that shall be examined later. "A Mississippi Autumn" also does this, particularly with reference to the use of "swain" in line 22. This term, in relation to the dissonance between the vocabulary and the realities of rural Southern life, cannot be more jarring than it is. In fact, this latter poem is a curious mixture of specifics and abstractions that sits uneasily and fails to gel into something precisely effective.

Yet these are not the only themes, although they are the major ones that occur, with some variations. They demonstrate, in essence, the common ties that work with the subject, landscapes (urban and rural), and the various technical aspects of the poems that help make them an identifiable body of work. In doing so, not all the poems are successes: many fail, and it is instructive to understand why.

To a large degree the poems fail for the same basic reasons that many of Lovecraft's other poems fail. "Quinsnicket Park," in particular, is marred by mechanical versification and lifeless imagery. Unlike the dictum, "much work makes light reading," it seems apparent that this poem, like "On Receiving a Picture of Swans," has seen little effort given to the revisory process, so that it remains quite close to the condition of a first draft. In the lines "'Tis Spring; the buds deck ev'ry forest bough, / While honest rustics labour with the plough" (ll. 15–16), note the colourlessness of "deck" and of "honest rustics," which uses an abstracted, poetic diction that draws away from any hint of freshness or vividness in the imagery. This poem is blazoned with many examples of the use of this lifeless poetic diction: "the feather'd songsters" (l. 17), "vernal scene" (l. 18), "leafy bow'r" (l. 43), and "reedy pool" (l. 47) all spring to mind. Yet these problems occur elsewhere. We read of the "teeming field and fruitful vine" (l. 5) in "A Mississippi Autumn," for example. So it helps us, then, to look more closely at many of the reasons why the poems fail.

There is, for starters, a racism that, whilst not all-pervasive, occurs with enough frequency to mar. Note the contrast of "aliens" and the emphasised *"Saxons"* of line 16 of "Templeton." As well, there is the positive racism expressed through the capitalisation of "Sons" in "Such rock-ribb'd hills our own *New-England* gave / To mould her Sons as rugged and as brave" (ll. 21–22). This privileges the New Englanders as being more important than others, unnamed and implied. Yet this is not the only reason for failure.

There is wooden diction. In "Quinsnicket Park" we read "Whose shady glens the years dissolve away" (l. 11). In "A Mississippi Autumn" we read "The season 'neath the lash of autumn bleeds" (l. 4). And in "[On Newport, Rhode Island]" we read "An *Alciphron* in all its Parts was made." These are all grammatical inversions. They arrest the flow of thought, and the reader's attention is broken, particularly in careful, close reading: there is always the chance of them being glossed over when skimmed. "On an Unspoil'd Rural Prospect" is also beset by this flaw, particularly in lines 25 and 26: "Here the encumb'ring weight of age / Its bitterest force a while resigns." This example, while admittedly rare, is glaring enough to break the flow of the poem at that point for the careful reader. And, as a result, its jarring tone mitigates the more general successes of the poem.

"Templeton" is marred typographically by the reversion to the eighteenth-century uses of both capitalisation and italics. This is echoed in a similar typography in "[On Newport, Rhode Island]," with similar effects. This is one specifiable occasion where we can say with certainty that the poem appears to have been written with the express aim of invoking the past, the eighteenth century, judging from the typography, the diction, and the prosody. And, as a result, it fails to become a living poem in its own right.

With "Quinsnicket Park," "At length the force of thankless toil to feel" (l. 23) looks back to the streamlet last mentioned in line 21 as the subject, and the inversion of "to feel" "the force of thankless toil" arrests the forward momentum of the reader's attention. A later example clearly demonstrates this problem with the grammatical inversions: "In yonder reedy pool we half expect / Some timid Nymph or Satyr to detect" (ll. 47–48). Note the unintentional ambiguity—do we detect them, or do they detect us in turn? Grammatical inversions are one particular problem of Lovecraft's diction, making it seem, for the most part, that he was forced into a straitjacket of a rigidly defined allowable rhyme.

With "On Receiving a Picture of the Marshes at Ipswich," the metronomic qualities of the rhythm fail to alleviate the boredom that develops in the reader. While bad enough on this small scale, over the length, say, of "A Mississippi Autumn" the effects are truly stultifying. Interestingly, it appears that, with "Templeton," there is the beginning of a thaw in the strictness of the iambic pentameter of Lovecraft's heroic couplets. Five times, the first foot of the line is inverted: we read "Pleas'd with the Beauties" in line 5, "Nods in Content" (l. 10), "Look to the North!" (l. 19), "Ancient *Monadnock!*" (l. 23), and "Stand thou, Great Sentinel" in line 27, occurring in almost a sixth of all the lines. This points toward a loosening of Lovecraft's line, dispelling the general woodenness of his earliest adult poems.

There is also the preservation of outdated and bloodless references to mythology. In "Quinsnicket Park" we read "Ye sylvan Dryads! turn the harass'd mind / From talk of towns to themes of rural kind" (ll. 1–2). Later on, there are the "fruitful orchards, by Pomona blest" (l. 81). These references occur also in "On an Unspoil'd Rural Prospect," where the poem references "the naiad band" in line 17 and "the dryads of the wood" in line 18. By this time, however, the archaic quality has diminished slightly, so that it is not as jarring as in the earlier poem. It is as if the naiads and dryads of these two lines are more metaphorical, given the grammar of their occurrence.

There is, in general, a wooden prosody. Both "A Mississippi Autumn" and "Templeton" are marred by having every couplet conclude on an end-stopped line, as well as most of the initial lines of the couplets, so that there is no rhythmical sense of progress, just a stilted and staccato succession of lines. This occurs in the vast majority of Lovecraft's heroic couplets, yet, where in the best of these poems they lend a form of stately cadence, in most they simply result in a series of monodic statements. Yet even this can be alleviated by the skilled use of prosodic and tropaic devices, as in "A Garden," which is comprised completely of end-stopped couplets, yet which escapes the staccato effect by emphasising the non-narrative nature of the lyric.

There are clichés also. "Quinsnicket Park" has its "azure lakes and verdant pastures" (l. 9), and its "shady glens" (l. 11). "A Mississippi Autumn" has both its "annual round" (l. 16) and "The fragrant roses, and the feather'd train" (l. 21). There is the "stately Elm, and stout-limb'd Oak" of "Templeton."

And there is, also, a degree of padding. In "Quinsnicket Park," lines 7–8, we read "Quinsnicket! haven of the weary'd heart; / Close to the busy town yet far apart": the second line of the couplet consists entirely of drab, lifeless padding that does not add but detracts from the poem. Here, the whole line is padding, not just one or more words or phrases. "Templeton" is marked by the high proportion of nouns that are modified by adjectives, and this helps weaken the vividness and immediacy of the poem, helping to render it stale and lifeless. The ending couplet is the strongest and most vivid of all, because of the lack of all but one adjective: "Stand thou, Great Sentinel, tho' Nations fall— / In thee New-England triumphs over all!" (ll. 27–28).

The occasional use of hyperbole can render the effects of that trope more problematic than otherwise. In "A Mississippi Autumn" we read "Some hail the end with welcome and relief, / Some cling with tears of unavailing grief" (ll. 27–28). Is the grief not tempered by the return of spring and summer? Similarly, the occasional simile fails to work. In the same poem, we read of how "Like holy candles, dimly burning by, / The tow'ring reeds will watch the summer die" (ll. 43–44). Holy candles do more and other than watch summer die, and, in this instance, the trope jars.

This is not to say that there cannot be scattered highlights, particularly among the earlier poems. In "Quinsnicket Park," "tiny torrent" (l. 19) surprises, and is particularly memorable through its use of the alliterated *t*. "Leaps in the sun" (l. 20; referring to the "tiny torrent"), though verging on the hackneyed, is nonetheless an arresting image. "Bewitching distance!" (l. 37) works through the use of assonance of the short *i* sound. In "A Mississippi Autumn," "Where once was verdure, leaves of brazen hue" (l. 11) sparks with the brief consonance of the letter *v*; there are also the later occurrences of "mystic madness" (l. 15), "loving laughter" (l. 22), and "Late-ling'ring summer from the eastern sky" (l. 19); note here the combination of the alliteration of the *l* sound, and the sigmatism.

Of course, not all the poems fail, and the reasons for these successes will be partially examined, but there is one point worth making first. In "Quinsnicket Park" a passage toward the beginning is worth quotation:

> Yon tiny torrent, fed by swollen springs,
> Leaps in the sun, and o'er the mountain sings;
> Thro' fields below, the streamlet flows along
> With greater amplitude, but less of song;
> At length the force of thankless toil to feel,
> And strain incessant at the whirling wheel.
> Thus with mankind, the sweetest days are first;
> From youthful lips the songs spontaneous burst:
> Maturer years a graver aspect give,
> And men become more wretched as they live. (ll. 19–28)

What is interesting here is the moral that Lovecraft has derived from the image of the stream; this is rare in his work, and here it helps to strengthen our interest in the poem. Although "On Receiving a Picture of the Marshes at Ipswich" ends with a moral, "Judge not the world by wealth of outward show, / But test the firmness of the soil below!" (ll. 9–10), which alleviates the dreariness of the preceding eight lines, it is marred by the general dreadfulness in the execution of the poem. And there is a sense of a lesson, almost of a

moral, in "Providence," but it has nothing to do with morality as
such: the poet writes that Providence is "of the soul of me, / And
always at my side!" (ll. 51–52). Yet, for the most part, Lovecraft fails
to derive moral or ethical lessons from the poems. This point is of
interest precisely because it helps to demonstrate one failing of the
topographical poems. Most of these poems lack any real purpose
beyond their immediate theme. Most do, in turn, help defamiliarise
the landscapes presented within, and most, as a result, are little
more than dry verse, rather than living poems. It is time, then, to
look at why those that live do so.

As partially noted, in the discussion of the scattered highlights,
some of the poems succeed for reasons antithetical to the reasons
for the failures. For example, "New England" lacks the contractions
that help create the more archaic air of such works as "Quinsnicket
Park." There are only four in whole poem: "o'er" (l. 3), "toss'd" (l.
10), "treach'rous" (l. 11), and "flow'rs" (l. 14). In "A Garden" there are
only three: "hedge-encompass'd" (l. 10), "o'er" (l. 15), and "shrivell'd"
(l. 16). "The East India Brick Row" is notable for the absence of all
but one grammatical inversion, one that is unobtrusive, in line 37. In
all, this poem comes the closest of all the topographical poems in
using a language that is predominantly free of Lovecraft's usual poetic diction. And, as such, must be considered as among his very
best poems in general.

Also, there is a degree of movement away from iambic pentameter in some poems. "Providence" uses the quatrain to great effect, and the alternating rhymes help work against the
predominance of the couplet form in his poetry. "New England" is
also a case in point. It has a strong use of anapaests, especially in
first three quatrains. It would help to look at the rhythm of the first
line to demonstrate this point:

When the   January tempest sweeps across the barren hill,

Note how the opening anapaest lends a forward momentum to the
poem, a momentum which is maintained by the other anapaests
scattered through the four quatrains. Similarly, note the rhythm established in the first line of "A Garden":

There's an ancient, ancient garden that I sometimes see in dreams

Consider the following line of the same poem: "As I walk, and wait, and listen, I will often seek to find" (l. 11). Note the use of multiple caesuras, especially the initial two masculine ones followed by the feminine one, and how the next syllable after that third caesura receives a secondary stress. "On an Unspoil'd Rural Prospect," further, is written in iambic tetrameters, and works as a result.

Yet, although "[On Marblehead]" is written in iambic pentameter, Lovecraft uses both metrical substitutions and inversions to vary the meter and to lessen the metronomic aspects of the meter. He substitutes, occasionally, anapaests for iambs; one example is "aethereal sky" in the last foot of line 8, another the "myriad sails" in foot 3 of the following line. Read aloud the opening couplet and feel the way that the variation in both lines' opening feet give a sense of rhythmical counterpoint: "What wonders now engag'd my ravisht sight, / Mellow and magick in the golden light?" Note, too the effects of the secondary stresses upon "now" in the second foot of line 1, and "in" in the third foot of the second line, the latter, especially, directly after the unmarked caesura. Related to this is the use of the tertiary stress in the second foot of the last line, line 56: "And Time trips lightly in his mildest moods!" Note especially how the assonance of "Time" and "mildest" is offset by that of the related *i* sound in the more lightly stressed "trips" and "in."

The fullest use of these measures is probably in "The East India Brick Row." The first quatrain can serve to demonstrate this:

> It is so long they have been standing there—
>   Red brick, slant roofs, above the harbour's edge;
> Chimneys against a fragment of salt air,
>   And a green hill ascending ledge by ledge.

Note how, in line 3, the line starts with the sudden "Chimneys," which not only breaks with the pattern established in the preceding two lines, but which also runs counter to the next line, which defers the stresses until the third syllable and second foot, in "And a green hill." In this case, the latter pattern both speeds up the rhythm of the line's beginning and defers the reader's sense of that rhythm, by making the sensual pleasure of the primary stress both

later and more concise than normal. This works alongside the variations in stress in the first two lines, the secondary stress on "is" in
the first foot of the first line, and the tertiary stresses on "Red" and
"slant," both adjectives (thereby throwing greater emphasis upon
their accompanying nouns) and both in feet separated from their
fellows by strong, marked caesuras.

As noted earlier, there is the use of alliteration, assonance, and
other devices to develop some interest in the poems. These patterns
of sound occur at infrequent intervals and are striking because of it.
They help create a sense of lapidariness in the poems. "A Garden"
has sigmatism in its first lines: "I see sometimes in dreams / ...
sunlight plays and glows with spectral gleams" (ll. 1–2). "New England" has "the barren hill" (l. 1), echoing "the marrow-piercing chill"
of the following line. In the line "the cold New England country
seems a sort of frozen hell" (l.4) there is the alliteration of the hard *c*
and the *s* sounds mixed with the voiced *z*, as if the sound is frozen
solid within that exact word. And in "But when the North awakes
in spring, and white gives way to green" (l. 13), the *w* is mixed with
the consonance of *n* sounds in "spring" and "green." "Providence" has
its share. Prominent among them is the *st* sounds in "Steep alley
steps" (l. 33). In "[On Marblehead]" there are numerous occurrences
of these sound patterns. The repetition of the terminal *t* sound in
the words "ravisht sight" of the first line both emphasises the line
ending and the rhyme with "light" in line 2, but it also engages the
sensual aspect of speech, in the process of being pronounced. Line 2
has "Mellow and magick," line 4 "vivid verdure," and "branches" and
"evening Breeze" in line 6: all in the first half-dozen lines. "[On a
Scene in Rural Rhode Island]" has "Traveller's Tread" in line 2, and
there is repetition in the phrase "Dome beyond Dome" (l. 3) that is
reminiscent of "A Garden." Similar to that "Dome beyond Dome" is
the "spring on spring" (l. 11) in "On an Unspoil'd Rural Prospect."
And there is further repetition in "The East India Brick Row." In
line 18, we read "our lives, our past, our land"—which, further
linked by the alliteration of the *l* sound in "lives" and "land," works
particularly well by effacing to a degree the emphasis of the repeated "our" by virtue of its being an unstressed syllable. Finally, in
the earlier "A Garden," in the first line, the repetition of "ancient"
and, in line 14, of "grey" helps set the emotional mood of the poem.

The emotion and mood both work toward these poems' successes, given the importance of emotion for the lyric.

Both emotion and emotional states are represented in the topographical poems. In "New England," line 8, we read of "cruel stars," and, in line 9, of how "mad, malignant billows rage." This language evokes in the reader an emotional state, and it demonstrates, further, the emotional state of the narrator. The poem is also effective in its use of "hell" as the terminal rhyme of all four quatrains. "A Garden" evokes emotion through the imagery of the desiccated, withered garden. Note the effectiveness of the imagery in the following line: "Where the gaudy-tinted blossoms seem to wither into grey" (l. 3). The final couplet also works effectively to bring a strong degree of poignancy to the poem: "Then a sadness settles o'er me, and a tremor seems to start: / For I know the flow'rs are shrivell'd hopes—the garden is my heart!" (ll. 15–16). This poem is anomalous in all the topographical poems: it is at once both a dream-narrative and an allegorical examination of the poet's emotional state. "The East India Brick Row" has, perhaps, the fullest expression of emotion in the topographical poems. By working with Lovecraft's strong aesthetic attachment to older, colonial architecture, it serves to convey its primary purpose quite well: to be a passionate plea for the preservation of old warehouses for aesthetic purposes. It should be remembered that, in Lovecraft's prose, he was the master of language, tone, and diction, and this same mastery is evident here.

There is, finally, the use of tropes that help work toward the poems' advantages. "Providence," particularly, uses anthropomorphism to good effect: the "centuried domes of shining gold / Salute the morning's glare" (ll. 5–6) is one, and the "gambrel roofs / [that] Keep watch" in lines 23 and 24 is another, and the overall effect is to help vivify the poem. "The East India Brick Row," although sparing in the use of tropes, uses anthropomorphism to great effect in the penultimate quatrain, in lines 43–44. "I think," the poet writes, "the harbour streets will always wear / A puzzled look of wistful emptiness." Note how the assonance of the *w* leads into the central portion of the trope, and how "A puzzled look" is emphasised through sight, through reading, at the initial position of its line. In these ways, then, and others, some of the poems generally succeed, and some succeed to a greater degree than others.

The topographical poems of H. P. Lovecraft vary in effectiveness and value. For any number of poems like "A Mississippi Autumn," "[On Newport, Rhode Island]," or "On Receiving a Picture of the Marshes at Ipswich," there are poems, like "A Garden," "Providence," "New England," or "The East India Brick Row" that ought to be counted among his more meritorious poems. There is the occasional poem, such as "[On Marblehead]" or "On an Unspoil'd Rural Prospect," in which he approaches this level of meritoriousness, only to have it fall aside; in the case of "[On Marblehead]," there is tendency toward the prominence of the same contractions that help mar the other, earlier poems, and the use of heroic couplets reminds us too heavily of his earlier failures. Yet though, in this case, the reversion to his archaic instincts and the heroic couplet help work against the poem, there is a sense of development, both technically and in his diction as well. But, on the whole, as Lovecraft develops as a poet, so does his verse. By examining the topographical poems in some detail, we come to understand Lovecraft's wider corpus, his verse in general, and why some succeeded as Lovecraft matured as a poet. This process of looking at the poems, encompassing, at first, the themes, then the reasons for the poems' failures and successes, has been a limited exercise. Far more can be written, and from a stricter framework of theory. Yet, overall, what we have seen here is, really, the beginning of a critical examination of the poems, as opposed to the far larger body of critical work dealing with the fiction.

The Theme of Distance in the Tales of H. P. Lovecraft

Lorenzo Mastropierro

[The following is the author's translation of a portion of his monograph, *Il tema della distanza nei racconti di H. P. Lovecraft* (Pineto: Dagon Press, 2008).—ED.]

Introduction

Reading Howard Phillips Lovecraft's short stories for the first time, it seems as if, at the end, there is always something missing. One may affirm that his stories have a pyramidal structure, in which the many elements constituting the base concentrate, as one reads, in the conclusion, forming a concluding climax. But as the peak of the pyramid is reached, very few questions are actually answered, nothing is definitely revealed; the real happenings remain wrapped in mystery, and the dreadful creatures are only visible in blurred outlines. Nonetheless, there is a "suspension of disbelief": the imagination is shaken by an infinitude of frightening theories that whirl in the reader's head.

Furthermore, although the tale just read has by no means put the lid to the story, one cannot resist starting another one, which is also bound to have no precise conclusion. After all, the tale has achieved its desired effects.

One goes on reading, story after story, in search of a revelation that does not exist. The reader clings to those fleeting clues that, on the one hand, partly solve a question, but on the other hand raise many others. And when the book is closed, the imagination opens up. Nothing is revealed, but *something* has touched the reader's heart.

This *something* can be found, for example, in the depths of the sepulchre in which Harley Warren descends ("The Statement of Randolph Carter"), in what happens at Martin's Beach ("The Horror at Martin's Beach"), and in what comes out of R'lyeh's jaws ("The Call of Cthulhu"), in the narration of "Dagon"'s protagonist, or in what Ammi Pierce and the group of policemen see in Nahum Gardner's farm ("The Colour out of Space"). But what is it exactly?

A question of this kind cannot find any answer. Or, on the contrary, it has many answers, as many as the reader's imagination can conceive. However, it is possible to identify a common element just where, paradoxically, something to identify is missing: that is, the lack of knowledge. Knowledge is absent in all Lovecraft's stories, indeed, as well as the understanding of mystery, the explanation for the enigma and the identification of the creature. And where knowledge is missing, its nemesis dominates: the *Unknown*, the alien, the unfamiliar. As this paper will show, it was Lovecraft's belief that the *Unknown* was a synonym for awful, terrifying.

I will not dwell upon the classical accusation of xenophobia against Lovecraft (which is, however, of great importance), but it is very easy to find this fear for diversity in many aspects of the writer's life. As a logical consequence, then, the unknown and what is veiled under it are considered equivalent to frightening. Nonetheless, it is erroneous to look at this element—the *Unknown*, namely—as the only possible explanation for the horror in H. P. Lovecraft, although it is a fundamental part. A complete comprehension of the sense of fear in his work can be achieved only by taking into account at least an interrelation between two elements, the *Unknown* and other fundamental elements of his literature. The work of a man like Lovecraft must necessarily admit several interpretations, all potentially valid. It would be sufficient to shift perspective in one's analysis to gain new, numerous elements to correlate one with the other and, consequently, several new interpretations and inferences.

This work searches for the exact "place of origin" of Lovecraft's horrors, considering it as the second interpretative element that must be connected to the *Unknown*. As one can easily imagine, in this case the research is impossible, because an exact collocation is lacking: there are no physical places, no precise marks on earth or space's map from which that "beating of black wings" originates. The few places that are clearly named are only metaphoric and cannot be considered, then, as actual places of birth of the horror. In a way, if the sources of the horror were clearly defined, probably the stories would be less attractive and interesting. In the abstract, however, it is possible to identify an element, a theme, as a frequently repeated place of origin of horrors: that is, *distance*. It is in the theme of *distance* that this analysis, in my opinion, finds the fulcrum of the fear transmitted by H. P. Lovecraft's short stories.

The theme of *distance* is developed here by analyzing three different sub-categories, each one exemplified by a short story: *distance from reality* in "Dagon," *distance in time* in "The Call of Cthulhu," and *distance in space* in "The Colour out of Space."

I will start, then, by explaining what *distance* and the *theme of distance* exactly are, opening with the same question that has been raised at the beginning: what is the horror in Lovecraft and, chiefly, *where* is it *from*?

The Theme of Distance

To understand the sources of Lovecraft's horrors it is necessary to arrange them within the ambit of his philosophical thought, namely "mechanistic materialism." In Lovecraft's opinion, the universe was nothing but a mechanism, moving in accordance with principles that mankind cannot entirely understand, or, even worse, solely according to chance. This thought derives, among other things, from some of the scientific discoveries of his century, which gave him the certainity that "it is *damned unlikely* that anything like a central cosmic will, a spirit world, or an eternal survival of personality exist. They are the most preposterous and unjustified of all the guesses which can be made about the universe" (SL 4.57).

Therefore, if there is something still not explainable by means of scientific method, it surely has nothing to do with a sort of "central cosmic will." Everything can be reduced to a mathematical calculus or to a chemical formula, and the only thing that seems to be in step with progress is a form of optimism originated by it.

But despite all this, Lovecraft was sure that "Art has been wrecked by a complete consciousness of the universe which shews that the world is to each man only a rubbish-heap limned by his individual perception" ("Lord Dunsany and His Work"; *CE* 2.61). In some way, in spite of his "love of the abstract truth and of scientific logick" (*SL* 1.110), he recognized that scientific advances proceeded only to the detriment of fantasy: the more science widened its boundaries, the more imagination tightened.

In consequence of this, he felt the necessity of the *Unknown* with which he could feed on his imagination and his art. Furthermore, as a weird fiction writer, he needed something frightful, unexplainable, with which he could also express his artistic vein. The solution was potentially simple, since Lovecraft knew well that "the oldest and strongest kind of fear is fear of the unknown" ("Supernatural Horror in Literature," *CE* 2.82), and thus, it was enough to throw himself in the shady areas not yet illuminated yet by the light of knowledge:

> for though the area of the unknown has been steadily contracting for thousands of years, an infinite reservoir of mystery still engulfs most of the outer cosmos, whilst a vast residuum of powerful in-herited associations clings round all the objects and processes that were once mysterious; however well they may now be explained. (Ibid., *CE* 2.83)

It was in these gulfs, so distant form scientific comprehension, that Lovecraft found the *Unknown* he needed. After the identification of the last refuges of Inexplicable, the conversion of them into the places of origin of his horrors was the next step:

> uncertainty and danger are always closely allied; thus making any kind of an unknown world a world of peril and evil possibilities. When to this sense of fear and evil the inevitable fascination of wonder and curiosity is superadded, there is born a composite body of keen emotion and imaginative provocation whose vitality must of necessity endure as long as the human race itself. (Ibid., *CE* 2.83–84)

Therefore, Lovecraft's universe was one in which mankind is only a momentary incident in the infinite sequence of unknown ancient eras; the earth with its laws is nothing but a speck of dust compared to the immensity of unexplored sideral voids, and the optimistic an-thropocentrism of men reveals itself to be a mere illusion. And here is where the "Cthulhu Mythos" come into play: even though Love-craft never conceived them directly (he spoke at the most of "Yog-Sothothery" or of "The Arkham Cycle"), the term "Cthulhu Mythos" refers to a series of themes, deities, settings, creatures and atmos-

pheres shared by a certain number of stories which have not consequential connections in plot except for the references to the above-
mentioned elements. Moreover, a lot of Lovecraft's correspondents
contributed to widen the "mythos," writing stories about them and
adding new elements. Obviously, this study does not consider not the
"Cthulhu Mythos" in this wider sense, since the number of authors
who have partecipated in amplifying the cycle is quite extensive, but
it concentrates on the work of its creator and best writer.

In these tales, the protagonists, moving in settings in which the
real world and the fictional one mix themselves in an almost imperceptible manner, run across a tear in daily life, in normality, through
which they succeed in glimpsing the supreme horror that lies beyond the unknown. The characters discover, in this way, the truth
Lovecraft hides under the thin veil of the protagonists' certainties,
destroying their optimistic outlook on life.

Moreover, Lovecraft, in order to gain better freedom of action in
the writing out of his fiction, placed his horrors in an alternative geography of New England, tracing a nightmare version of the region
in which the impossible lies over the possible. Thus, he could provide new refuges to the *Unknown* in his beloved lands, without going too far from the surrounding ambient. He added imaginary cities
(such as the mysterious Arkham, the crumbling Innsmouth, or the
ancient and secluded Kingsport), invented geographical elements
and institutions (like the Miskatonic river and Miskatonic University), animating with new dark strength the drowsy New England.

It is in these territories that Lovecraft's protagonists take their
trembling steps. As he wrote in his 1934 essay "Some Notes on Interplanetary Fiction": "The characters of a story are essentially projections of ourselves; and unless they can share our own ignorance
and wonder concerning what occurs, there is an inevitable handi-
cap" (*CE* 2.180). They are mostly autobiographical characters, or at
least belong to aristocratic and learned families of the sort that
Lovecraft felt himself to be a part: distinguished men with a good
education; professionals, professors, archaeologists, and scholars,
people moved by an almost scientific curiosity that leads them toward a point of no return. However, these characters are never the
true protagonists of his stories: they lack a defined psychological
characterization and they are quite similar one to the other. Actu-

ally, they act only as intermediary of the real protagonist, the very fulcrum of the story: "The true 'hero' of a marvel tale is not any human being, but simply a *set of phenomena*. Over and above everything else should tower the stark, outrageous monstrousness of the one chosen departure from Nature" (Ibid., CE 2.179). In another essay he added: "Atmosphere, not action, is the great desideratum of weird fiction. Indeed, all that a wonder story can ever be is a *vivid picture of a certain type of human mood*. The moment it tries to be anything else it becomes cheap, puerile, and unconvincing" ("Notes on Writing Weird Fiction"; CE 2.177). So the real protagonists are the feelings, the atmosphere, what the character brings in his heart and what happens in his mind when he gradually realizes the truth of Lovecraft's universe at the final disclosure. And what they feel when they find themselves in front of the puzzling revelation, the utmost truth, is not terror, horror, bur rather *awe*: a mixture of fear and respect, intense dread and subjection, the feeling of consternation that one experiences when faces something greater than himself, well over his capacity of comprehension.

Now, one might wonder what these horrors are and what their origin is. In this case too, Lovecraft did much more than create a simple series of "monsters"; he imagined a complete pantheon of terrible divinities, entire alien races, dreadful worships and worshippers that diverged from the traditional representations of horror creatures: the tentacled Cthulhu, the formless Azathoth, the eerie Nyarlathotep, the Old Ones, and the Fungi from Yuggoth; they are only some examples of the vast and original bestiary born from his fervent imagination. But even here, a careful analysis could demonstrate how these creatures are nothing but a means, a medium to express an awesome message, namely the real source of horror. It is not their simple presence to incite the awe but rather what their presence means: they are incontestable proof of the existence of something unknowable, they are metaphor of the impenetrable obscurity that surrounds the feeble light of man's knowledge, they represent the very essence of the Unknown that undermines the foundation of the laws of Nature, as man knows them:

> The true weird tale has something more than secret murder, bloody bones, or a sheeted form clanking chains according to rule. A certain atmosphere of breathless and unexplainable dread of outer, *un-*

known forces must be present; and there must be a hint, expressed
with a seriousness and portentousness becoming its subject, of that
most terrible conception of the human brain—*a malign and particular suspension or defeat of those fixed laws of Nature* which are
our only safeguard against the assaults of chaos and the daeligmons
of unplumbed space. ("Supernatural Horror in Literature," *CE* 2.84;
my emphasis)

Therefore, the one who finds himself on the brink of this precipice
that opens on to the *Unknown* cannot do anything but feel fear and
awe.

So it is in this perspective that the *theme of distance* comes into
play: if, in Lovecraft's opinion, "horror and the unknown or the
strange are always closely connected" ("Notes on Writing Weird
Fiction," *CE* 2.176), it is *strangeness* that he recognizes as the fertile
ground on which his horror could originate and from which it could
arrive: "What must always be present in superlative degree is a
deep, pervasive sense of *strangeness*—the utter, incomprehensible
strangeness of a world holding nothing in common with ours"
("Some Notes on Interplanetary Fiction," *CE* 2.181).

Thus, it is in the *distance from reality, distance in time,* and *distance in space* that Lovecraft finds the right dimension of *strangeness:* it is from millions of aeons, from endless black space, and even
from a different perception of reality which the frightful *Unknown*
comes.

Lovecraft, in his stories, places a metaphoric red line beyond
which the *Unknown* lies. It marks the utmost limit over which
nothing remains the same; life and its laws—as the characters know
them—fade away in the oblivion of death or madness. Returning
back is useless because, once the protagonist has seen what lies beyond the brink, everything changes its meaning or even loses it. Life
itself becomes intolerable, and there is no way out. Even approaching that limit is pernicious, since something could be seen and realized, and permanent wounds could be branded in mind.

Luckily, that line is very *distant* from us; there are several million years between, endless light-years, and also mental sanity and
conventions. But it is not enough. Chance could interfere and
shorten these distances, it could let us come too near the line and
thus consign us, casually and fatally, to a terrible doom. In fact,

Lovecraft did not by accident make of Chance his major divinity, the most dreadful: "the blind idiot god Azathoth, Lord of All Things, encircled by his flopping horde of mindless and amorphous dancers, and lulled by the thin monotonous piping of a daemoniac flute held in nameless paws" ("The Haunter of the Dark," *DH* 110). In conclusion, Lovecraft's stories can be regarded as an unwitting path across *distance* toward an unthinkable horror—a horror that his characters, induced by Chance, come upon.

As I have said, this study will analyze three of his major works ("Dagon," "The Call of Cthulhu," and "The Colour out of Space") in order to follow these unlucky protagonists in their paths, seeing how the *theme of distance*, respectively, *from reality, in time*, and *in space*, represents a main element, source, and medium to transmit awe and horror in Lovecraft's work.

Distance from Reality: "Dagon"

Sometimes, in Lovecraft's tales, the horror could be just round the corner, the awful discovery could lie right under his character's nose. But fortunately, very often they ignore it, they do not notice the presence of the horror or, if they face it, they do not recognize it. There is a *distance* that protects and separates Lovecraft's characters from this horror, a resistant barrier that makes the incursions of what resides beyond the boundary line non-effective. This *distance* is composed by their conventions, by their firm beliefs about reality, and also by their finite sensory capacities; in this shelter they take refuge and stay with their eyes closed in front of the dark light of the lands beyond the line.

But this is not always true: it could happen that, because of a strange game of Chance, these barriers dissipate, the strong certainties of the characters weaken, and the *distance* that divides them from horror shortens. They begin to see everything in a different way; some doubts may insinuate into their beliefs, slowly cracking them slowly so that they may crumble; and so, Lovecraft's characters find themselves, unconsciously, beyond the line of no-return. Nothing can be done then, there is no turning back.

This is, more or less, what happens to the unnamed character of "Dagon." Although the deity that gives the name to the story is not Lovecraft's creation, but appears several times in the Old Testament as a Philistine fish-god, "Dagon" is considered by critics a cardinal work in Lovecraft's fiction. In fact, the story contains the seeds of the "Cthulhu Mythos" and holds the major elements of his cycle or, from a more general point of view, of his narrative: a terrible divinity emerging from an unknown abyss, as a metaphor of the dark corner of mind, a dream-setting, and the superimposition of an "alternative" reality on that of the protagonists. Besides, as to emphasize the *distance* from reality, the story was inspired by a dream.

"Dagon" (D 14–19) was written, together with "The Tomb," in the summer of 1917. These two stories mark the restarting of Lovecraft's fiction writing after a long period of poetry and essay writing. It was first published in the *Vagrant*, W. Paul Cook's amateur journal, in 1919; professionally, it appeared in *Weird Tales* in 1923: it represents the first Lovecraft's short story published on that magazine.

The story is an account written in the first person by the unnamed protagonist of the reported event. At the outset, after expressing his decision to put an end to his life at the conclusion of his narrative, the narrator admits his drug addiction, his only way to endure life after his terrible adventure. This element gives the reader the first alarm about the truthfulness of the report (could a statement by a drug addict, pre-announced as unbelievable, be true?), but at the same time it advises us about a possible bewilderment that drugs may have caused on the perceptions of the character, on the perceptions of his memoirs, becoming *distant* perceptions from the normal way of sensing reality.

Moreover, the narrator explains that the reader will "never fully realise" his story, even if it was narrated in detail: of course, for the one who stands on this side of reality, before the line, separated by *distance*, it is impossible to understand one who goes beyond the border; in fact, the protagonist sees reality through different eyes, and nothing could allow him to explain to the reader what he sees.

After this dazzling premise, the narrator starts expounding his adventure: he was a supercargo of a ship that, while sailing in "one of the most open and least frequented parts of the broad Pacific," is seized by a German cruiser during the First World War. After a five-day imprisonment, the protagonist succeeds in escaping from his captors and flees alone on board a small boat with the necessary provisions.

And it is now that the drift from reality begins:

> When I finally found myself adrift and free, I had but little idea of
> my surroundings. Never a competent navigator, I could only guess
> vaguely by the sun and the stars that I was somewhat south of the
> equator. Of the longitude I knew nothing, and no island or coast-
> line was in sight. The weather kept fair, and for uncounted days I
> drifted aimlessly beneath the scorching sun; waiting either for some
> passing ship, or to be cast on the shores of some habitable land. But
> neither ship nor land appeared, and I began to despair in my soli-
> tude upon the heaving vastnesses of unbroken blue.

The castaway finds himself immersed in a surreal environment, lost
in an "unbroken blue," *distant* from reality; a drift condition not
only psychological but also physical: the few alimentary resources
weaken his body, while the scorching sun clouds his mind.

In this situation, "the change happened." The narrator has no
perception of the environmental transformation because he is sleeping a "troubled and dream-infested" slumber. It is meaningful that
the change happens during his sleep: this element could make the
reader doubt the actual awakening of the narrator, since what the
castaway sees after the slumber is really a nightmare landscape:

> When at last I awaked, it was to discover myself half sucked into a
> slimy expanse of hellish black mire which extended about me in
> monotonous undulations as far as I could see [. . .]. The region was
> putrid with the carcasses of decaying fish, and other less describable
> things which I saw protruding from the nasty mud of the unending
> plain. [. . .] There was nothing within hearing, and nothing in sight
> save a vast reach of black slime; yet the very completeness of the
> stillness and the homogeneity of the landscape oppressed me with a
> nauseating fear.

It seems that, because of a strange intervention of Chance, the small
boat on which the castaway sailed now finds itself on a huge portion of the ocean floor that has been thrown to the surface in consequence of an "unprecedented volcanic upheaval."

The narrator acknowledges the impossibility of explaining and
describing everything "in mere words," not only because the event
cannot be expressed but also because it cannot be entirely understood by those who stay on this side of the *distance*. By now, the

main character finds himself in a region far away from reality; the relationships with it seem to be broken, and no element allows the reader to recognize and link that land of ooze with something familiar: "So great was the extent of the new land which had risen beneath me, that I could not detect the faintest noise of the surging ocean, strain my ears as I might. Nor were there any sea-fowl to prey upon the dead things."

As soon as the soil becomes enough dry to walk upon it, the protagonist begins an exploration, heading toward the only distinguishable element of the region, a high hummock. During the route, the reader realizes, with the castaway, that even the visual perceptions of the landscape are different and confused:

> That night I encamped, and on the following day still travelled toward the hummock, though that object seemed scarcely near than when I had first espied it. By the fourth evening I attained the base of the mound, which turned out to be much higher than it had appeared from a distance; [. . .] I began to see that the slopes of the valley were not quite so perpendicular as I had imagined.

Could not these elements mean that the journey toward the boundary line, through *distance*, is not only physical but mental too?

After a nightmare-populated sleep—as if they were a kind of warning—the narrator continues his walk under the moonlight, climbing the hillock. Oppressed by "the unbroken monotony of the rolling plain," he gains the summit of the hummock, namely the "red line" that cannot be crossed, the ultimate limit beyond which there is no turning back: "I felt myself on the edge of the world; peering over the rim into a fathomless chaos of eternal night." Here is where that strange, almost scientific curiosity for the unknown and unknowable intervenes, so characteristically present in the protagonists of Lovecraft's stories. The castaway, "urged on by an impulse" which he "cannot definitely analyse," decides to descend downstream and to cast a glance beyond the line, marking, in this way, his destiny: "I scrambled with difficulty down the rocks and stood on the gentler slope beneath, gazing into the Stygian deeps where no light had yet penetrated" At this point, the line has been surpassed, the *distance* has been left behind. He finds himself in front of horrors which have no correlations with "his" reality, both

from a mental viewpoint—with sensations he "cannot express"—
and from a physical viewpoint, since the monolith he sees downstream, gives "a distinct impression that its contour and position
were not altogether the work of Nature. [. . .] for despite its enormous magnitude, and its position in an abyss which had yawned at
the bottom of the sea since the world was young." A closer analysis
confirms or even emphasizes that sense of extraneousness. The in-
scriptions and sculptures traced on its surface reproduce elements
"unknown to the modern world," defined by the narrator as "grotesque beyond the imagination of a Poe or a Bulwer," as if he wants
to demonstrate that even the most lively imagination cannot succeed in conceiving such a thing, far beyond human conception.

"Awestruck at this unexpected glimpse into a past beyond the
conception of the most daring anthropologist," the castaway finds
himself faced with the utmost horror, the last revelation, which an-
nihilates *distance* and demolishes every barriers. Now his doom is
decided: "I think I went mad then." A frightful and scaly creature
slides out from a dark little river near the monolith and, producing
several disgusting cries, throws itself at the gigantic piece of stone,
embracing it. From now on, it is impossible to distinguish reality
from fiction; both mix with each other in an alternative state of
consciousness difficult to define in no other way but *distant*: "Of
my frantic ascent of the slopes and cliff, and of my delirious journey
back to the stranded boat, I remember little. I believe I sang a great
deal, and laughed oddly when I was unable to sing. I have indistinct
recollections of a great storm some time after I reached the boat."

After the astonishing flight, the castaway is, in some way, picked
up by an American ship in the middle of the ocean and put in
safety, awakening in a San Francisco hospital. In this last part of the
story, every certainty about the truthfulness of the event is dissi-
pated and doubts replace the few notions the reader considered
true. The tale of one who has returned from *distance* is now a "de-
lirium" listened to with "scant attention"; even scientists and eth-
nologists are "hopelessly conventional" from the narrator's point of
view. The rescuers know nothing of any land upheaval in the Pacific, and even the protagonist starts doubting of the whole matter:
"Often I ask myself if it could not have been a pure phantasm—a
mere freak of fever as I lay sun-stricken and raving in the open boat

after my escape from the German man-of-war." The only certainty the reader has now is given by conventions, by the beliefs about reality and by conventional conceptions: the narrator is mad. A sentence that leaves no escape, both to him who can do nothing but doubt himself, and for the reader who cannot judge in any other way because of a narrow-minded viewpoint, separated, protected, and limited by *distance*.

For the protagonist, the oblivion of the death is what remains: living in a world that cannot understand him is unbearable. Besides, the end of the tale and of the narrator gives a finishing stroke not only to him but even to the last confidence in the veracity of the story: "The end is near. I hear a noise at the door, as of some immense slippery body lumbering against it. It shall not find me. God, *that hand!* The window! The window!" This is surely a hallucination; it is the madness inside the narrator's head that seizes him and leaves to him no way out. This is what fate reserves for the ones who go behind *distance*. And readers remain with nothing but doubt.

Distance in Time: "The Call of Cthulhu"

In Lovecraft's cosmology, mankind is nothing but a twinkling of an eye compared to the grand age of the Earth. A transitory instant then, preceded and followed by infinitude of eras.

Notwithstanding, human beings live in their blind optimism, relying on their strong conviction of being the dominant race, now and in ages to come. They ignore horrors that preceded and follow them, unaware of being a nullity in the infinitude of time. There is a *distance* of several thousand million years that, as a barrier, separates Lovecraft's characters from a terrible truth, an aeons-old horror that is not dead, is not extinct, but is simply sleeping, awaiting a time when a casual intervention of Chance shortens *distance* with the present day and gives it the opportunity of emerging from the abyss of time in which it rests. Lovecraft, in his tales, through the intervention of accident, opens some fissures in that barrier and permits his characters to see through the cracks; this small glance is enough to bring those who glimpse, in this case too, to madness or to the oblivion of death. Francis Wayland Thurston, in "The Call of Cthulhu," discovers the horror that lies beyond the "red line" and, even though he does not face it directly, the sole awareness of the truth in Lovecraftian universe leaves him no escape.

"The Call of Cthulhu" was written in 1926, probably some months after Lovecraft's return to Providence from New York, even though the idea of the story traces back at least to 1920. It was first published in *Weird Tales* in 1928, after being rejected by its editor, Farnsworth Wright, and it is regarded today as one of the best of Lovecraft's stories. In fact, all the fundamental characteristics of his cycle and his artistic maturity find full completion in this work: a personal pantheon and a whole alternative mythology, a narration that privileges an almost "scientific" point of view, an extensively developed and complex plot, and a fully grown cosmic horror, namely a form of horror entirely extraneous to human anthropocentrism.

"The Call of Cthulhu" (*DH* 125–54) starts with an opening paragraph that already contains the fulcrum of the tale and, from a more general point of view, of Lovecraft's poetics:

> The most merciful thing in the world, I think, is the inability of the human mind to correlate all its contents. We live on a placid island of ignorance in the midst of black seas of infinity, and it was not meant that we should voyage far. The sciences, each straining in its own direction, have hitherto harmed us little; but some day the piecing together of dissociated knowledge will open up such terrifying vistas of reality, and of our frightful position therein, that we shall either go mad from the revelation or flee from the deadly light into the peace and safety of a new dark age.

Since the story is a written account of the protagonist, a manuscript "found among the papers of the late Francis Wayland Thurston, of Boston," this oppressive passage immediately dips the reader in an atmosphere of immobilisation and impotence, which permeates the whole work. The narrator continues:

> Theosophists have guessed at the awesome grandeur of the cosmic cycle wherein our world and human race form transient incidents. They have hinted at strange survivals in terms which would freeze the blood [. . .]. But it is not from them that there came the single glimpse of forbidden aeons which chills me when I think of it and maddens me when I dream of it. That glimpse, like all dread glimpses of truth, flashed out from an accidental piecing together of

separated things.

So it is immediately evident that the protagonist has already glanced beyond *distance*, and that, by now, he is lost in abysses of the mind with no remedies. But it is equally evident that, in this case, the kind of *distance* overstepped is quite different compared to the one analyzed in "Dagon": the glance has been cast at "forbidden aeons," at a terrible past, beyond endless ages that disguise an intolerable truth.

After becoming heir and executor of his late grand-uncle, who died in mysterious circumstances, Francis Wayland comes into possession of the box containing his uncle's documents and an odd clay bas-relief. The horror represented on the clay tablet is hardly describable, as if the ability to describe it is lacking to the imagination: "A pulpy, tentacled head surmounted a grotesque and scaly body with rudimentary wings; but it was the *general outline* of the whole which made it most shockingly frightful." Besides the strange image represented, what is puzzling about the bas-relief is that, despite the fact that it is "obviously of modern origin," "its designs" are "far from modern in atmosphere and suggestion," for it features a " cryptic regularity which lurks in prehistoric writing."

The writing accompanying that object is composed by two parts: a document entitled "CTHULHU CULT" and a series of press cuttings and notes about strange dreams and episodes of insanity. Standing yet before the line, before the *distance*, the narrator is afflicted by a narrowness of views and cannot do anything but think that his uncle has "become credulous of the most superficial impostures," for the eccentric set of oddities contained in the box.

The earlier part of the manuscript explains how the professor came into possession of the bas-relief: Henry Anthony Wilcox, a young and eccentric sculptor, presented himself with that weird work, asking "for the benefit of his host's archaeological knowledge in identifying the hieroglyphics on the bas-relief." As a result of the harsh reply of the professor, since the tablet was manifestly fresh, the young answered in an impressive way: "It is new, indeed, for I made it last night in a dream of strange cities; and dreams are older then brooding Tyre, or the contemplative Sphinx, or the garden-girdled Babylon." Here, the dream has that value so typical in Lovecraft's work: dream is conceived as messenger, as a means and connection with worlds and states of consciousness *far* from *reality*, *time*, and *space*. They are able to open links with what lies beyond *distance*, because they travel by a route cleared of the limitations of mind and of the conscience. And so, Wilcox, who is gifted with "psychical hypersensitivity," indispensable for gaining these kinds of "vibrations," acts as a connection between our time and the horror represented in the bas-relief.

The dreams are caused by the emergence of R'lyeh, the dead city in which the Great Cthulhu awaits sleeping, as a result of a casual earthquake. The intervention of this external element in our time does not disturb only Wilcox's dreams, but it afflicts all the minds provided with the necessary hypersensitivity to open this kind of horrible connection.

It is interesting to note how "average people in society and business" are not affected by Cthulhu's dreams, since they lack the indispensable sensibility and are the most attached to social conventions, and so the most *distant*.

In the second chapter, Inspector Legrasse takes part in a meeting of the American Archaeological Society because he needs the benefit of the scientists' archaeological knowledge in identifying a very ancient statuette, representing the monster Cthulhu, found during a raid on a supposed voodoo ceremony:

> One sight of the thing had been enough to throw the assembled men of science into a state of tense excitement, and they lost no time in crowding around him to gaze at the diminutive figure whose utter strangeness and air of genuinely abysmal antiquity hinted so potently at the unopened and archaic vistas. No recognised school of sculpture had animated this terrible object, yet centuries and even thousands of years seemed recorded in its dim and greenish surface of unplaceable stone.

The statuette represents a sort of connection with what lies beyond *distance:* it is a messenger of horrors that hide themselves in the dark past of the earth, unquestionable testimony of mysterious civilizations concealed in the mists of time. The "men of science" know it, and it is exactly this that shocks and frightens them; they feel the defeat suffered by their knowledge inflicted by the unknown:

> The aspect of the whole was abnormally life-like, and the more subtly fearful because its source was so totally unknown. Its vast,

awesome, and incalculable age was unmistakable; yet not one link did it shew with any known type of art belonging to civilisation's youth—or indeed to any other time. [. . .] The characters along the base were equally baffling [. . .] They, like the subject and the material, belonged to something horribly remote and distinct from mankind as we know it; something frightfully suggestive of old and unhallowed cycles of life in which our world and our conceptions have no part.

The unknown becomes here synonymous with frightful, terrible, developing in present-day people a kind of awe that draws its strength from *distance in time* and from what stands beyond it. The more the distance in time increases, the more the distance from our world enlarges; and the more the distance from our world increases, the more the awfulness rises.

After the general dismay, Inspector Legrasse starts relating his story. During the frightful operation, many worshippers are captured; the information about the cult drawn from the prisoners reveals itself to be very upsetting and unexpected:

They worshipped, so they said, The Great Old Ones who lived ages before there were any man [. . .] Those Old Ones were gone now, [. . .] but their dead bodies had told their secrets in dreams to the first men, who formed a cult which had never died. [. . .] it had always existed and always would exist.

Clearly, Legrasse and his men do not succeed in realizing the range of these elements, nor they could do so: their way of seeing the matter separates them from the cultists and prevents them from a complete understanding. In fact, it is interesting to note that "only two of the prisoners were found sane enough to be hanged," while the majority of the worshippers are regarded as foolish, mad. Only one thing becomes clear to the policemen, a perception that changes to a shocking certainty: "Mankind was not absolutely alone among the conscious things of earth."

It is equally clear that the cult has nothing to do with voodoo or with the witch-cult: "It was not allied to the European witch-cult, and was virtually unknown beyond its members." This passage is salient because it marks a clean separation with classic "witchcraft" and, from a more general point of view, with everything within the

ambit of human beliefs: here, the Evil is not earthly, it is not hu-
manized, it is not the Devil of human religion. The Evil here is *beyond time*, so much behind characters' age that mankind did not
exist. Thus, an Evil that is not intrinsically hostile to human beings,
but is terrible because immensely superior to them, overwhelming
beyond comparison, and dreadfully indifferent toward humanity,
regarded as a mere nothing.

The narrator, after reading the manuscripts about Wilcox's
dreams and Legrasse's raid, is caught by that scientific curiosity
which characterizes all Lovecraft's protagonists:

> The matter of the cult still remained to fascinate me, and at times I
> had visions of personal fame from researches into its origin and
> connexions. [. . .] for I felt sure that I was on the track of a very real,
> very secret, and very ancient religion whose discovery would make
> me an anthropologist of note.

It is a sort of scientific obligation, an almost moral obligation toward
knowledge. But with Lovecraft, knowledge gains a new value compared to the one it has in *weird* literature. Indeed, in classic horror
fiction, knowledge and wisdom are indispensable weapons with
which the Evil must be fought: the werewolf can be defeated only
being aware of his vulnerability to silver; Professor Abraham Van
Helsing succeeds in beating Count Dracula only because he knows
well his vampire nature and his weak points. But with Lovecraft,
the knowledge of the horrors that surround his characters leads toward sure oblivion. There is no possibility of defeating what lies beyond distance, and the knowledge of it can only make us feel more
impotent.

With the last part of the story comes the conclusion, in which
the various pieces of information are linked together, exhibiting the
terrible truth that Lovecraft places behind the veil of time. With
the new data obtained by the finding of the newspaper article, the
narrator realizes that something horrible has happened; *distance* has
been almost canceled, and he feels shaky on the border of that line
he knows he must not surpass: "Was I tottering on the brink of
cosmic horrors beyond man's power to bear? If so, they must be
horrors of the mind alone, for in some way the second April had
put a stop to whatever monstrous menace had begun its siege of

mankind's soul."

So the menace of these "cosmic horrors" is not a direct threat of mankind's extinction but rather a "horror of the mind." The danger is avoided for now; Great Cthulhu has returned back in his nightmare-city and he will sleep there for the next million years. But the attack on the mind has been accomplished, and Cthulhu reveals himself to be nothing but the messenger of "cosmic horror," and not "cosmic horror" itself: the message that the awful creature brings is a direct menace to man's mind, to his anthropocentrism and to his optimistic certainty and confidence in his species. And so, the narrator trembles with fear, realizing that the solitude of man in universe, as well as his mental sanity, is threatened.

And it is not over: when the narrator finally obtains the diary of Gustaf Johansen, its reading takes him over the limit. By now, the fear of the Unknown is intolerable, and he cannot think of what lurks "behind life in time and in space" without a shiver:

> I cannot attempt to transcribe [the diary] verbatim in all its cloudiness and redundance, but I will tell its gist enough to shew why the sound of the water against the vessel's sides became so unendurable to me than I stopped my ears with cotton. Johansen, thank God, did not know quite all, even though he saw the city and the Thing, but I shall never sleep calmly again when I think of the horrors that lurk ceaselessly behind life in time and in space, and of those unhallowed blasphemies from elder stars which dream beneath the sea.

Thus, the narrator has seen beyond the threshold, over the maximum limit: life and reality now seem to him like a thin veil, a curtain that protects humanity from the awesome truth behind it, from its appalling actors and from its senseless scripts. So, in Lovecraft's narrative, human beings are regarded as nothing but unarmed spectators, who are advised to stare only at the curtain rather than to see that horrendous "opera" that is the universe and to realize their role into it.

After this visit in a such forbidden land, everything is seen under a new dark light; nothing has the same meaning as before; life is useless and the world is a lie: "I have looked upon all that the universe has to hold of horror, and even the skies of spring and the flowers of summer must ever afterward be poison to me. But I do not think my life will be long. As my uncle went, as poor Johansen went, so I shall go. I know too much, and the cult still lives." At the end, the narrator seems to understand the mistake he has committed, pushed by curiosity and aided by Chance. Knowledge has revealed itself fatal: "Let me pray that, if I do not survive this manuscript, my executors may put caution before audacity and see that it meets no other eye." Caution before audacity, and thus, ignorance before knowledge. This is the final message that the protagonist wishes to give us as heritage: it is better not to know and to live under the darkness of ignorance than under the awful light that illuminates the horror beyond *distance*.

Distance in Space: "The Colour out of Space"

If the past hides in its mist unimaginable monstrosities, space is, in the Lovecraftian universe, their very cradle. In the sidereal void beyond our small planet, in universes that cannot be even imagined by humanity, in distant worlds infinite light-years away, Lovecraft places his unmentionable horrors, lying in ambush. And, if even whole sciences cannot do anything but submit to the unknowable out of space, his characters cannot even bear its sole thought, so different, *distant* it is.

This is, in short, the core of the theme of *distance in space*, which in "The Colour out of Space" finds one of its greatest exemplifications. The story was written in March 1927 and was first published in September of the same year, in *Amazing Stories*, the first American science fiction magazine. The publication of the tale in that magazine is an ulterior confirmation of the coeval tendency of Lovecraft in conceiving stories more and more inclined to science fiction. That tendency, begun with "The Call of Cthulhu," tends to mix wisely the classical elements of *weird* narrative with a more scientific point of view, since he knew well that

> Inconceivable events and conditions form a class apart from all other story elements, and cannot be made convincing by any mere process of casual narration. They have the handicap of incredibility to overcome; and this can be accomplished only through a careful realism in every *other* phase of the story, plus a gradual *atmospheric or emotional building-up* of the utmost subtlety. ("Some Notes on Interplanetary Fiction," CE 2.178–79)

"The Colour out of Space" is a sort of finishing line of this new style, so that Lovecraft himself defined the tale as an "atmospheric study" rather than a real horror story (SL 2.114).

Beyond the disquisitions about style, this short story is regarded as one of the better works of the author: although it can be included only marginally in the "Cthulhu Mythos," because of its setting near Arkham, the tale succeeds perfectly in expressing that sense of inexplicable mystery emerging from space and the distressful defencelessness that oppresses the characters.

In "The Colour out of Space" (*DH* 53–82), it is again an unnamed narrator who relates the terrible story of Gardners' farm. During his first inspection of the area, although he did not know the "blasted heath," he feels something strange; he notices that "Upon everything was a haze of restlessness and oppression; a touch of the unreal and the grotesque, as if some vital element of the perspective or chiaroscuro were awry." Therefore, there is something indecipherable, unintelligible, but existing and concrete; a sensation that can be felt but not understood. And while he is walking very close to the "blasted heath," he feels "an odd reluctance about approaching." So strong is the spontaneous repulsion to see that gray land filled with dead trees that at twilight the narrator wishes "some clouds would gather, for an odd timidity about the deep skyey voids above had crept into [his] soul." So the sight of the "blasted heath" causes an indefinite feeling of dismay that, however, insinuates an ancestral fear toward the unknown, toward the *distant*.

Despite the warning of the Arkham citizens about old Ammi, regarded as a fool, the narrator decides to go and to listen to the strange story of the Gardners and their farm. Thus, also in this case, even though the narrator has not lived through the happenings, he suffers equally the effect, simply in consequence of hearing the story. This means that, with Lovecraft, however dreadful the creatures and their appearance may be, the horror is not generated by them but rather by the bewilderment of consciousness, by a mental, a symbolic path, a course of denied certainties and revealed truths.

"It all began, old Ammi said, with the meteorite": this is the opening sentence with which the tale starts and so, immediately, the cause and the origin of the whole matter are clarified. Everything begins with something beyond time; in "The Call of Cthulhu" it is the bas-relief; here everything starts with something coming out from distant skies. In both cases, the horror has origin in the Unknown.

The scientists who arrived to study the object, after a long series of inconclusive analysis and tests, realize that "it was nothing of this earth, but a piece of the great outside; and as such dowered with outside properties and obedient to outside laws." The overthrow of science is inevitable, and the gap that separates them from comprehension is so wide that, when the meteorite completely disappears, since it quickly deteriorates, the scientists "felt scarcely sure they had indeed seen with waking eyes that cryptic vestige of the fathomless gulfs outside; that lone weird message from other universes and other realms of matter, force, and entity." A sin of pride then, committed by the "men of science," as a metaphor of all sciences and of mankind who so optimistically relies on them: what cannot be understood and explained does not even exist. And when they hear about a strange illness that has poisoned the Gardners' ground and vegetables and has spread among farmers, the scientists "stayed away in contempt," since "there was really nothing for serious men to do in cases of wild gossip, for superstitious rustics will say and believe anything."

Not only the harvest, but also Gardner family seems to have suffered the influence of the meteorite; they become weaker and more taciturn. Moreover, it seems that something ineffable and indefinite wanders around the farm, and the family perceives "a feeling of vague disquiet":

> The entire Gardner family developed the habit of stealthy listening, though not for any sound which they could name. The listening was, indeed, rather a product of moments when consciousness seemed half to slip away. [. . .] The Gardners took to watching at night—watching in all directions at random for something . . . they could not tell what.

So, in order to give space to "another" perception, their consciousness seems to retire with all its bonds: in this way they try, with normal senses, to perceive something imperceptible by its very nature.

This searching for something that cannot be found causes the health of the family to deteriorate little by little, both physically and psychically: they claim to see, by night, the dying trees and the farmland shine from the odd colour that typified the core of the meteorite—the same indescribable colour that tinted the strange vegetables grown rotten in the farm. Madness is the obvious outcome of all that, and it would not keep them waiting: first Mrs. Gardner and then Thaddeus, one of the sons, is afflicted.

And it is not over; after the first cases of insanity, the livestock commences to die in a very frightful way: they turn gray and brittle, and then fall to pieces before they die. Nobody succeeds in understanding the cause of the illness, since the livestock had no contacts with the infected ground, grass, or vegetables. Moreover, living in pens or paddocks, "no bites of prowling things could have brought the virus, for what live beast of earth can pass through solid obstacles?"

With that "of earth," Lovecraft seems both to restrict voluntarily the investigation field and, at the same time, to suggest to the reader an alternative research field: the solution must be sought in something out "of earth," however unbelievable it may be.

The only explanation—logical explanation—that old Ammi and the late Nahum could conceive is that of "divine" punishment: "It must all be a judgment of some sort; though he could not fancy what for, since he had always walked uprightly in the Lord's ways so far as he knew." But this is not a divine "judgment"—Lovecraft makes that clear; this is nothing but the sheer realization, however monstrous it may be, of the law of the jungle, in which the predator eats the prey: man finds himself playing the role of the unarmed prey, hunted by a predator about which he knows nothing, and in a jungle bigger and more dangerous than he can imagine, namely the endless universe. In this way, the transposition is realized, the inversion of Evil's place of origin: previously, the evil forces resided down below us. In classic Gothic fiction, places such as dungeons, catacombs, jails, and underground crypts abounded; they were always hideaways of something evil. Moreover, Hell itself was placed in the bowels of the earth. But in Lovecraft, and particularly in "The Colour out of Space," the Evil comes from above, from sidereal space, from the sky, classically regarded as the metaphor of Heaven, as the abode of the supreme Good. Therefore, the "judgment" comes from the sky, of course, but it is surely not "divine."

When old Ammi finally goes to see what has happened to his neighbours, he realizes that, in consequence of the madness of Mrs. Gardner and the disappearance of the other sons, even the pillar of support of the family, Nahum Gardner, has bent under the weight of misfortunes; his mind has surrendered: "The stoutest cord had broken at least, and the hapless farmer's mind was proof against more sorrow." Madness is here regarded as the sole way out: there is no other solution for Lovecraft's characters when the evil is the raw truth, reality. Thus, when reality, the normality of what surrounds them, reveals itself to be so terrible, the only remaining solution is the abnormality of insanity.

But, despite it all, the last words of the mad Nahum contain the truth:

> "Nothin' ... nothin' ... the colour ... it burns ... cold an' wet ... but it burns ... it lived in the well ... I seen it ... a kind o'smoke ... jest like the flowers last spring ... the well shone at night ... Thad an' Mernie an' Zenas ... everything alive ... suckin' the life out of everything ... in that stone ... it must a' come in that stone ... pizened the whole place ... [...] I seen it the fust time this week ... must a' got strong on Zenas ... he was a big boy, full o' life ... it beats down your mind an' then gits ye ... burns ye up ... [...] Zenas never come back from the well ... can't git away ... draws ye ... ye know summ'at's comin', but 'tain't no use ... [...] it come from some place whar things ain't as they is here ... one o' them professors said so ... he was right ... look out, Ammi, it'll do suthin' more ... sucks the life out ..."

Then Ammi decides to go to the Arkham police station in order to announce the event. In spite of his protests, he is obliged to take a group of officers to the Gardners' farm, together with a doctor and a veterinarian. The investigations in the house and in the well do nothing but confirm the horrors without a logical explanation as to happened in that farm. Later, in the darkness of the night, they find themselves in facing the Colour coming out from the well; their explanation about it, however tacit it may be, is unanimous: "It must be somethin' from away off in the sky like the men from the college last year says the meteor stone was. The way it's made an' the way it works ain't like no way o' God's world. It's some'at from beyond." By now it is clear: it is something coming "from beyond."

Moreover, when a darker cloud obscures the moon, the men, sheltered in the farmhouse, succeed in getting a better view of the odd colour assembling, becoming larger, and then flowing "directly into the sky." In this way, the colour confirms its origin, returning to where it has come from: it is not a Lucifer, fallen down from the sky to bring mishap and compelled to stay on Earth; the colour has no God that prevents it from coming back in the skies. It has come, has brought madness and death, has fed on everything alive, and now returns unmolested to heaven. This is the utmost confirmation that skies are the cradle of horrors unknown to human beings, and the unlucky witnesses have its proof in front of their eyes:

> Then without warning the hideous thing shot vertically up toward the sky like a rocket or meteor, leaving behind no trail and disappearing though a round and curiously regular hole in the clouds before any man could gasp or cry out. No watcher can ever forget that sight, and Ammi stared blankly at the stars of Cygnus, Deneb twinkling above the others, where the unknown colour had melted into the Milky Way.

The men, after realizing that even the house in which they are standing gleams with that odd colour, run away, leaving the collapsing farmhouse far behind. The next day, "five eldritch acres of dusty grey desert" is all that can be found of the farm; an expanse of poisoned ground on which nothing could ever grow.

At the end of the story, the narrator himself is stunned, he feels a sort of awe as a result of the revelations he has known, he glimpses the range of the matter but he does not understand it all, he cannot. What remains to him is "an odd timidity about the deep skyey voids above" and a great many doubts and perplexities:

> What it is, only God knows. In terms of matter I suppose the thing Ammi described would be called a gas, but this gas obeyed laws that are not of our cosmos. This was no fruit of such worlds and suns as shine on the telescopes and photographic plates of our observatories. This was no breath from skies whose motions and dimensions our astronomers measure or deem too vast to measure. It was just a colour out of space—a frightful messenger from unformed realms of infinity beyond all Nature as we know it; from realms whose mere existence stuns the brain and numbs un with

the black extra-cosmic gulfs it throws open before our frenzied eyes.

Therefore, the doubts are numerous but the certainty is one: the littleness of man toward the infinitude of cosmos, cosmos of which man does not even imagine, beyond every possible estimate.

In conclusion, once again the menace is not tangible, is not immediate, is not material; the life of human beings is not in direct danger. The colour reveals itself to be nothing but a messenger, but it is not a messenger of evil, malignity. Its arrival represents rather a challenge to all human thought, to mankind's optimistic vision of the universe and its role in it. The colour is regarded as the proof, in Lovecraft's cosmology, of the existence of something beyond the Unknown, something not intrinsically hostile to his characters but dreadfully different to them. This message totally destroys man's anthropocentrism and places him on the same level as an ant, an insignificant ant that could be squashed by a distracted foot, unintentionally and without wickedness. And this awful message comes from beyond space, beyond *distance*.

Conclusion

"Dagon." "The Call of Cthulhu." "The Colour out of Space": three short stories that differ in plot, setting, characters, but which, being three of Lovecraft's most significant works, contain extracts that explain the whole poetic of the writer.

In choosing them as exemplary cases, it is obvious that these short stories may have some features in common, features that can be also ascribed to all Lovecraft's fiction.

So, after the analysis of the individual cases, I will go on to identify those features that the tales share, with the aim of finding the essence of Lovecraftian horror through their similarities. A horror that, as I have tried to demonstrate, comes from beyond *distance*.

The first element to analyze is certainly Chance; it accompanies all the characters' troubles and is partly their cause. In "Dagon," Chance can be seen in the choice made by the German soldiers to attack exactly the ship of the protagonist, or when the protagonist's boat is wrecked exactly on that part of the seabed that would emerge afterwards. In "The Call of Cthulhu" one may claim that the majority of occurrences in the entire story happen by chance. If in the emergence of R'lyeh from the sea depths one may notice a kind of planning (was it the alignment of stars that caused the earth-quake and the seaquake that made the dead city reemerge?) , the same planning cannot be found in its following sinking. It is cer-tainly by chance that Thurston finds the press-cutting that describes the adventures of the *Emma*. Finally, in "The Color out of Space," it is only by chance that the meteorite falls in the outskirts of Ark-ham, in Nahum Gardner's estate. It is equally accidental that the supervision task of the narrator is right in the blasted heath, where the new water basin should be built.

Although there is no doubt that Chance often offers the possi-bility to go beyond *distance*, it is equally undeniable that the char-acters constantly find themselves face-to-face with the *Unknown* mainly because of their own choices—choices that they make out of curiosity. There is a kind of imperative in the characters or narra-tors, indeed, that obliges them, in all three stories, to investigate the *Unknown*, groping in the dark of the unknowable. While the casta-way of "Dagon" convinces himself that he must explore the stretch of dark mud only because he wants to find a solution to an unusual situation, he is not persuaded by necessity but by curiosity, as when he decides to go downhill in order to analyze the huge monolith more closely. In "The Call of Cthulhu" it is Thurston himself that admits his curiosity, which compels him (scientific obligation or moral one?) to investigate the cult, after having realized the truth-fulness and the importance of the matter. In "The Colour out of Space," finally, it is only the diligence in his work that pushes the narrator to hear Ammi's story, although the whole community of Arkham has marked him as an old fool and therefore unreliable.

Finally, as I have shown in the course of this analysis, although there are three different typologies of *distance*, the results of cross-ing them are the same: the annihilation of conventional ways of thinking, and the consequent exile from society, the oblivion of madness or death. And this happens not only to those who have personally faced what is beyond *distance* (the castaway of "Dagon," Gustaf Johansen, Ammi Pierce, the Gardners), but also to those who have dealt with it only indirectly (Francis Wayland Thurston, the narrator of "The Colour out of Space"). The common fate of the characters is a result of the fact that beyond that metaphoric red line, which can be distant from reality, in time or in space, always resides the *Unknown*, with all consequences that this bears.

Taking into account these three key concepts of the analyzed stories, it is quite easy to catch a glimpse of the ideas that constitute the basis of Lovecraft's cosmic horror. These ideas are extremely clear in the already-quoted introductory lines of "The Call of Cthulhu":

> The most merciful thing in the world, I think, is the inability of the human mind to correlate all its contents. We live on a placid island of ignorance in the midst of black seas of infinity, and it was not meant that we should voyage far. The sciences, each straining in its own direction, have hitherto harmed us little; but some day the piecing together of dissociated knowledge will open up such terrifying vistas of reality, and of our frightful position therein, that we shall either go mad from the revelation or flee from the deadly light into the peace and safety of a new dark age.

The *Unknown* leaves no way out, it surrounds humanity with its "black seas of infinity," as the night sky around the moon. It is not necessary to experience it directly, because a casual, unexpected awareness would be enough to annihilate. And all sciences, inspired by their proud desire of knowledge, distribute to every person a part of the infinite darkness that they can glimpse through their telescopes. But human beings are too insignificant to keep even a small fragment of the endless unknown that surrounds them; it is no use searching for answers where only questions can be found; there is no redemption in faith, just as there is no faith in redemption. And thus, is there no hope in Lovecraft's universe? Yes, perhaps there is. But only in a utopian "new dark age."

I would like to make a final remark about Chance, because I consider it fundamental in Lovecraft's short stories. It underlines in a very cynical way that what is beyond the *Unknown* has no precise reason to harm humankind; its damage is not intentional and it does not represent any kind of cruelty toward human beings. With Lovecraft, the struggle between Good and Evil is absent, because of the inequality between the two: if one force is immensely superior to the other, to the point that the latter can be ignored, can we talk about battle? The readers of Lovecraft, and his characters too, know well the sense of disarming impotence and frustrating inferiority that derives from this. And this is the essential sentiment of cosmic horror.

Finally, this is the origin of fear in Lovecraft's fiction: the abysmal difference, *distance*, between his characters and the universe that surrounds them—which can be the sidereal void, an inconceivable past, or the unknown labyrinths of the mind. It is a *distance* full of horrors.

Briefly Noted

Kenneth W. Faig Jr. has published a volume of his selected essays on Lovecraft, *The Unknown Lovecraft* (Hippocampus Press, 2009), focusing chiefly on the obscurer corners of Lovecraft biography, where research can still yield valuable results. Among Faig's more significant articles are discussions of Lovecraft's paternal and maternal ancestry, his involvement in the world of amateur journalism, and essays on such of Lovecraft's colleagues as Dudley Newton and R. H. Barlow. Articles on the biographical relevance of such stories as "He," "The Silver Key," and *The Dream-Quest of Unknown Kadath* are also included. The volume is a fitting commemoration of more than thirty years of scholarship by one of the pioneering authorities on Lovecraft.

Lovecraft's Avatars: Azathoth, Nyarlathotep, Dagon, and Lovecraftian Utopias

Brandon Reynolds

Most scholarship regarding the issue of religion in H. P. Lovecraft's writing has tended to examine the question of religion from the perspective of either highlighting the religious undertones in his work or arguing that there are none, that in fact Lovecraft is not concerned with religious issues at all. August Derleth's superimposition of his own Catholic worldview upon Lovecraft's existing mythology seems to be chiefly responsible for this debate. In contrast, most other scholars have argued that Lovecraft was an atheist for whom religious questions had little or no importance, a view for instance that Dirk W. Mosig advanced in "The Great American Throwaway" and "H. P. Lovecraft: Myth Maker." In fact, however, a closer look at religion in Lovecraft's novels, short stories, poems, and letters shows him to have been a writer deeply concerned with the problem of religion. Lovecraft's early writing shows a fascination with what he called paganism, which led him to explore the Greek pantheon. While he tended more and more toward atheism as his life went on, nonetheless his work continued to show a tension between his desires for two very different utopias, one a pagan-based utopia of which the fish-god Dagon is a primary representative, and a second anti-religious utopia that can be achieved only by the destruction of mankind, which is best represented by the figures of Azathoth and Nyarlathotep. In order to understand Lovecraft's ideas about religion more thoroughly, we need to consider the interaction between his desires for paganism and atheism and to trace more closely how that interaction plays out over the course of his life and writing.

According to Lovecraft's essay "A Confession of Unfaith," his brief "pagan phase" reached its apex in 1897:

> When about seven or eight I was a genuine pagan, so intoxicated
> with the beauty of Greece that I acquired a half-sincere belief in
> the old gods and nature-spirits ... Once I firmly thought I beheld
> ... these creatures dancing under autumnal oaks; a kind of "religious
> experience" as true in its way as the subjective ecstasies of any
> Christian. If a Christian tell me he has *felt* the reality of his Jesus or
> Jahveh, I can reply that I have *seen* the hoofed Pan. (CE 5.146)

Here, Lovecraft's differentiation between Christianity and paganism
relies on the simple concept of tangibility; that is, visual proof of
religion, which he claims paganism has and Christianity does not.

Because of his devotion to the anachronistic gods of ancient
Greece, Lovecraft spent his early life lamenting over the loss of pagan (non-Christian) religion in the world around him and dedicated
much of his early fiction and poetry to the glorification and preservation of these dying belief systems. "A Confession of Unfaith" reveals this tendency: "my pompous book called *Poemata Minora*,
written when I was eleven, was dedicated 'To the Gods, Heroes,
and Ideals of the Ancients' and harped in disillusioned ... sorrow of
the pagan robbed of his antique pantheon" (CE 5.146). The *Poemata
Minora* that Lovecraft alludes to here is a small collection of five
classical poems that he wrote in 1902. It includes: "Ode to Selene or
Diana," "To the Old Pagan Religion," "On the Ruin of Rome," "To
Pan," and "On the Vanity of Human Ambition."

All five poems in Lovecraft's *Poemata Minora* contain a distinct leaning toward paganism. However, the following passage
from "To the Old Pagan Religion" best encapsulates Lovecraft's sorrow at the loss of pre-Christian faith:

> Olympian Gods! How can I let ye go
> And pin my faith to this new *Christian* creed?
> Can I resign the deities I know
> For him who on a cross for man did bleed? (*AT* 11, ll. 1–4)

It is clear that the narrator worships the gods of ancient Greece
within the context of this poem. There is also an obvious question
of assimilation posited as well. Can the narrator indeed renounce his
beliefs in favor of the "new" Christian faith? The final stanza of the
piece provides us with the answer:

Fast spreads the new; the older faith declines.
The name of *Christ* resounds upon the air.
But my wrack'd soul in solitude repines
And gives the Gods their last-receivèd pray'r
                                        (*AT* 11–12, ll. 13–16)

The lament over the loss of paganism here, though emotional and heartfelt, is very unrealistic. By writing the "last-receivèd pray'r" line, Lovecraft is arguing that the gods of the Greek pantheon no longer exist in light of the ascension of Christianity. The conquest is too complete, as if Christianity has physically destroyed young Lovecraft's pagan gods and they can no longer be resurrected or deified. But while Christianity is indeed the more popular of the two belief systems, nothing is in fact preventing the narrator from maintaining his original pagan faith.

Although the narrator of "To the Old Pagan Religion" was content to let the gods of ancient Greece fade into the past, Lovecraft himself was not. Eighteen years after he wrote about the "destruction" of the Greek pantheon, Lovecraft once again attempted to resurrect it in his 1920 collaboration with Anna Helen Crofts entitled "Poetry and the Gods." The story opens with the protagonist Marcia "alone with strange thoughts and wishes . . . which floated out of the spacious twentieth-century drawing room . . . and eastward to far olive-groves in Arcady which she had seen only in her dreams" (*D* 349). Because Marcia feels "separated . . . from . . . the strange home in which she lived . . . where relations were always strained" (*D* 349), she reaches for "some healing bit of poetry" (*D* 349) and promptly lapses into a deep sleep.

Marcia, while dreaming, "cried to the rhythmical stars, of her delight at the coming of a new age of song, a rebirth of Pan" (*D* 351). Marcia's elation at the "rebirth of Pan" is rewarded by the appearance of the Greek god of poetry and literature. Hermes deems Marcia a "prophetess more lovely than the Sibyl of Cumae when Apollo first knew her" (*D* 351). Hermes' transformation of Marcia from mortal woman to prophetess has a singular motivation, revealed in the following monologue:

Thou has truly spoken of the new age, for even now on Maenalus, Pan sighs and stretches in his sleep, wishful to awake and behold about him the little rose-crowned fauns and the antique Satyrs. In thy yearning hast thou divined what no mortal else, saving only a few whom the world rejects, remembereth: *that the Gods were never dead*, but only sleeping ... but neither man nor giant shall defy the Gods forever ... in sleeping the Gods have grown kind, and will not hurl him to the gulf made for deniers of Gods. Instead will their vengeance smite the darkness, fallacy, and ugliness which have turned the mind of man; and under the sway of bearded Saturnus shall mortals, once more sacrificing unto him, dwell in beauty and delight. (D 351–52)

Although the reemergence of the Greek pantheon here takes place within a hypothetical dreamscape, paganism is depicted as beneficial to mankind. While the preceding passage is utopian in that it (naively) promises an eternal state of "beauty and delight" upon re-dedication to the slumbering gods of ancient Greece, the concept of mortal death is also notably absent. This pagan resurgence takes place on earth. These new disciples of Saturnus can presumably see and interact with the gods they are sacrificing to in exchange for a blissful existence. Both physical and visual proof of the existence of pagan deities are certainly present.

However, the utopia set forth here is not wholly positive. An air of menace hovers around the line "neither man nor giant shall defy the Gods forever." It hints at an act of assimilation that must be undergone by mankind prior to residing in this Grecian paradise. Although the narrator promises no divine retaliation against our race directly, he does mention later that the "shadow of false faiths will soon be gone and the Gods shall once more walk among men" (D 355), as all other systems of belief other than the pagan gods of Greece will be destroyed. Lovecraft's pagan utopia thus requires four elements: the reawakening (literal or symbolic) of dormant pagan deities, the physical (or visual) tangibility of said deities, the assimilation of mankind into their specific belief system, and the absence of any opposing religion. These four specific elements are best embodied in the fish-god Dagon and his devout followers.

The fish-god Dagon is originally a biblical deity of the Philistines. Dagon made his brief debut for Lovecraft's short story "Dagon" in 1917. The story itself is unremarkable and brief. Readers only glimpse Dagon as a "vast, polyphemus-like and loathsome" object that "darted like a stupendous monster of nightmares" (*D* 18). The details surrounding Dagon's followers are vague as well, citing only a "pictorial carving . . . supposed to depict . . . a certain sort of men . . . paying homage at some monolithic shrine . . . under the waves" (*D* 17–18).

S. T. Joshi amusingly contends in *H. P. Lovecraft: A Life* that Lovecraft "conceived only a relatively small number of . . . plots or scenarios and spent most of his career reworking" (Joshi 159) them. Joshi's assertion that Lovecraft tended to "recycle" his plots certainly proves true in "The Shadow over Innsmouth" (1931), which elaborates on all the aspects of the Dagon pseudomythology only hinted at in the 1917 version of the story.

When the narrator, Robert Olmstead (who according to Joshi is "never mentioned by name but identified in the surviving notes" [*Life* 496]) arrives at Innsmouth, he encounters his first evidence of Dagon and his cult: "the bus had come to a sort of open concourse . . . with churches on two sides . . . once white paint was now grey and peeling, and the black and gold sign on the pediment was so faded that I could only . . . make out the words 'Esoteric Order of Dagon'" (*DH* 318). Olmstead then deduces that this ruined structure "was the former Masonic Hall now given over to a degraded cult" (*DH* 318). The occupation of former churches by the followers of the fish-god Dagon symbolizes paganism rising above Christian opposition.

The origin of the Esoteric Order of Dagon's presence in Innsmouth—and thus the elimination of Christianity—can be traced to its founder, Captain Obed. After Olmstead fills ninety-six-year-old Zadok Allen with multiple bottles of Innsmouth's finest hard liquor, the old man more than willingly divulges Innsmouth's history of paganism:

> "Never was nobody like Cap'n Obed—old limb o' Satan . . . says they'd orter get better gods . . . gods as ud bring good fishin' in return for their sacrifices . . . told abaout an island east of Otaheité . . . They was a little volcanic island near thar, too, whar they was other ruins . . . all wore away like they'd been under the sea onct, an' with pictures of awful monsters all over 'em . . . the natives araound thar had all the fish they cud ketch, an' sported bracelets an' armlets an' head rigs made aout o' a queer kind o' gold with picters o' . . . fish-like frogs or frog-like fishes that was . . . in all kinds o' positions like they was human bein's." (*DH* 329–30)

Zadok Allen's monologue provides crucial background to Dagon's followers. In addition to the original locale of the Order of Dagon (written here as "Otaheité," i.e., Tahiti), it reveals that the cult achieved its takeover of Innsmouth by offering a "divine" answer to Innsmouth's severe shortage of fish. The members of Dagon's order show their devotion through the act of sacrifice and are given a near-boundless supply of food. The carvings on the undersea monolith (whose contents are now fully described) can be seen as a prophecy of the transformation that is overtaking those denizens of Innsmouth who belong to the Esoteric Order of Dagon.

Another key encounter with a non-native of Innsmouth reveals how its citizens of assimilate into Lovecraft's pagan ideal. Through a conversation with a teenage grocer, Olmstead learns a number of key facts about Innsmouth and its reclusive population:

> Certain spots were almost forbidden territory . . . one must not, for example, linger much . . . around the pillared Order of Dagon Hall at New Church Green . . . their creeds were heterodox and mysterious, involving hints of certain marvelous transformations leading to bodily immortality—of a sort—on this earth . . . their appearance—especially those staring, unwinking eyes which one never saw shut—was certainly shocking enough; and their voices were disgusting. It was awful to hear them chanting in their churches at night, and especially during their main festivals or revivals, which fell . . . on April 30th and October 31st. (*DH* 320–21)

The form of worship here is much more extreme because the members of Dagon's order undergo grotesque bodily transformations (made clear by the narrator's description of their inhuman "unwinking eyes" and "disgusting voices"). The reward for this sacrifice of humanity—a gesture of worship to Dagon—is the promise of eternal life. Zadok Allen tells Olmstead that "we all had to take the Oath o' Dagon" (*DH* 337) and that "all in the band of the faithful . . . shud never die, but go back to the Mother Hydra an' Father Dagon what we all come from onct" (*DH* 337). Therefore, the physical devolution of the townspeople of Innsmouth can be seen as a grotesque form of assimilation into Dagon's religion.

The third and fourth elements Lovecraft's pagan utopia, the re-awakening of dormant pagan deities and an element of physical or visual tangibility, reside in mankind's origins. In "The Shadow over Innsmouth," these origins are directly linked to the physical regression of Dagon's followers. Key information regarding these aspects of the Esoteric Order of Dagon is once again relayed to Olmstead by the drunken Zadok Allen: "seems that human folks has got a kind o' relation to sech water-beasts—that everything alive come aout o' the water onct, an' only needs a little change to go back agin ... them as turned into fish things an' went into the water *wouldn't never die*" (*DH* 331). This passage implies that all human life originated from the sea at one time or another. But the reawakening of Dagon does not actually involve the deity itself. Instead, his followers return to the sea after their transformation is complete. By rejoining Dagon and Mother Hydra beneath the surrounding ocean, the members of the Esoteric Order of Dagon enjoy immortal life and simultaneously establish their fish-god as Innsmouth's primary deity. The physical return to Dagon's undersea kingdom by the newly transformed members of the order is a tangible reward for religious worship (physical in the act of transformation, visual in the return to the ocean that allows them to behold their god) of Dagon's pagan belief system. The eradication of Christianity combined with the physical assimilation of Innsmouth's human inhabitants through the "Oath of Dagon" and the ultimate return as immortals in the "lair of the Deep Ones ... amidst wonder and glory for ever" (*DH* 367) completes the ideal representation of the four elements of Lovecraft's pagan utopia.

Despite the clear return to paganism in "The Shadow over Innsmouth," Lovecraft was already an avid subscriber to the atheistic philosophy that had become synonymous with his life by this time. Hints of this viewpoint permeate the Esoteric Order of Dagon and its members. The reward of "earthly immortality" promised to all those who faithfully take Dagon's oath makes the concept of afterlife unnecessary. By achieving immortality without experiencing physical death, the members of Dagon's order have already achieved their ideal state through their physical degeneration. This disavowal of the afterlife (and any deity that may preside over it) along with Lovecraft's proposition that man should return to a perpetual state of nothingness comprise Lovecraft's second utopia.

Though we have seen Lovecraft's early advocacy of non-Christian religion, his continued spiritual evolution transformed him into a devoted atheist who made increasingly blunt attacks on faith, humanity's dependence on organized religion, and mortal notions of the afterlife. The period between 1916 and 1921 is of particular interest in Lovecraft's new view of the world. According to Joshi's *H. P. Lovecraft: The Decline of the West* (which presents his chronicle of Lovecraft's philosophical evolution), Lovecraft "read Nietzsche, Haeckel, and Elliot" (16) in 1919 and therefore "felt at liberty to condemn the various mythical philosophies of the time in tones of withering scorn" (16). Joshi cites the "three main principles of mechanistic materialism" (7) that originated in Hugh Elliot's *Modern Science and Materialism* as: "the uniformity of law, the denial of teleology," and "the denial of any form of existence other than those envisaged by physics and chemistry, that is to say, other existences that have some kind of palpable material characteristics and qualities" (7).

The influence of Elliot's materialism on Lovecraft's religious views can be seen in the biting satire of Lovecraft's 1920 poem "On Religion":

> Would that we all might innocently dream
> In primal bliss by Lethe's flow'ry stream;
> 'Neath fancy's glow a fairy would survey,
> Nor glimpse, beyond, the with'ring light of day;
> Drink from the perfum'd tide a pleasing draught,
> And breath the scent that lotos'd zephyrs waft,
> While others, not so blest, lift tearful eyes
> To the bleak cycle of the godless skies! (*AT* 240, ll. 1–8)

This segment of the poem could mirror Lovecraft's own religious evolution from pagan to atheist. However, the two philosophies highlighted in this passage present a contradiction. The first half of the segment again laments the lack of paganism in the world. The second half is a mock-revelation of the "truth" that no god exists and that the nature of the world is nothing but a "bleak cycle" in which mankind is indeed alone in the universe and cries to "vacant air." The lines "would that we all might innocently dream" and "while others, not so blest" are of particular interest because they create a dichotomy between a small circle of pagans who are relaxing comfortably by the river Lethe and the rest of mankind, whose religion and faith in a supreme being has no validity. While this may be another of Lovecraft's attempts to claim pagan supremacy, "On Religion" ultimately shows a Lovecraft unable to make up his mind because of the aforementioned contradiction between those select few pagans who will enjoy a lush afterlife within their pantheon and (presumably) everyone else, whose God does not exist.

Contradictions aside, there is a connection between Lovecraft's atheism and the insignificance of the human race within his universe. An early example can be found in an extract from one of Lovecraft's letters to the Kleicomolo correspondence cycle, written on August 8, 1916: "might not the total destruction of humanity, and of all animate creation, be a positive *boon* to nature as a whole? How arrogant of us ... whose very species is but an experiment of the *Deus Naturae,* to arrogate ourselves an immortal future and considerable status ... the best thing a man might do is annihilate himself!" (*SL* 1.24). Lovecraft's atheism surfaces here through his argument that immortality is little more than a status symbol brought on by mankind's arrogance, while his referral to our species as an "experiment" indicates our overall insignificance within his worldview. Lovecraft clearly disdains humanity's attempt to transcend its lowly status through belief in the afterlife and therefore offers annihilation as the only beneficial solution to avoid this delusion of importance.

Lovecraft's second utopia involves the eradication of the entire human race. Lovecraft expands on the desires he expressed in "Nietzscheism and Realism" (1921), a collection of extracts taken from letters to his future wife, Sonia H. Greene: "universal suicide is the most logical thing in all the world—we reject it only because of our primitive cowardice and childish fear of the dark. If we were at all sensible we would seek death—the same blissful blank which we enjoyed before we existed" (*CE* 5.71). In simpler terms, Lovecraft's atheistic ideal for mankind involves one key principle: mankind's apocalyptic destruction. This ideal is best characterized by two specific deities in Lovecraft's pantheon: the Demon Sultan Azathoth and his avatar, the shape-shifting Nyarlathotep.

Nyarlathotep made his debut in the story of the same name in 1920. Although Nyarlathotep acts as the messenger and avatar of superior beings residing in the cosmos, he too has cosmic origins that are revealed in the events that herald his coming to earth: "out of the abysses between the stars swept chill currents that made men shiver ... everyone felt that the world and perhaps the universe had passed ... to ... gods or forces which were unknown ... and it was then that Nyarlathotep came out of Egypt" (*MW* 32). Nyarlathotep's arrival in conjunction with the takeover of the universe by "unknown forces" is no coincidence. In fact the link between the forces now in control of the cosmos and Nyarlathotep reveals his specific role:

> I remember when Nyarlathotep came to my city ... my friend had told me of ... the impelling fascination and allurement of his revelations ... my friend said they were horrible ... what was thrown on a screen in the darkened room prophesied things none but Nyarlathotep dared prophesy ... I saw hooded forms amidst ruins ... I saw the world battling against blackness ... against ... destruction from ultimate space ... beyond the worlds vague ghosts of monstrous things ... and through this revolting graveyard of the universe the ... monotonous whine of blasphemous flutes from ... beyond time ... whereunto dance slowly ... and absurdly the gigantic, tenebrous ultimate gods—the blind, voiceless, mindless gargoyles whose soul is Nyarlathotep. (*MW* 33–34)

Nyarlathotep is the prophet of the universal apocalypse at the hands of unnamed "Ultimate Gods." Since these gods are in spheres of existence beyond earth and without sight, voice, and mind, Nyarlathotep comes to earth in their stead to bring the message of Armageddon. Still, Nyarlathotep does not actually bring the end of days upon mankind, but rather displays a terrifying inevitability at the hands of deities who reside in space.

Though he is seen here as the prophet of the apocalypse, Nyarlathotep has versatile functions within Lovecraft's fiction. In "The Dreams in the Witch House" (1932), Nyarlathotep reprises his role as a messenger, this time in the guise of a hooded figure dressed in black. Walter Gilman takes up residence in the "Witch House," so named because it was once home to Arkham's most notorious witch, Keziah Mason. Gilman contracts a violent fever caused by graphic nightmares involving the long-deceased witch and her rat-like familiar known only as "Brown Jenkin." We learn later that the realms of hyperspace depicted in his nightmares actually exist. However, it is Gilman's first real-life encounter with the ancient woman that reveals Nyarlathotep's specific function:

When [Gilman] awaked he could recall a croaking voice that persuaded and threatened. He must meet the Black Man, and go with
them all to the throne of Azathoth at the centre of ultimate chaos
... he must sign in his own blood the book of Azathoth ... what
kept him from going with her and Brown Jenkin and the other to
the throne of Chaos where the thin flutes pipe mindlessly was the
fact that he had seen the name "Azathoth" in the *Necronomicon*.
And knew it stood for a primal evil too horrible for description.
(*MM* 272–73)

Here we are introduced to the relationship between the supreme god
Azathoth and the messenger Nyarlathotep. In order to venture into
what Lovecraft calls "ultimate chaos," Gilman must sign Azathoth's
book, not coincidentally offered on earth to Gilman by Nyarlathotep,
as Azathoth is inaccessible to him in his kingdom of "ultimate chaos."
Later in the story, Lovecraft gets more specific in his description of
Nyarlathotep by labeling him a "deputy or messenger of hidden and
terrible powers—the 'black man' of the witch-cult, and the 'Nyarlathotep' of the *Necronomicon*" (*MM* 286). Description of this type is
reminiscent of Nyarlathotep's debut as a Nostradamus figure predict-
ing the final hours of the universe. Though Lovecraft stresses in multiple stories that Nyarlathotep, though all-knowing, is but a
messenger for the all-powerful Azathoth, who resides in unseen
realms, the fact that he can freely travel to earth whereas his master
cannot undermines Azathoth's supposed supremacy because of his
inability to venture beyond his kingdom.

Azathoth is the most powerful and malignant of all Lovecraft's
fictional beings. However, when compared to his earthly avatar
Nyarlathotep and his theater of apocalyptic delights, Azathoth is
actually rather passive. Instead, he is more an ideal than an active
agent. Lovecraft argues in "Nietzscheism and Realism" that universal
suicide—which he defines as the return to a state of "blissful" nothingness—should be willingly accepted by mankind for our own
benefit. The kingdom in which Azathoth resides has certain characteristics that associate it with the concepts of total destruction and
nothingness that comprise the above definition.

Consider the following extract from *The Dream-Quest of Unknown Kadath*, written in 1926–27:

If in our dreamland [Kadath] might conceivably be reached ...
there were, in such voyages, incalculable local dangers; as well as
that shocking final peril which gibbers unmentionably outside that
ordered universe, where no dreams reach; that last amorphous
blight of nethermost confusion which blasphemes and bubbles at
the centre of all infinity—the boundless daemon sultan Azathoth
... who gnaws hungrily in inconceivable, unlighted chambers beyond time amidst the muffled, maddening beating of vile drums
and the ... whine of accursed flutes; to which detestable pounding
and piping dance ... absurdly the gigantic ultimate gods ... whose
soul and messenger is the crawling chaos Nyarlathotep. (MM 308)

While Azathoth dwells beyond the reaches of time and space, this
extract from *The Dream-Quest of Unknown Kadath* (in which the
monstrosity debuts) provides a detailed description of the desolation surrounding Lovecraft's "daemon sultan." Azathoth dwells in an
absolute nothingness that Lovecraft labels the "center of infinity."
Azathoth himself is also "amorphous," lacking definite, tangible
form even within his kingdom.

An additional excerpt (simply titled "Azathoth") from Lovecraft's 1929–30 poetry collection, *Fungi from Yuggoth*, provides additional insight into Azathoth, his surroundings, and his relationship
with the Messenger God Nyarlathotep:

> Out in the mindless void the daemon bore me,
> Past the bright clusters of dimensioned space,
> Till neither time nor matter stretched before me,
> But only chaos, without form or place.
> Here the vast Lord of All in darkness muttered
> Things he had dreamed but could not understand,
> While near him shapeless bat-things flopped and fluttered
> In idiot vortices that ray-streams fanned.
>
> They danced insanely to the high, thin whining
> Of a cracked flute clutched in a monstrous paw,
> Whence flow the aimless waves whose chance combining
> Gives each frail cosmos its eternal law.
> "I am His Messenger," the daemon said,
> As in contempt he struck his master's head. (AT 73)

The passage details the formless, blank nature of Azathoth's dwelling in which the monotonous droning of his cracked flute "gives each frail cosmos its natural law." Azathoth is the creator of the structure of our universe, the Lovecraftian origin of existence. Furthermore, his "messenger" (in this case an unnamed Nyarlathotep) is none too pleased with his position of servitude and thus strikes Azathoth's head in contempt.

Azathoth and Nyarlathotep represent a cause-and-effect relationship that encapsulates Lovecraft's atheistic ideal of "universal suicide." Nyarlathotep is the causal element, the evil prophet who shows mankind its inevitable end in a terrifying theater show. But his role on earth is assigned to him by his master. Nyarlathotep's coming—along with the inevitable apocalypse that it signals—is the means by which mankind will ultimately be destroyed and thus return to the state of perpetual nothingness that is Azathoth's realm at the "center of infinity."

My purpose here has not been by any means to establish H. P. Lovecraft as a religious man. His abrupt transition from his "half sincere" belief in pagan gods to a belief in a cold, cyclical cosmos shows a man unwilling to accept anything other than these two extremes. In either case, the future is unsurprisingly bleak for the human race. Within Lovecraft's universe, we are given two choices: physical degeneration into Innsmouth's fishlike people coupled with an eternal undersea existence for the rebirth of paganism, or complete and utter destruction of everything for the sake of achieving a "blissful" existence of nothingness.

Works Cited

Joshi, S. T. *H. P. Lovecraft: A Life.* West Warwick, RI: Necronomicon Press, 1996.
———. *H. P. Lovecraft: The Decline of the West.* 1990. Berkeley Heights, NJ: Wildside Press, [2001].

Acknowledgments: I would like to thank Mark Wallace for his valuable contributions to this article.

Self, Other, and the Evolution of Lovecraft's Treatment of Outsideness

Massimo Berruti

As a necessary premise, one has to define the notion of *outsideness* as it appears and is meant in Lovecraft's fiction and nonfiction. Lovecraft employs the word "outsideness," often accompanied by the adjective "cosmic," in several of his theoretical and aesthetic writings. For example: in "[Notes on Weird Fiction]" (*CE* 2.172), in "Notes on Writing Weird Fiction," where it is associated with the notion of "cosmic alienage" (*CE* 2.176), and in the autobiographical "Some Notes on a Nonentity," where "cosmic outsideness" is specifically referred to as a peculiar thematic quality of Lovecraft's literary production, together with "dream-life" and "strange shadow" (*CE* 5.210). Thus outsideness is a Lovecraftian neologism and it stands for alterity, otherness, and their manifestations, their tokens rationally unexplainable occurring in the Lovecraftian *oeuvre*. In fact, these manifestations can be events, characters, landscape or architectural descriptions, etc., for which the human reason is unable to account: they may assume the form, on the discourse surface, of Cthulhu's resurgence from R'lyeh as well as of the description of the architectural "anomalies" of R'lyeh itself ("The Call of Cthulhu," 1926), of humanity's encounter with the Great Race ("The Shadow out of Time," 1934–35), of tons of rats migrating along the walls of an antique abbey ("The Rats in the Walls," 1923), of the music of a cello which unveils portions of an unfathomable Great Beyond ("The Music of Erich Zann," 1921), of the mind-blowing "photograph from life" (*DH* 25) of a ghoul in the catacombs of Boston ("Pickman's Model," 1926), etc. They all represent manifestations, different on the surface level, but homogeneous in that they reflect a stable theme at the deep level: the alterity irrupting in the human dimension and, according to the modalities with which the subjectivity of the involved characters perceive and face it, disrupting such a dimension.

My critical hypothesis is that it is possible to separate (based on the viewpoints that will become clear in the course of this article) Lovecraft's fiction into two macro-periods: pre- and post–"Call of Cthulhu," i.e., before and after the "exile" in New York City (1924– 26), periods that, for the purpose of synthesis and clarity, will be labeled "phase 1" (from "The Tomb," 1917, to the New York tales inclusive) and "phase 2" (from "The Call of Cthulhu" to "The Haunter of the Dark" and the collaborations/ghostwritings of Lovecraft's last active year, 1936).

It is my conviction that the Lovecraftian literary poetics following the return from the New York "exile" undergo a substantial mutation, especially with reference to the modalities with which the characters' subjectivities perceive—and therefore describe—the manifestation of the Other, the Different, or, to use the Lovecraftian term, of the outsideness into which they bump.

What is the nature of this change in Lovecraft's poetics? It is a complex and multifaceted one, and a very crucial one in the evolution of his *weird* production toward its purest and most distinguished form, one that will affect deeply the developments of the fantastic genre *tout court:* the *non-supernatural cosmic art.*[1] This definition actually involves not only a lot of literary and narratological issues, but a shift even in the philosophical background backing the fiction, with a convinced adhesion to the principles of *cosmicism.*

The Levels of Evolution in the Treatment of Outsideness

The ways in which the manifestations of outsideness are perceived, coped with, and described in Lovecraft's fiction depend on the sub-

---

1. Lovecraft himself employs this expression in a letter addressed to Frank Belknap Long on February 27, 1931: "The time has come when the normal revolt against time, space, & matter must assume a form not overtly incompatible with what is known of reality—when it must be gratified by images forming supplements rather than contradictions of the visible & mensurable universe. And what, if not a form of *non-supernatural cosmic art,* is to pacify this sense of revolt—as well as gratify the cognate sense of curiosity?" (*SL* 3.295–96).

jectivity of the characters that the narrating voice calls into action as *filters-focalizers* of those manifestations. These characters are placed and built by the voice as fictional *masks* of the author, who reserves to himself an absolutely privileged, demiurgic role in the fictional world. Thus the above-mentioned evolution of Lovecraft's poetics among the two phases involves not only the features of outside-ness's representations, but, inevitably, also the subjectivity of the characters, since it is precisely *through the filter of their subjectivity that outsideness's manifestations find a textual representation* and, ultimately, come to *signify*. It is then certainly fruitful to precede the study of the evolution of outsideness among the phases with one of the subjectivity of the fictional characters, and tools like semiotics may prove useful in the process—applied not only to the fictional texts but also to the nonfiction: since the representation of fictional *personae* is a key factor in all Lovecraft texts (in essays and above all the letters[2]).

---

2. In fact, that Lovecraft enjoys using different "masks" and fictionalizing his own "self" appears clear also in his letters. Airaksinen remarks that "Too many of his friends are pen friends with whom he plays the game of false identities. For instance, he likes to use false names and descriptions to sign his letters. He is a 'Granpa' [*sic*] and 'Ludovicus Theobaldus Junior'. He has no 'I'. This is why he is able to describe his feelings of horror so convincingly" (33). Also according to Sondergard, even in the use of the nickname "Grandpa" one can detect Lovecraft's tendency toward autosemiotization in his nonfiction: "the relatively young author who signs his letters 'Grandpa' is another facet of the constructed self recognized and replicated throughout Lovecraft's fiction. Rapid, premature aging is a frequent price paid by his characters for arcane knowledge" (101), and the author mentions "The Tomb" (1917) and "From Beyond" (1920) as convenient examples. Airaksinen (17–37) convincingly argues that at least two different "Lovecrafts" exist: the empirical author, and the writer of the letters and of the fiction. This consideration is meant to go beyond the "elementary distinction . . . often drawn between the author and the narrator of a text" (17). According to Airaksinen, Lovecraft the empirical author consciously builds a fictitious "mask" of himself both as the author of the letters and as the author of the fiction (the latter two almost never coincide): "To argue that by reading the letters we learn about the man behind them is unwarranted. On the contrary, the letters can be understood *as his fictional autobiography*. Hence, we can say that this 'I' is a fictional entity, his own creation. . . . We should not naively read the letters as veridical reports on the author. Many people fic-

The evolution of Lovecraft's poetics regarding outsideness among the two phases stems also from a shift in the *dialectics between self and other*. It already appears clear that the evolution of the aesthetic treatment of outsideness assumes several different forms and can be discussed on a multiplicity of levels. It represents a complex topic, of which now the main guidelines will be touched upon. In particular, it must be clear that what evolves is *not* outsideness in itself from the viewpoint of the forms and contents of its manifestation, but the *perception* of these forms and contents by the filtering subjectivity, whose evolution thus provokes an utter modification in the ways in which *outsideness is made to signify*.

Here will be discussed the four macro-levels in the evolution of outsideness that can be taken into account for a productive analysis: literature, philosophy, characterization, representation. However, it must be of course taken for granted that these levels are not strictly separable but overlap continuously as they refer to a shared macro-process.

1.   Literary Level: the evolution from a mythical (epic) to a scientific (novelistic) discourse

This level leads to the evolution from a supernatural *weird* fiction to a non-supernatural cosmic art, where the supernatural element is banished in favor of an analytical and rationalistic approach. Moreover, this scientific attitude has a strong materialistic and mechanistic nuance.

With the term "discourse," I mean the use of language for communicative purposes, in specific contextual and generic situations, which can be considered discourse situations. The mythical discourse employed in the first phase of Lovecraft's literature involves the resort to supernatural elements and to the technique of *distanciation*. This evolution can be traced upon the distinctions envisioned by Mikhail Bakhtin in his discussion of the epic and novelistic elements.

An important corollary of this conflict between mythical and scientific discourse emerges in the theme of censorship: in the first phase, the mythical discourse imposes the mark of ignorance on the discovered truth. The facts must stay within the boundaries of a

---

tionalize themselves" (18–19; my italics).

private discourse: scientific curiosity may be allowed, but the results of the consequent surveys are not to be made public. The contrast with the approach of the scientific discourse of the second phase is blatant, where the main goal of the discourse is that of making its discoveries public and available for the general advancement of human knowledge at large. What is involved is a plain conflict between the necessity to maintain the secrecy of knowledge and the necessity to ensure its diffusion. The dialectics between secrecy and publicity of knowledge is a quite problematic issue. In a tale of the first phase like "Facts concerning the Late Arthur Jermyn and His Family" (1920), we not surprisingly read: "Science, already oppressive with its shocking revelations, will perhaps be the ultimate exterminator of our human species—if separate species we be—for its reserve of unguessed horrors could never be borne by mortal brains if loosed upon the world. If we knew what we are, we should do as Sir Arthur Jermyn did; and Arthur Jermyn soaked himself in oil and set fire to his clothing one night" (*D* 73). However, in the opening of the tale I consider the initiator of the second phase, "The Call of Cthulhu," we read:

> The most merciful thing in the world, I think, is the inability of the human mind to correlate all its contents. We live on a placid island of ignorance in the midst of black seas of infinity, and it was not meant that we should voyage far. The sciences, each straining in its own direction, have hitherto harmed us little; but some day the piecing together of dissociated knowledge will open up such terrifying vistas of reality, and of our frightful position therein, that we shall either go mad from the revelation or flee from the light into the peace and safety of a new dark age. (*DH* 125)

The intrinsic dangerousness of truth—and of its revelation to the large public—is a topic Lovecraft will always be aware of: however, the comparison between these two openings only apparently reveals a conflict, since while in "Jermyn" the voice cannot find any solution to the revelation of truth besides self-destruction, in the second tale another possibility is left besides insanity: that of the refusal of the knowledge, a "voluntary ignorance" that leads to a new Middle Age in which minds are kept in a providential obscurity. The mythical discourse does not allow the publicity of knowledge:

the *Necronomicon* is kept under lock and key and watched, sheltered jealously by the heralds of the official science (like Dr. Armit-
age in "The Dunwich Horror," a very interesting tale for its
dialectics between myth and science). In the first phase, the scientists do not seem so much practitioners of modern and post-
Galilean sciences as wizards prey to superstitions (in "Jermyn," the
scientists' behavior toward the mummy of the ape-woman does not
really appear as "scientific"[3]). Lovecraft's discourse is, in phase 1,
fighting the democracy of knowledge (and, coherently, also political
democracy): science is repressive and elitist, because it defends the
Anglo-Saxon community of WASPs to which Lovecraft devoted all
his hopes for the preservation of Western civilization. In the early
phase Lovecraft believed in racial hierarchy, and thus applied the
same hierarchical approach to (the distribution of) knowledge. In
phase 2, knowledge is finally made public by a human character
who understands the fundamental value of the democratization of
knowledge: let us think of William Dyer and his group's expedition
to Antarctica, or of Nathaniel Peaslee and his decision to popularize
his memoir—after earlier publications of neutrally scientific accounts of the same experience—about the mind-exchange with the
alien of the Great Race.

2.   *Philosophical Level: the evolution of the dialectics between Self and
     Other, from one of irreconcilable conflict to one of compromise,
     acceptation, and reciprocal scientific interest*

This is a crucial issue in the evolution of the treatment of outsideness in Lovecraft, so much so that it entails also the evolution of
outsideness from morally and aesthetically "evil" to "good" or at least
"acceptable."

     In what ways do the dialectics and relationships between self
and other evolve from the first to the second phase? Why is this
element so crucial in the evolution of the treatment of outsideness's
manifestations?

     The ways in which the shift takes place are really manifold and
heterogeneous, involving many different themes and their represen-

---

3. "Members of the Royal Anthropological Institute burned the thing and
threw the locket into a well, and some of them do not admit that Arthur
Jermyn ever existed" (*D* 82).

tations, a fact that shows the capillarity and centrality of the issue.

In the first phase, which approximately ends with "The Call of Cthulhu" and *The Case of Charles Dexter Ward* (1927), these being two transition tales toward the second phase, the relationship between self and other is dominated by the following processes, logically consequent and in some cases even simultaneous:

a. (unauthorized) *intrusion:* typically, but not exclusively, of the other onto the dimension of the self;

b. *assimilation:* of the self into the dimension of the other;

c. *merging, fusion:* which leads to destructive consequences for the integrity and survival of the self;

d. *prevarication:* of the other over the self.

As noted, the forms in which these processes take place are manifold, but they all entail an inevitable conflict between self and other: the other appears under the masks of any intrusion of the rationally inexplicable into the human dimension. It is already meaningful that Lovecraft cannot see any other "vestige" for the other but under these hostile-to-man ways. Of the countless possible passages that could demonstrate my argument, some extremely well-known and over-quoted, I choose one so far mostly overlooked by Lovecraft commentators. In "The Rats in the Walls," the narrator even reveals that, during his and his group's descent along the stair below the cellar in Exham Priory, everyone noticed that "the passage, according to the direction of the strokes, must have been chiselled *from beneath*" (*DH* 41; Lovecraft's italics). This notation resembles a reference to the inner *malignity* of outsideness, to the fact that the other craves for the destruction of the self: the other must not be looked for, it even digs its own way toward the surface and toward the destruction of the self, which cannot escape this destiny, being represented as a victim of the other's plots.

In the first phase, manifestations of outsideness may be decayed corpses in a burial ground luring the living through an attempt at psychic possession ("The Tomb"), a ghoul concealed in the catacombs under Boston ("Pickman's Model"), a storm of rats scurrying along the walls of an ancient priory ("The Rats in the Walls"), a gigantic fishy creature emerging from the slimy sea and obsessing the protagonist far beyond his physical escape ("Dagon," 1917), etc. In the second phase, analogous figurative elements are chosen to depict the occurrence of outsideness's manifestations: what changes, as we will see, is the perception and the filtering that the characters' subjectivity applies to these manifestations, actually modifying their appearance, impact, and ultimately their signified for the human perceiver (who is the only perceiver that counts in Lovecraft's literature).

One introductory question that the interpreter should posit, and to which no answer has been provided up to now in Lovecraftian studies, concerns the original source of the encounter between self and other: is the "first step" in the process made by the self or by the other? In other words: which goes toward the other? In both phases, the contact between self and other appears as inevitable: in fact, the other never ceases to attract and fascinate the self. The relationship is ambiguous: the self senses terror and repulsion toward the other, but also a strong drive to go further and effect the "union," or at least, the encounter and confrontation. It is really like an attraction/repulsion dialectics: fascination and amazement (and, in phase 2, also thirst for knowledge)—which push toward an encounter—are ambiguously mixed with horror and repulsion, with the instinct of self-preservation that lacerates the subject and also lures it toward a withdrawal. The conflict between these contrasting drives is also what renders the self-other dialectics particularly complex and tantalizing in Lovecraft's fiction.

In phase 1, the contact and confrontation between self and other inevitably lead to a *prevarication* of the other on the self. And it must be noted that the irruption and the attack of the other against the dimension of the self may stem either from a *physical* invasion from outside (i.e., in the case that the other resides *outside* the physical borders of the self), or from the inside of the self (i.e., from within the physical borders of the body: see "Dagon," "The Outsider," "The Rats in the Walls," where the harbingers of outsideness can be interpreted as creatures depicted—and given substance—by the characters' interiority). I believe it is not particularly relevant, even to achieve a thorough understanding of Lovecraft's poetics, to establish the provenance, whether internal or external, of the forces of outsideness, since in Lovecraft the manifestations of the other are always revelatory, whatever form they assume or source they are produced by: what really matters in terms of their signification is the *perception* that the characters' subjectivities experience when forced to cope with them. Certainly, the fact that the source of outsideness and thus of the horror often lies in the inside leads to a representation of the human interiority as a "psychological geometry," i.e., as a labyrinthic architecture, as a confused and chaotic (i.e., not clearly signifying) mixture of overlapping elements, from which ancestral horrors may surface almost in a physical way, finding the route to resurrect at light.

Often this "irruption → attack" phenomenon takes the form of a fusion/merging of the two dimensions, through a process of cancellation of the borders that brings destructive consequences for the self. This fusion can be either physical or spiritual: physical, for instance in "Jermyn," where the sexual intercourse between a member of the human race and one of the primates is alluded to, and spiritual, for instance in "The Music of Erich Zann" (1921), in which the union occurs between a human being, the titular musician, and the weird notes produces by his cello. What is shared by the different representations of the fusion is their effecting of a condition of chaos, disorder, and lack of harmony, all especially abhorred by Lovecraft as the signs of the ultimate decadence of civilization and reason: the only possible contact with the other leads to chaos and disorder, which destroy harmony and reason in the human dimension. This is why most of the humans depicted in the stories of the first phase end up insane or suicidal, or die, or *regress to a primitive state* ("The Lurking Fear" and "The Rats in the Walls"). These two stories are also extremely revelatory of Lovecraft's horror for everything that is merging and confusion: in "The Lurking Fear," the physical unions between consanguineous members lead, over the generations, to a progressive degeneration and regression along the evolutionary scale. This is the description of the last "product" of this abominable degeneration of human beings:

> . . . a filthy whitish gorilla thing with sharp yellow fangs and matted fur. It was the ultimate product of mammalian degeneration; the frightful outcome of isolated spawning, multiplication, and cannibal nutrition above and below the ground; the embodiment of all the snarling chaos and grinning fear that lurk behind life. (D 199)

Outsideness is manifested also in the lack of harmony and order, as in Exham Priory's twilit grotto, whose floor is made up of a blasphemous mix of bones, architectural styles, and skeletons belonging to creatures from different stages on the evolutionary scale. The physical chaos is indeed also a harbinger of moral and psychological chaos. In phase 1, that of the mythical—and not yet scientific—discourse, cultural and biological diversity, far from representing a value or a topic to research, generates a sense of *error* that easily converts into a sense of *horror*.

Why does the merging of self and other have, among its consequences, that of effecting a condition of disorder and chaos? This is because outsideness, in Lovecraft, means also *alienity*, and thus the self's merging with it leads to an *incongruous and blasphemous matching of the self with the different-from-the-self.* Outsideness is manifested in the uncontrolled irruption of the different into the semiotic dimension of the self, after which they start to live together, while an abusing other imposes its nature on the self, in a sort of noxious hug.[4] The semiotic nature of the self gets dissolved in this merging with the different. The self loses its boundaries, and its semiotic growth is interrupted: since its physical integrity is endangered and ultimately made impossible, the self *stops to signify.* The merging with the other is a process that leads both to *mixing and, consequently, the loss of identities.* This problem is well represented by an entity like Nyarlathotep. This deity embodies an effective synthesis of the chaos and disorder of outsideness for a multiplicity of reasons: not only is Nyarlathotep often represented as residing in black pits, but he is often depicted as the god of camouflage and deceit, one deprived of a stable identity, who is continuously changing. He is sometimes defined as "faceless god," "crawling chaos," "multiform and unlocalized": all features where confusion and disorder play a major role, and where it is impossible to isolate a clear and stable identity. Lovecraft has also devised another powerful figure sharing at least one of Nyarlathotep's features in regard to the identity issue: the creatures known as "night-

---

4. This is of course reminiscent of Lovecraft's early abhorrence of all forms of fusions: of foreign races with the WASPs, of immigrants' blood with that of the Anglo-Saxon, but also of different architectural styles, a tendency that was endangering the survival of his beloved colonial style in New England.

gaunts," who share the random Nyarlathotep's characteristic of being faceless. Thus chaos and outsideness may stem from such different sources as the absence (Nyarlathotep, night-gaunts) or mixing (mongrels, interbreeding) of identities, and the lack of order and harmony.

The recurrent theme of the *blasphemous merging* and the chaos it conveys may be represented by several different "pairs": interbreeding, the merging of different human races (such as Caucasians and African Americans), of creatures from different stages of the evolutionary scale, of architectural styles, etc. Other categories of the eventual eruption of the narrative conflict stemming from this self-other matching can be found in the association of modernity vs. antiquity, of light vs. darkness (often the deities from outside, in the first phase, are depicted as dwelling in dark/black realms of obscurity, as Nyarlathotep), of reason vs. superstition/religion. All these categories are meant to stay clearly separate, and to respect their reciprocal borders: whenever the boundaries get overstepped, the narrative conflict typical of Lovecraft's first phase (and of most mythical discourses, according to Bakhtin) erupts.

The human regression to a primitive state represents a specific case of the disorder/chaos problem discussed above, one that often recurs in the stories of the first phase: phenomena like crossbreeding, merging of different races, miscegenation (disorder in the genetic inheritance that inevitably reemerges in the modern descendants of a cursed spawn[5]), together with that of atavistic regression (an impossible union between the self and an other that is now represented by the dimension of the past) are employed by Lovecraft to show the destructive consequences of the fusion between self

---

5. In the first phase, Lovecraft often gives to the manifestations of outsideness the character of the inevitable descent of the guilts of the ancestors upon their modern descendants: the faults of the past come back, sometimes literally as a genetic patrimony inscribed in the DNA, to haunt the contemporaries when they commit the mistake of recreating a contact with them, through the attempt—more or less intentionally—to *reactivate* or *escape* them. It is *inevitable*, Lovecraft says, that the guilts of our ancestors (i.e., of our past) affect us and demand of us their tribute of horror: in other words, it is not possible to dodge the other that is in us, so much so that it is even coded into our DNA.

and other. Chaos may take the form of the horrible fusion between a human and an ape ("Jermyn"), of consanguineous unions ("The Lurking Fear"), and of the regression to a primitive cannibalistic state ("The Lurking Fear," "The Rats in the Walls"). Lovecraft's discourse involves therefore a harsh criticism against primitivism, a philosophical attitude that was widely debated during the modern history of Western thought (starting from the eighteenth-century Enlightenment) and was actually the central topic of countless literary works over the two centuries preceding Lovecraft.[6] In his decision to join in his fiction the debate over the consequences of primitivism, Lovecraft was influenced not only by literary or historical sources, but also by the reading of Thomas Henry Huxley's "Man's Place in Nature" (1863). In his Darwinian treatise, the English biologist claimed that the contemporary, civilized man had savage origins, in particular that the human race had, among its ancestors, semi-bestial creatures such as manlike apes. And Huxley placed a question: should the modern artist and philosopher feel degraded by the incontrovertible fact that they directly descend from some brutish and subhuman savage creature, whose intelligence is barely enough to make it superior to a fox? According to Huxley, the answer should be negative. According to Lovecraft, no doubt it would be positive: suffice to read, among a number of possible sources, just a single tale: "Arthur Jermyn," with its man(self)-ape(other) hybridization leading to the catastrophe for its modern descendants, since the blasphemous merging activates the genes of bestiality, violence, and savagery in the human DNA.

Also, the act of cannibalism related in "The Rats in the Walls" (and alluded to in "The Lurking Fear"[7]) may be interpreted as a

---

6. Most of these works (not limited to the fantastic genre, but also involving the adventure and "popular" ones), let us note incidentally, shared Lovecraft's worried warning about the disastrous consequences of a merging of self and other, of Western civilization and primitive cultures—if not of the human race and non-human animal species. This is also the reason why, while the first phase of Lovecraft's fiction can be considered more "traditional," the second one—with its turning over of the perspectives on the self-other dialectics—configures a significant innovation for the genre of the literary *weird*.

7. "cannibal nutrition above and below the ground" (*D* 199).

powerful image employed by Lovecraft to depict the abhorred fusion of self and other, as well as the loss of the self: the form is now that of taking possession of the *body* of the other, that of fusing one's self into the other to such an extent that even the physical barrier is erased. An act like cannibalism is a sort of supreme form, of sublimation of chaos and of outsideness, an act that cannot but generate in Lovecraft an "inundating cataclysm of voiceless horror" ("The Lurking Fear" [*D* 199]). Paul Montelone remarks that the employment of the eater/eaten dichotomy is indeed revelatory of the depiction of a universe dominated by chaos, as well as of the ultimate inanity of existence:

> The eater/eaten dichotomy, which instantiates itself in most brutally in his [Delapore's] devouring of Norrys, becomes in its last stage of the narrative an emblem for existence, for that hideousness of life wich Lovecraft imperfectly realized in "Jermyn." ... Schopenhauer [also] uses the eater/eaten dichotomy as a way of demonstrating the pain of life and accordingly as support for pessimism.... Delapore spontaneously translates acts other than literal ingestion into the terms of eater/eaten dichotomy. The war "ate" his son, the Yanks "ate" his family homestead, the fire "ate" the family secret. In other words, he is using the dichotomy as a way of representing the pain of his own life. But the representation does not stop with this. It is taken just one step further. (24–25)

In the first phase, the other is depicted as a gnawing worm that dwells within the self and, metaphorically, devours it: from this, the eater-eaten metaphor stems. From the encounter with the other—an encounter made even more inevitable when the other is depicted as dwelling within the self—the Self realizes the non-sense and the sorrow of life, the inanity of existence (Schopenhauer): in phase 1, Lovecraft's is a harsh pessimism.

The loss of identity brings along psychological horror,[8] alienation

---

8. Airaksinen agrees that "the ultimate horror is connected to the loss of the self. This happens to Lovecraft and his heroes, although none of them succeeds in explicating it. How could they? They are in the process of getting lost and thus losing themselves. The situation does not make it any easier to tell what is happening. A nonentity, who knows what he or she is, is a paradox ... How could that which is nothing speculate on and

and amorality (let us think of the ironic despise for morality displayed by a character like Herbert West), insanity, but also *loss of the body:* when the borders between self and other are blurred, the body's physical delimitations are also threatened. The self *gets separated from itself.* The encounter with the other provokes the scission from one's semiotic self: contact is lost with it. The only possible consequence is that the self goes searching for the lost identity, and for its own now alienated body. Indeed the contact with the other leads to the *alienization* of the self.

This is the philosophical reason behind themes like cannibalism and genetic regression: the self tries to repossess the body, an attempt destined to a tragic failure, since it is not by eating the other's body that the self can regain its own. It is not by regressing to a primitive state ("The Rats in the Walls"), or by "possessing" the body of consanguineous members ("The Lurking Fear"), or by giving life to corpses ("Herbert West—Reanimator"), or by having an ambiguous psychic intercourse with them ("The Tomb") that the self can find again the body, by now irremediably lost in the magma of the other. The stories of the first phase illustrate the doomed-to-fail effort of the self to cope with the loss of identity consequent to the irruption of the other into the self's own dimension.

The analysis is further complicated by the fact that in his first phase, with the literary representations of the fusion between self and other, Lovecraft also gives voice to a loss of the self that somehow reflects also a liberation from inhibitions: the loss of identity leads, in a sense, also to the surpassing of the physical and biological limits of the self. But what is discovered, in this annihilation of inhibitions, is confusion, chaos, a destructive eruption of the instincts into sheer disorder: exactly what Lovecraft abhorred. In the second phase, on the contrary, contact with outsideness still leads to a liberation of the instincts; but the approach is totally different, since the perception of the same event by the filtering subjectivity has totally changed. In the second phase, the liberation of the instincts must be positively quested for, since it is now perceived as the release from the inhibitions that limit freedom and the full expression

communicate what is going on?" (31). Employing the term "nonentity," Airaksinen pays homage to Lovecraft's autobiographical essay "Some Notes on a Nonentity" (1933; *CE* 5.207–11).

of the potentialities of the mind (let us just think of the non-Euclidean geometries depicted in many of the mature tales), it is perceived as the possibility—or better, the illusion—of defying and defeating the "galling limitations of time, space, and natural law which forever imprison us and frustrate our curiosity about the infinite cosmic space beyond the radius of our sight and analysis" ("Notes on Writing Weird Fiction," *CE* 2.176).

In the first phase, anything related to the manifestations of outsidess, being so dangerous for the survival and integrity of the self, is seen in Lovecraft's fiction as potentially dangerous, something that must be marginalized, suffocated, and eventually eliminated, often through the action of the figure of the *insignis vir*, the performer of atrocious acts that are necessary in order to reestablish the violated *status quo* and sweep all the destabilizing forces away. There is no comprehension or interpretation possible: no compromise or mediation between self and other; only conflict can emerge from their encounter.

This is of course a conservative and traditional perspective on horror literature, the one of the classic Gothic tale and of most genre writers prior to Lovecraft. His production of the first phase follows this pattern and constitutes a warming-up for the innovative elements that will appear in the second phase and that will contribute to effect the Copernican revolution Lovecraft introduces in the *weird*.

In the second phase, in fact, Lovecraft embraces a more critical and ironic perspective over traditional horror, and comes to devise a self-other dialectics that leaves room for dialogue and confrontation.

Lovecraft's characters undergo a huge evolution in their perception of the manifestations of outsideness. The discourse of the narrators becomes scientific because, gradually and with some transition passages starting from the writing of "The Call of Cthulhu," the self of the characters starts to perceive the other no longer as an entity to be marginalized and rejected, no longer as a source of error/horror, but as one of rational astonishment and scientific interest. The self develops an interest in the other because *Lovecraft's fiction becomes aware that not only merging—and destruction—are possible between self and other*, but also a respect of the reciprocal boundaries that leads to *rational curiosity*, to the awareness that scientific investigation can be pursued having the other as its object. This epochal shift is precisely what takes place in the later Lovecraftian output and in works such as *At the Mountains of Madness* (1931), "The Shadow over Innsmouth" (1931), and "The Shadow out of Time" (1934–35). This evolution follows a new consideration of the manifestation of the other from the viewpoint of the characters' subjectivity: in phase 1, the irruption of the other was effected by *supernatural entities* (as in traditional Gothic and weird fiction), and especially had, as its protagonists, deities that were not subjected to physical, biological, or natural laws (they were indeed super-natural). And in that case, outsideness was to be fought and feared, and Lovecraft's approach was that of a writer of supernatural literature. The evolution of his characters' perception[9] leads them to consider the harbingers of outsideness no longer as supernatural deities, but as *extraterrestrial beings*, i.e., non-supernatural creatures, simply non-terrestrial ones. This "ontological" shift leads Lovecraft's art toward a non-supernatural, cosmic, and scientific discourse: since the harbingers of outsideness are now extraterrestrials, they have to be approached and investigated through *scientific* tools (of course, natural and human sciences fall short in this attempt, but this does not imply that human beings should not try: in that case, they will resort to non-human, non-terrestrial sciences) and through *irony*—a rational tool *par excellence*. And on the meta-literary level, of course Lovecraft shifts from the "epic" to the "novelistic" frame (not accidentally, it is in his second phase that he conceives and writes the lengthiest works and those that most resemble the status of novels). In "The Rats in the Walls," a linguistic spy helps to clarify the transition, since Lovecraft even employs the expression "epic of the rats" (*DH* 31): the manifestation of the rats (i.e., of outsideness) is therefore considered an epic-mythical event, a supernatural one that may then respond to the canons of the Bakhtinian "epic discourse." In the stories of the second phase, the manifestations of outsideness are not "epic-

---

9. The role played by the characters' perception in the evolution of Lovecraft's outsideness is crucial: it is in fact plain that *all the manifestations of outsideness occur only and just when the human perceiver is there to register them*. This is a trait that remains constant between phase 1 and 2 of Lovecraft's output.

mythical" events anymore, but *scientific facts* to be scanned with the microscope and dissected with the scalpel.

Schematically:

Phase	Role of outsideness	Literary discourse	The harbingers of outsideness
1	The Different = the *evil horror* to be fought	Mythical; Epic; Supernatural fiction	Supernatural deities not subjected any natural law[10]
2	The Different = the *unknown element* to be made known and integrated	Scientific; Novelistic; Non-supernatural cosmic art	Extraterrestrials subjected to (non-terrestrial) natural laws

Therefore, it is not outsideness that changes its nature from phase 1 to phase 2: the old nomenclature, including Yog-Sothoth, Azathoth, Shub-Niggurath, Nyarlathotep, the *Necronomicon*, etc., remains there and no intrinsic evolution takes place.[11] The change affects

---

10. The sheer devising of the names by which Lovecraft labels these entities points to their supernatural/mythical nature, thanks to the clear reference to Egyptian and Greek mythologies: "Nyarlathotep," "Azathoth," "Yog-Sothoth," "Shub-Niggurath," etc., among others, remind us of Egyptian deities such as Thoth, Horus, etc. In a phase 1 tale like "The Rats in the Walls," in order to oppose Nyarlathotep (deity of darkness and deceit), the narrator is able to employ only references to Horus and Thoth, the gods of rationality: Delapore refers in fact to Nigger-Man as darting like a "winged Egyptian god" (DH 44), whereas the major winged Egyptian gods were Horus (the hawk-god, adversary of evil entities) and Thoth (the deity of rationality). In phase 1, only the mythical discourse applies to outsideness: a discourse of sheer, brutal contraposition between the rational (Horus, Thoth) and the supernatural/chaotic (Nyarlathotep). No compromise is possible: the different (the immigrant, the irrational, the degraded, the non-civilized, the primitive, etc.) must be eradicated, and the only possible tools to do so are classical reason, order, and harmony.

11. Let us reflect for instance on the figure of Nyarlathotep as herald of outsideness: in the first phase, for example in "The Rats in the Walls," he is triggering horrors (the rats) that lead to the destruction of the protagonist Delapore. In the second phase, as in *The Dream-Quest of Unknown Kadath* (1926–27), Nyarlathotep is still depicted as a protean and deceitful harbinger of chaos, but no longer as a supernatural divinity, as Randolph Carter will be allowed to meet him, talk with him, and even discuss and make agreements.

only the subjectivity of the characters (or Lovecraftian masks; see below)—a change that leads to a new perception of the different: what, previously, was perceived as horror/chaos that must be fought, turns into an *object of scientific inquiry*. The shift configures the transition toward, first, a relativistic and anti-anthropocentric perspective, and later, to the surpassing even of this phase and the final introduction of a theme like *alien socialism* or *humanism*, perhaps the highest pinnacle achieved by Lovecraft's fiction in its innovative effort.

Perspectives are overturned: in phase 1, outsideness is perceived as negative also because, thanks to the encounter with it, the self discovers the nonsense and the horror of its own real nature. In the stories of phase 1, typically the character discovers the truth about his horrible past and his real nature, is shocked by the revelation, and thus goes insane or dies, sometimes even regresses to a primitive or subhuman state: there is *no rational way to cope with the horror of the discovery*; Lovecraft's discourse is not scientific. The reason is that the self's *perception is still immature*: the character lies in a not fully semiotic state, he does not produce signs and meanings properly, and thus his perceptions are flawed and biased. He is still in the *infantile step of his semiotic development*. In phase 1, after the encounter with the other, the search of the self for its lost identity, body, and ultimately of its sense is doomed to fail, since the subject still lies in a childhood of reason: he believes in ghosts and in the supernatural, *he is immature from the semiotic viewpoint because he is unable to recognize the alterity of the other*. The self of the subject is more or less forced to try to incorporate/dominate the other and make it its own: the inevitable effect of this inopportune mixing and merging is the loss of the self. Aspiring to possess the other, not only the self fails, but also loses itself.[12] If the self is not active in the

---

12. It should be also noted that, in the first phase, the self's attempt to possess the other involves the linguistic level also: of course this attempt fails, so much so that the language of the self is degraded to a state of incomprehensible confusion and chaos (reflecting the same process that occurs for the self's own identity and physical body). One may just think of the nonsensical blabbering that Delapore utters at the end of his regression process in "The Rats in the Walls": the self tries to describe the other using a language that it does not master, and that becomes totally incomprehen-

fusion process, it is the other that leads it: the two poles of the dialectics try to incorporate each other, assuming on one's self the practices of the other.

In the stories of phase 2, on the contrary, the *very same discoveries* made by the self generate acceptation: the self's recognition of its hideous nature and provenience does not entail horror, insanity, repulsion. The self comes to realize (since it has now grown to a more mature semiotic state) that the sheer fact that the encounter with outsideness has the power to unleash hideous revelations *does not necessarily imply that outsideness is "evil" or must be fought*. In phase 1, this was the flawed perception of the self: it was aware of a somehow intrinsic evil of the other, as a result of an immature state of perception. The encounter with the other was the key event provoking the hideous discoveries on the part of the self, for instance that the human race has a low and irrelevant position in the economy of the universe: since it was still semiotically immature, a phase-1 self considered its mission that of perpetrating the illusion

---

sible, since the "unnamable" is not describable. On the other hand, in the second phase the voice of the self recognizes its own insufficiency and incapability to describe/name the other (i.e., to possess it linguistically), and accepts this limitation, since it is moved by a scientific attitude: Heisenberg's uncertainty principle had stated that modern natural science could not claim any pretension to perfection, it had to admit its limits and its incapability to account for all the dimensions of existence. Science, as language, has to recognize its epistemic limits. Therefore, in phase 2 Lovecraft's scientific discourse does not show the mythical presumption to dominate otherness and possess its language: it is a discourse that does not claim to exhaust all the descriptive possibilities of the other, but just to approach the other with the necessary distance and scientific, linguistic "respect." "The Call of Cthulhu" is again an emblematic work in the accomplishment of this transition: the subject is Thurston, and the linguistic chaos of the human language in front of the manifestations of outsideness (a chaos that, in phase 1, had no solution: see "The Rats in the Walls") leads to *acceptation:* the language—or the attempt to reproduce it through the human language, i.e., human reason—of the other is no longer a source of insanity and death: "R'lyeh" and "Cthulhu" are transcribed into our characters, and the evil couplet from the *Necronomicon* ("That is not dead which can eternal lie, / And with strange aeons even death may die") is *translated into English*. This is a fine example of the scientific approach of the second phase at work also on the linguistic level.

that the human species occupies a privileged place in the universal scheme and, even worse, in the plans of a benign demiurge. This was the biased perception that automatically triggered a negative consideration of outsideness. In phase 2, on the contrary, perception has matured and the self has learned to accept its ontological inferiority and the inanity of its myths of greatness (not by chance, the previous one was the mythical phase of the self), truths all revealed by the encounter with the other: the self now adopts a more mature and, above all, properly *scientific* attitude. This should be, in Lovecraft's view, the transition from the infancy to the adulthood of the semiotic self, but also of Western civilization *tout court*.

Moreover, while in phase 1 the character seems to be totally passive in the face of the manifestations of outsideness, which display the uncontested power to condition the fate of the character in full—and the character cannot even try to subtract himself from outsideness's influence—in the second phase another aspect of the maturation of the character concerns his capability to choose voluntarily, to discern between acceptation and refusal of what the other proposes: while in "The Rats in the Walls" Delapore is unable to choose consciously and defend against the attack of outsideness and of his own genes claiming their tribute on him and not leaving any possible alternative (so that he regresses to a primitive state and turns into a cannibal: he cannot but follow the drives inscribed in his genetic code[13]), in phase 2 the regression to a horrible primitive state by a character like the protagonist of "The Shadow over Innsmouth" (1931) is the *result of an intentional choice* and of a conscious acceptation of his own past: he decides to accept the call of his genes and return to the sea, in order to join the descendants of

---

13. Delapore ends his account with these words, which some interpreters have considered a puerile attempt at rejecting accusations, but in whose literal sense I instead believe: "When I speak of poor Norrys they accuse me of a hideous thing [having eaten his body], but they must know that I did not do it. They must know it was the rats" (*DH* 45). Literally, it *was* Delapore eating Norrys's body; but of course he is right when he blames the rats, since he was just driven to eat Norrys by the "scurrying" rats in the walls, the messengers from outsideness who provoked his insanity and his yielding to the calls of his genetic code. The other made Delapore a victim in order to destroy his self.

his old ancestors, a race of half-human and half-fish creatures bearing the unmistakable "Innsmouth look."[14]

Another example of the evolution of the perception of outsideness may help to clarify this notion: while in phase 1 the absence/mixing of identities consequent to the encounter between self and other originates "mythical" horror (let us recall the figures of Nyarlathotep and of the night-gaunts, or the "Jermyn" story as well as the New York tales), in the second phase *the very same mixing* is a source of scientific curiosity and investigation: in "The Shadow out of Time" the mind-exchange process between Prof. Peaslee and the extraterrestrial member of the Great Race triggers a true "cultural exchange" between the human and the alien races, separated by incalculable distances in space and time but animated by a very similar scientific attitude and thirst for knowledge. These are decisive changes: while in phase 1 the discovery of the hideous nature of the single individual (especially because the individual is involved in phase 1, not the entire human race: see section 4 of this article) entails horror, insanity, destruction, in phase 2 the discovery of the irrelevant position that the human race occupies in the cosmic scheme of things bears totally different consequences. And even the discovery, made by the Miskatonic expedition in Antarctica in *At the Mountains of Madness*, that earth-life was concocted as "jest or mistake" (*MM* 22) by the Old Ones filtered from the stars aeons ago represents of course a shocking revelation, one that causes the character to lose "peace and balance" (*MM* 28), but not one that makes Prof. Dyer go insane or regress to a cannibalic state. Dyer is a "white" Lovecraftian mask (see next section of this article), he is a

---

14. Once he realizes that he bears this look himself, the unnamed protagonist *intentionally* chooses to join his fishy fellows: he would have other options, but he chooses to embrace the other that lies in himself: "I shall plan my cousin's escape from that Canton madhouse, and together we shall go to marvel-shadowed Innsmouth. We shall swim out to that brooding reef in the sea and dive down through black abysses to Cyclopean and many-columned Y'hanthlei, and in that lair of the Deep Ones we shall dwell amidst wonder and glory for ever" (*DH* 367). The intentionality of this choice is perhaps even reinforced by the fact that this last sentence is a clear parody of Psalm 23:6: "Surely goodness and mercy shall follow me all the days of my life: and I will dwell in the house of the Lord for ever."

"man of science," his self is semiotically mature and he has learned to embark on the contact with the other—and the revelations the process entails, no matter how "bleak"—with a scientific approach.

Again with reference to "The Shadow out of Time," it can be noticed how the very theme of "mind exchange" reaches a maturation that even in the short novel *The Case of Charles Dexter Ward*, a transition story toward phase 2, was not achieved in full. In this latter story, the wizard and necromancer Joseph Curwen (dead for more than a century, in 1771) resurges to psychic life exploiting the body of his modern descendant Charles Dexter Ward, which Curwen overcomes and invades, taking possession over the young man's psychic faculties. In this case, it is the other that tries successfully to invade the self, and the relationship that the process entails between the two poles is still based on conflict: there is fight and contrast, though the two dimensions live together for a while in a state of forced "cohabitation." In phase 2, this theme of forced cohabitation is present in "The Shadow out of Time," but its treatment is significantly different: the exchange self-other, though still superimposed by the other over the self, occurs in a peaceful and "productive" way for both partakers, and with openly scientific and cultural goals as objectives.

Another analogous case: the genetic regression and the interbreeding, that in "The Rats in the Walls" and "Jermyn" provoke horror, insanity, and death, in "The Shadow over Innsmouth" cause amazement, "scientific" marvel, and intellectual curiosity in the protagonist, who is brought to a serene acceptation of his destiny—again inscribed in his DNA, just as for many protagonists of the phase 1 stories—as a member of the human-fish interbred race.

We can therefore provisionally conclude that in the second phase the subject matures, refines his reason and capacity to discern, becomes semiotically adult and understands that, in order to "signify," he does not need to dominate the other: it is enough to learn to respect it. Of course, this semiotic maturation of the subject's self does not alter the substance: the manifestations of outsideness still remain as the literary heralds and harbingers of the deep inanity of human experience, of its irrelevance on the cosmic scale, of the bleakness of the universal laws and of the ultimate nonsense and purposelessness of human experience: what changes is the way in which the self renders this outsideness/alterity signifying. If, while semiotically immature, in phase 1 the self perceives this same alterity as destructive (the self is anthropocentric and intends to dominate the other), in phase 2 the self becomes aware that *just recognizing its own inferiority and its own limits it makes itself signifying*, since it assigns to itself the most appropriate meaning (that of being a transient and puny self, whose experience in the lifeworld is not destined to leave a mark in the history of a mechanistic and indifferent universe dominated by the laws of chaos): it is only by achieving this awareness that *the self really starts to signify*.

A clear consequence of the evolution described above is its transition, on philosophic and aesthetic grounds, from a more traditional, Gothic-like anthropocentric perspective to a full-fledged cosmicistic and relativistic one. This is the direct consequence, and the inevitable premise, for Lovecraft's literary shift toward a non-supernatural cosmic art: only through the endorsement of a relativistic perspective on the philosophical ground is it possible to inform the literary treatment with the scientific discourse. And the other way around: the scientific discourse, with the neutral attitude it entails, leads necessarily to a reconsideration of the moral implications of the object, the nature and the results of the analysis: nothing is morally or metaphysically good or evil anymore, when described and studied within a scientific perspective. In Lovecraft's view, the object of the scientific interest turns somehow positive, even only for the fact that the very same token was previously considered morally evil (in the immaturity of the mythical discourse applied to it) and also because it now arouses a rational curiosity that ultimately leads to the acquisition of some truth (and for Lovecraft truth, no matter how hideous and debasing, is always a positive achievement).

Cosmicism takes on the characters of a mechanistic and materialistic philosophy. The manifestations of outsideness are revealed as the tokens of an *outer reality* that shocks human certainties and perceptions (the five senses are fallacious in the interpretation of these manifestations), the laws of human sciences, and of course human philosophical convictions (for instance, the anthropocentric perspective in literature and philosophy is shown as groundless: the very notion of the supposed centrality of the human race and history on the cosmic scale is to be discarded as a puerile fantasy). Lovecraft achieves this literary effect by embracing a cosmic perspective on the narrated material, and by abandoning the biased and ultimately irrelevant human viewpoint on the lifeworld, which comes to be depicted as a mechanistic domain where there is no room for the divine, the supernatural, a notion like a preordained "fate" and any benevolence by a superior demiurge toward the human race. These are the key philosophical tenets of Lovecraft's *cosmic art*, whose poetics will prove revolutionary for the later development of the weird genre.

Still, one question remains unanswered: *why* does Lovecraft effect this shift toward a non-supernatural cosmic art? Why this significant change in his literary poetics? The answer is complex and requires more space than this article allows. For now suffice it to say, with reference to the specific scope of this paper, that in his second phase Lovecraft decides to cease depicting outsideness as supernatural for an aesthetic reason: he comes to realize that the supernatural *has lost the power to affect his emotions*. Or at least, the supernatural is no longer able to generate emotion as much as the representation of the sense of illusion provided by the violation of the galling limitations of time and space, as the literary depiction of the (temporary) interruption of the laws of nature and of their dominance on humankind.[15] In the second phase of his fiction, Lovecraft decides to represent the sense of liberation from the bounds that Nature imposes over humanity, from the limitations to which human beings are tied by their incapability, for instance, to live in more than three dimensions, to travel in time, to move in-

---

15. In a letter to E. Hoffmann Price dated August 15, 1934, Lovecraft clarifies this point: "No one ever wrote a story yet without some real emotional drive behind it—and I have not that drive except where violations of the natural order . . ., defiances and evasions of time, space, and cosmic law . . . are concerned. Just why this is so I haven't the slightest idea—it simply *is* so. I am interested only in broad pageants—historic streams—orders of biological, chemical, physical and astronomical organisation—and the only conflict which has any deep emotional significance to me is that of *the principle of freedom or irregularity or adventurous opportunity against the eternal and maddening rigidity of cosmic law* . . . especially the laws of *time*" (*SL* 4.18–20).

stantly in space, to be simultaneously in more than one place, to experience existence with more numerous and refined senses. This is part of the Copernican revolution mentioned by Leiber, and it pushes Lovecraft's fiction many steps forward in comparison to the other writers of coeval and past times. And of course it is hardly to be denied that this revolution represents the *literary* reflection, thanks to the introduction of a "horror of relativity," of Lovecraft's absorption of the *scientific* revolution that took place in the first decades of the twentieth century with the advances in physics and other fields achieved by scientists such as Albert Einstein, Max Planck, and Werner Heisenberg.

However, this process leading from a supernatural to a non-supernatural cosmic art represents just an intermediate phase in the aesthetic maturation of Lovecraft's fiction. The further step, from the aesthetic and thematic viewpoints, is constituted by the shift toward the *alien socialism* mentioned above, whereas the relativistic, anti-anthropocentric perspective is even surpassed in favor of an almost brotherly sense of similarity and community between totally different beings (as a human and an Old One or an extraterrestrial of the Great Race might be) *through intellect*. In fact, in spite of how *different* and alien some creatures may be, they are after all *men*, just thanks to the existence in them of logic and of coherent and creative mental processes. Just like humankind, then, the civilizations of the extraterrestrials—in spite of their alterity—are subject to the cycle of creation and destruction, development and dissolution that marks, materialistically and mechanistically, the (human) community in an absolutely chaotic and unpredictable way.[16] I propose to define this new theme (appearing from 1931

16. Emblematic at this level is the well-known quotation from *At the Mountains of Madness*, whereas the narrator William Dyer utters this sentence, toward the end of the story and after having perused the cardinal steps in the history of the civilization of the Old Ones (steps that appeared so dramatically similar, in their inevitable cyclicity, to those of any human civilization): "... poor Lake, poor Gedney ... and poor Old Ones! Scientists to the last—what had they done that we would not have done in their place? God, what intelligence and persistence! What a facing of the incredible, just as those carven kinsmen and forbears had faced things only a little less incredible! Radiates, vegetables, monstrosities, star spawn—whatever they had been, they were men!" (*MM* 96).

onwards) generated by the second phase of Lovecraft's poetics as
alien humanism or *socialism*, a theme that marks a period in which
the achievements of the second phase come to their most mature
consequences in the dialectics between self and other: the evolution
of the perceptive skills of the self, and its semiotic maturation, lead
to a process of *socialization* of the other, to its more effective inte-
gration into the self. It would perhaps be too hazardous to claim
that outsideness becomes now *insideness* (the fusion of self and
other still conflicts with scientific laws, both terrestrial and "other"),
but certainly the new self is now able to accept the other through
the recognition of the latter's non-supernatural nature as a value to
treasure, and not a threat to fight. So long as the other is considered
supernatural, as intrinsically *alien* to the self, the other scares, terri-
fies, and is the enemy that must be fought and marginalized (this is
the classic Gothic version of the problem, and even the Lovecraftian first phase). But from the moment when both Lovecraft
and his masks realize that the other represents the necessary pole of
a dialectics aiming at making *both poles* (self and other) *signify*, and
from the moment when Lovecraft and his masks realize the fundamental similarities that the poles share, then space is left for the acceptation and revaluation of the other.

The introduction and representation of the theme of *alien humanism* perhaps represents the most advanced achievement Lovecraft realized in his path towards the renovation of the *weird* genre.

In concluding this section, it must be definitely highlighted that,
taking into account the specific reference to the implications derived from the devising of a non-supernatural cosmic art, and considering the constant "negotiation" that his fiction entertains with
the tradition of the weird genre (often criticized and addressed in an
openly ironic way), Lovecraft's discourse appears clearly to place at
its center of interest the *discussion about the very foundations of the
fantastic genre in literature.* Lovecraft explores the means and limits
of this genre, and re-founds it on new bases, redefining the possibilities of this artistic expression. In this sense, the critical study of the
process leading Lovecraft to conceive and establish a new form of
weird literature—the non-supernatural cosmic genre—may help
demonstrate how one of the main traits of his literary discourse is
indeed that of *self-reflexivity*.

3. *Characterization Level: the evolution from a "black" to a "white" fictional mask*

Taking it for granted that "Discursive selves, permanent or provisional, proliferate in literature as much as in other modes of discourse" (Onega and Garcia Landa 10), Lovecraft's fiction shows the employment of several "fictional masks of *personae* which mediate between the authorial voice and the characters" (ibid. 26). In Lovecraft, the study of the nature of these masks and of the evolution of their subjectivity is particularly relevant because, as discussed above, it is just through the *filter of the characters' subjectivities* that the manifestations of outsideness are made to signify and undergo an evolution in their signification. In fact, it is just as a result of the character's perception that outsideness is even defined as such: the other would not *be* the other, without a self there that perceives the other as different ("opposed" in phase 1, "complementary" in phase 2, and "similar" in the *alien humanism*) from the self. These "masks" constitute literary alter egos of the writer, deliberately and wittingly devised in a way to make them resemble—or, in some cases, deny—personal traits of their creator.

In Lovecraft's fiction, several "masks" of the author appear, and are meant to be his more or less serious, detailed, and full-fledged representation. Just to mention a few: Randolph Carter (perhaps the most faithful, complex, and "serious" portrait Lovecraft devised of himself within his fiction, appearing in five fictional works), de la Poer or Delapore (in the surname "De la Poer" it is also possible to recognize a hint to the master of those times: E. A. Poe), Herbert West (a mask meant ironically as a portrait of the writer's "dark" side), William Dyer, Nathaniel Wingate Peaslee (these last two are "serious" projections Lovecraft devises of his own personality as a wannabe scholar in the natural [for Dyer] and economic [for Peaslee] sciences).[17]

These "masks," which can be found both in his fiction and non-fiction (especially in the nearly 100,000 letters of his enormous epistolary corpus), undergo an evolution as well between the first

---

17. It might also be interesting and illuminating to analyze this process of self-projection onto literary masks in terms of the Freudian notion of "transference."

and the second phase of Lovecraft's fiction. I propose to adopt a chromatic distinction in order to illustrate this evolution, that of a "black" mask in phase 1 leading to a "white" mask in phase 2.

The "black" mask could be defined as the psychologically deranged or obsessed character in the Poe (and traditional Gothic) manner: Delapore ("The Rats in the Walls"), Herbert West ("Herbert West—Reanimator"), Jervas Dudley ("The Tomb"), Arthur Jermyn ("Facts concerning the Late Arthur Jermyn and His Family"), the unnamed protagonist of "Dagon," Randolph Carter in "The Statement," etc. Let us briefly touch upon the figures of de la Poer (later Delapore during the story) and Herbert West, since these characters, though sharing the trait of being "black" self-portraits, represent two different types of masks: the "passive" and the "active" one in front of outsideness's manifestations.

Delapore is a "black" Lovecraftian alter ego: to define it as "black," suffice it to think of the mask's final regression to a cannibalistic state and his internment in a mental asylum. But Lovecraft enjoys combining the traits of an outsider to those of his personal ideal state: Delapore is an American, but of noble English heritage, refined manners, and vast culture, who takes abode in a Gothic-Romanesque abbey (Lovecraft's predilection for these architectural styles is well known) placed in England, with the only real company of beloved—and very sensitive—cats, his favorite one being called Nigger-Man, i.e., with the same name Lovecraft had assigned to a cat he had cherished during his childhood. On a personal and psychological level, Delapore is a character lacerated by a sense of loss and of "removal," since he has a British lineage but is forced to live in the United States. All these aspects are spies of Lovecraft's subjectivity: besides the obvious ties linking Lovecraft to Delapore on a personal level, the flesh-and-bones author feels in fact, as a refined Englishman forced to live on a "foreign" sole, a sense of loss too: of the beloved mother-country England, and of a colonial past Lovecraft sees as glorious or at least preferable to the prosaic, mechanized, and unimaginative time in which he lives. However, later Delapore deviates from Lovecraft's ideal figure (and in this resides the "blackness" of the mask) because the character is converted along the story into the latest descendant of a family of murderers and blasphemous cultists. Delapore is made look into a mirror and discover his real nature as totally different from the so-called "civilized," and lets himself be engulfed in a degradation toward a primitive state because of his inability to resist the sadistic-irrational drives encoded in his DNA and embodied by the iconic element of the rats in the walls. Delapore does not react nor oppose the destructive call of the other; he is passive in the face of the doom the other brings to him.

In his turn, Herbert West embodies Lovecraft's thirst for knowledge and scientific advance, but displays a black twist when he dedicates his scientific experiments to an evil goal: the reanimation of the dead. Herbert in fact is a practitioner of medical science who invents a fluid capable to bring the dead to life; his early successful experiments turn into disaster when the reanimated dead display an aggressive and sadistic nature. In turn, Herbert himself is converted into a murderer, overwhelmed by an uncontrolled drive to pursue his experiments, and goes so far as to kill people in order to get fresh corpses on which to inject his fluid. The figure of Herbert West is modeled upon that of Dr. Frankenstein, but represents also an ironically dark self-portrait of his author: Herbert is depicted as a sort of evil wizard, and described as a figure imperturbable until the very end in the face of his doomed fate. He is not in any way a "victim" of outsideness like Delapore, and not also an outsider—rejected by Nature—like the unnamed protagonist of the tale of the same title: Herbert is an "enforcer" of his own (i.e., stemming from himself) macabre tendencies.

These reflections on just two of the masks should already provide an idea on how complex is the relationship between Lovecraft and his alter-egos (and let us remember that up to now I have left the most elaborated of these figures, Randolph Carter, out of the discussion): Lovecraft's masks are definitely complex and various in nature. The study of their subjectivity is complex too, since these masks are not single-sided and monotypical reproductions of himself that Lovecraft inserts in his literature.

The "black" masks are moved by individual and private motivations along their quests[18] for, or "relationships" with, the other (regardless of whether the relationship was originated by them or by

---

18. Jervas Dudley explicitly refers to a "monomania" ("The Tomb" [D 6]).

the other). They need to clarify some obscure elements of their or their families' past, or simply the events involving them have just a private nature and do not concretely affect other individuals nor lead to discoveries affecting a range of individuals wider than their restricted circle of relatives and/or acquaintances. The "drama" is limited to a single individual or family, and the story of the "black" mask shows how the mask's or his family's lives (and only those) implode after the intrusion of the other into their own, private dimensions.

A passage in "The Rats in the Walls" may help clarify these points: Delapore, at the outset of his accounting (while, let us remember, he is already placed in the madhouse and recalls a past experience), states: "Neither my father nor I ever knew what our hereditary envelope had contained, and as I merged into the greyness of Massachusetts business life I lost all interest in the mysteries which evidently lurked far back in my family tree. *Had I suspected their nature, how gladly I would have left Exham Priory to its moss, bats, and cobwebs*" (*DH* 27–28; my italics). This typical utterance by a phase 1 "black" mask reveals much of its selfish and opportunistic attitude: the mask, in fact, perfectly knows, at this point when it is telling the story, everything that happened. Delapore claims that he would have avoided "exhuming" Exham Priory, had he known the horrors his action would have generated; but this is just because this "exhumation" has caused its (the mask's) insanity and ultimate self-destruction. It is an egoistic consideration about a very private consequence of its action.[19] On the contrary, from the "collective"

---

19. Airaksinen too agrees that selfishness represents one distinguishing trait of a specific phase of Lovecraft's characters, and convincingly links this trait to the "loss of identity" befalling them. In fact, from a philosophical point of view the loss of identity "is the ultimate evil in two different ways. First, the horror is simply the person's realization of the ultimate loss. He sees that what is dearest to him, his self, is going to be lost. This is a source of panic. The second, Schopenhauerian possibility is that the person loses his own individuality and thus is able to see the end of the world. This world is evil, hence the shock. We can call the first egocentric, and the second the cosmic view. When we think of the Lovecraftian philosophy of cosmicism, the second possibility must be chosen as the correct interpretation of his explanation of fear. Nevertheless, in some stories the first interpretation can be utilized too" (37).

viewpoint the exhumation of the abbey has had an extremely positive effect, since it ultimately led to finally place the word "END" on the horrors that, from centuries and countless generations ago, had been infesting the areas below the abbey and, above all, the population inhabiting its surroundings. Since Delapore is what I define a "black" mask, he is unable to see beyond his own private interest and advantage.

In the second phase, contextually with the appearance of the "white" mask, the motive emerges of the subject risking his own mental and physical survival in order to face the other and to make it "known" to the wider scientific community and the human assembly at large. The "white" mask has in fact a scientific attitude: William Dyer (*At the Mountains of Madness*) and Nathaniel Peaslee ("The Shadow out of Time")—and, at least partly, Francis Wayland Thurston of "The Call of Cthulhu"—represent the prototypes of the "white" mask, with their mature awareness of the universal function that their confrontation with outsideness achieves. Delapore is unable to think in their way: he just sees his own profit, his is not yet a scientific discourse. Delapore's self is still looking for its own full-fledged signification; this is why the subject reacts in an egoistic way in the face of the manifestation of outsideness.

The "white" masks' self, on the other hand, has achieved the awareness of its most proper signification: that of facing the other in order to give testimony of this facing to the entire human collectivity, through the resort to an authentically scientific discourse, allowing the realization of the signifying totality of the subject's self. The "black" mask is instead still enslaved by a mythical-supernatural view of the other, and its discourse cannot be but a private one.

In phase 1 the self is *victimized* by its relationship with the other: Delapore does not choose consciously to proceed in his investigation; he is manipulated and in a sense hypnotized and carried away by the other toward self-destruction. In the second phase, the characters' subjectivity has strengthened enough to guide the self toward a conscious choice to proceed, for knowledge and truth's sake, and for scientific objectives. There is also another aspect that helps explain, on the "white" mask's part, this conscious will to proceed in a potentially self-destructive inquiry: this mask has a tendency (missing in the "black" mask) to pursue the search for truth at any cost, since its "truth hunger" is unquenchable.[20] So much so that the "white" mask even has a tendency toward voluntary *self-immolation*, also as a way to sublimate its self. Let us remember here that Lovecraft even wrote an essay titled "Some Causes of Self-Immolation: Motives for Voluntary Self-Subjugation to Unpleasant Conditions by Human Beings" (1931), whose tenets and spirit—especially in the reflections on the "Exterior-gratification motive" as the one driven by "many phases of genuine intellectual, religious, and aesthetic martyrdom" that even lead to "most real self-denial to promote intellectual, aesthetic, and moral objects" (*CE* 5.81)—configure scientific research and the pursuit of truth as almost holy vocations for a restricted category of highly advanced and civilized human beings. The self-immolation motive in Lovecraft's "white" masks may be considered an element strengthening the idea that these masks represent the projections of the scholar "type" that Lovecraft himself wished to become.

One aspect that the "black" and the "white" mask share is their initial attitude toward the manifestations of outsideness: all these subjects display an ingrained rationalism and skepticism. The mental *habitus* of all these characters is always that of trying to find logical explanations capable of shedding rational light on the apparent illogicality of outsideness's manifestations.

So what are the differences? First, the fact that the "black" mask never joins its rationalism with an authentically scientific discourse and interest, while for the "white" mask this very same rationalism results in a strong popularizing, investigative, ultimately scientific attitude. Both masks attempt at explaining the irruption of outsideness by resorting to human reason, but their goal is consistently different: the "black" mask simply tries to preserve its own mental

---

20. This aspect further reinforces Lovecraft's own link with his white masks' attitude, since he had always assessed the appreciation of—and the search for—truth as "missions" of the highest intellectual and moral stance, no matter how depressing and unflattering the revelations may be. Among the many possible examples, let us mention these statements that Lovecraft uttered in two early letters: "To the scientist there is the joy in pursuing truth which nearly counteracts the depressing revelations of truth" (to the Kleicomolo, October 1916; *SL* 1.27) and the unequivocal "Truth-hunger is a hunger just as real food-hunger" (to the Kleicomolo, April 1917; *SL* 1.45).

safety, and in some cases physical survival; it also tries to *reject* outsideness with rational means in order to eliminate and destroy its sources. The "white" mask strives instead to find a rational explanation because its goal is to *come up with a plausible model* capable of accounting for the unexplainable in the presence of the scientific community and, ultimately, the human assembly at large.

Moreover, the "black" mask, because of its semiotic immaturity, is unable to accept the manifestations of outsideness because it perceives them as *supernatural*, i.e., as events that are not explainable through rational and natural laws *and thus have to be rejected*. The "white" mask, on the other hand, realizes that the manifestations of outsideness are not *beyond* Nature and its laws: they are simply beyond *terrestrial* natural laws, those recognized and popularized by human natural sciences. These manifestations do respect some natural laws; the only problem is that these laws are unknown to human science and episteme. They are the laws of another dimension, or possible world, that of Outsideness indeed: only by assuming a scientific, relativistic perspective can this realization not harm the human mind unveiling it. And as we have seen, this shift of perspective is achieved by Lovecraft's fiction and masks only in their second phase.

It is then possible to schematize as follows: the characters' subjectivity evolves from phase 1 to phase 2, from a mythical to a scientific discourse, and from a supernatural to a non-supernatural cosmic art. Therefore, in its turn, the Lovecraftian mask perceiving the outsideness and generating the shift in the outsideness's signification evolves as follows:

1. **"Black" mask (first phase):** Delapore, the Outsider, Herbert West, the protagonist of "Dagon," etc. The traits of these masks have been discussed in details above.

→

2. **"White" mask (second phase):** a scholar, a learned man, a scientist with a rational background and no belief whatsoever in the supernatural. He has great faith in science and reason, and in their capacity to explain existence, or at least to approximate an explanation. There is awareness of the epistemic limits of terrestrial sciences and

of the "tools" available to human beings in order to "know" (*in primis*, the five senses): this is why the "white" mask is willing to accept only a semblance of the truth. These masks do not have any "black" side: they display a strong sense of *morality* (unlike characters like West), as well as a strong sense of duty and of the relevance of their "civilizing" mission. They try to defend and preserve all civilizations (because they recognize the worth of their achievements) whether human or even alien (in the phase of *alien humanism*).

What is the mask that works as a liaison between the two phases, executing the transition? I believe it is Francis Wayland Thurston, the protagonist of "The Call of Cthulhu." He represents a still clumsy, unsure prototype of fully mature "white" masks such as Dyer and Peaslee. In fact, Thurston also has a thirst for knowledge and searches actively for truth, by enforcing an investigative process based on a rational "piecing together of dissociated knowledge" (*DH* 125). He brings on a scientific discourse, since he aims at finding the truth and making it public, communicating it to the human assembly; he remodels his intentions, aspirations, and discoveries, elevating them from the individual level to the cosmic one. His worries are typical of the scientific discourse of phase 2. But he is not yet a full-fledged "white" mask, since he lacks the cultural and scientific background of more mature figures, and above all because, in spite of the fact that his actions and intentions are already assimilable to those originating a scientific discourse, their *results* are still unfortunate: Thurston gets overwhelmed, destroyed, "eaten" just like Delapore by the contact with the other, he is still unable to cope successfully with the manifestations of the outsideness he so rationally and thoroughly investigates.

As a last word on this topic, it must be recognized that the situation of the Lovecraftian alter egos is not always easily schematizable as the previous discussion might suggest. There exists in fact a mask, the most multifaceted (probably because the most faithful to the original) one, that defies categorization: Randolph Carter. This mask goes through both phases, and apparently without being subjected to the evolution from "black" to "white." The specificity of this mask resides in the fact that Lovecraft wants it to embody a value he considers immortal, one he has always cherished no matter which phase his fiction was traversing: the value of *dream*. Carter is in fact an oneiric (anti)hero, and he embodies a passion/exigence on Lovecraft's part that trespasses the borders of the evolution of his poetics of outsideness—his passion for *dream*, an invariant factor so important for Lovecraft that it stays untouched and is preserved even through the stormy winds brought by the evolution of the poetics.

I have claimed that the evolution of the perception of outsideness on the characters' part is a crucial factor in the study of the Lovecraftian shift between the first and the second phase of his fictional production. I have extensively discussed this process above. What would be now left for further study and investigation is the problem of the range and intensity of the phenomenon of "reflexivity" of the creator on the characters: in other words, a study concerning the modes and the extent of the similarity between the evolution of the masks' subjectivity and that of their creator.

4. *Representation Level: the evolution from a "particular" to a*
    "universal" representation of outsideness

Lovecraft's literary discourse on outsideness's manifestations shifts from the representation of individual, isolated cases affecting single persons (in the mythical discourse, whereas a single hero or antihero, an *insignis vir*, or his family, are involved), to that of whole sophisticated and evolved alien communities dominating the universe, in which the revelations stemming from the encounter with the other generate reflections on the fate of all humankind (scientific discourse). Only in the second phase are the manifestations of outsideness messengers of truly cosmic realities and horrors. In the tales of the first phase, Lovecraft is still searching for that authentically new and revolutionary representation of outsideness and horror that he will start to grasp only with "The Call of Cthulhu." Also, the resort to a few structural elements of the Gothic tradition (including the "mice tale," the detective tale, the ghost tale, with hideous rumors, mysterious disappearances of people from villages, resort to macabre allusions, to the animal helper, to prophetic or threatening dreams), the necrophiliac tale ("The Tomb," "In the Vault"), the setting in the eerie castle (as in "The Rats in the Walls") or in the haunted house (as in "The Shunned House")—are to be interpreted as a warming up in preparation of more mature representations of Outsideness.

In this article, I have tried to elucidate several of the elements that allow the interpreter to speak about "scientific discourse" in the second phase of Lovecraft's output. One additional element may come at this level, considering how the *motivations* themselves push the narrators shift toward a more universalistic attitude in the second phase. In other words, the representation of outsideness in the second phase is truly cosmic and "scientific" because the narrator is now moved—in his investigation and its reporting—by an interest that is no longer individual and private. The urge pushing William Dyer to write an uncensored account of the Miskatonic expedition in Antarctica (*At the Mountains of Madness*)[21] is generated by the need to spread knowledge on a universal basis, one able to reach the entire humankind and hopefully save it from a likely doom; while the motivations pushing Delapore to tell about his experience with the rats from the madhouse, or Randolph Carter to write his "Statement" (1919), seem particular, specific to these sole individuals. In the stories of the first phase, also the prevalence of the Poe model is a telltale sign of Lovecraft's tendency to devise private motivations for his narrators. Their encounter with the other has mainly individual, not cosmic implications. For instance, Delapore writes because he is driven by the intention to reconstruct the history of his family, to avert the blame away from himself for the murder of Norrys, and probably also to expiate the sense of guilt deriving from the death of his son for the consequences of a war injury.

An interesting comparison can be made between the use of an apparently similar figurative element—the rat—in tales of the first and the second phase: "The Rats in the Walls" (1923) and "The Dreams in the Witch House" (1932). The iconic element stays the same: we have "normal" rats in the first tale, and they are messengers of Nyarlathotep and come from an outsideness that is ambiguously depicted as half-external and half-internal to the character (Delapore); in the second tale, there is one single rat, Brown Jenkin,

---

21. "I am *forced into speech* because men of science have refused to follow my advice without knowing why" is Dyer's exordium of his account (*MM* 3; my italics).

but a very uncommon one: his size is huge, he has a human face, and he possesses an evil will of his own that leads him to perform unnamable actions. It is hardly questionable that the figure of Brown Jenkin is the more "cosmic" one, and only through it does outsideness find its own cosmic dimension with regard to the motive of the rats.

In conclusion, the following scheme could be proposed as a general model of interpretation for the evolution of Lovecraft's treatment of outsideness:

Discourse phase	Protagonist subject	Subject's role	Subject's function
1. Mythical	Individual Anti-hero "Black" mask	He is alone in his confrontation with the Other. Represents only himself	His discoveries have an individual value. He is not invested of a collective mission/function. His quest is born for private reasons.
2. Scientific	Individual Hero— *Insignis Vir* "White" mask	He is the leader of a group, of which he is the spokesman. The group represents a microcosm of humankind.	His quest is "institutionalized": it is the quest for knowledge of the entire species. His mission reflects the advancement of a *collective reason*.

This article has striven to point out the elements of rupture between the two phases of Lovecraft's fiction, with particular reference to the treatment of the theme of outsideness. In all probability, a fruitful and productive further direction for research would be to explore the elements of continuity, which no doubt could be demonstrated to be abundant and consistent, especially in reference to the stability along the phases of the narrative techniques and of the textual strategies.

Works Cited

Airaksinen, Timo. *The Philosophy of H. P. Lovecraft: The Route to Horror*. New York: Peter Lang Publishing, 1999.

Bakhtin, Mikhail. "Epic and Novel" (1941). Rpt. in Bakhtin's *The Dialogic Imagination: Four Essays.* Austin: University of Texas Press, 1982.

Leiber, Fritz. "A Literary Copernicus" (1949). Rpt. in *Lovecraft Remembered,* ed. Peter Cannon. Sauk City, WI: Arkham House, 1998. 455–66.

Montelone, Paul. "'The Rats in the Walls': A Study in Pessimism." *Lovecraft Studies* No. 32 (Spring 1995): 18–26.

Onega, Susana, and José Angel Garcia Landa, ed.. *Narratology: An Introduction.* London: Longman, 1999.

Sondergard, Sidney L. "Mapping the Lovecraft Idiolect: Iterative Structures and Autosemiotization as Reading Strategies." *American Journal of Semiotics* 18 (2006): 87–106.

Briefly Noted

S. T. Joshi's exhaustively revised and updated bibliography of Lovecraft, now titled *H. P. Lovecraft: A Comprehensive Bibliography,* is scheduled to be released by University of Tampa Press in late summer or early fall. At 706 pp., the volume includes a full listing of Lovecraft's own publications (books, contributions to books and periodicals, works edited, etc.), an extensive catalogue of Lovecraft's works in translation (in at least 25 languages), and, most significantly, an abundant listing of Lovecraft criticism. Joshi's original bibliography (Kent State University Press, 1981) emerged at the very time when Lovecraft criticism was experiencing a tremendous upsurge, so that little of it was included in that work; the new listing should be of considerable aid to scholarship. The University of Tampa Press will also publish S. T. Joshi's annotated edition of *The Case of Charles Dexter Ward,* probably in 2010. However, the press is no longer able to continue the issuance of *Studies in the Fantastic,* two issues of which were published.

Some Notes on Lovecraft's "The Transition of Juan Romero"

Leigh Blackmore

"I yearned to shew what ought to be done"

Let us confess at the outset that this tale is a comparatively minor one of Lovecraft's. It tells of events which took place in the gold-mining country of the American West at the Norton Mine on October 18 and 19, 1894.

Lovecraft wrote the tale in 1919; he was then aged twenty-nine. He had resumed writing fiction (after an eight-year hiatus) with "The Tomb" (June 1917). In March 1919 his mother, Sarah Susan Lovecraft, was hospitalized at Butler Hospital in Providence. In September 1919 he discovered the work of Lord Dunsany, which was to influence him greatly for some years to come. (In November 1919 Lovecraft actually heard Dunsany lecture at an amateur convention in Boston.)

The one reference we have to "Transition" in Lovecraft's letters occurs in a letter of April 1920 to the Gallomo. Lovecraft says: "My next—'Juan Romero'—was written merely as a reaction from copying a dull yarn by Phil Mac. He had made such a commonplace adventure yarn from a richly significant setting, that I yearned to shew what ought to be done with such a setting" (*Lord of a Visible World* 69). ("Phil Mac" was the amateur writer Prof. Phillip B. Macdonald, who contributed several articles to magazines such as the *Vagrant*, the *United Co-operative*, and even to Lovecraft's *Conservative*. Lovecraft had previously taken Macdonald to task for belittling the importance of classical authors.) The paucity of references to the tale in Lovecraft's letters is another indication that he did not think highly of it, for in the case of most of his other stories he was eager

147

to regale his correspondents with details of his latest fictional accomplishment.

"Transition" has been little studied, not warranting even a mention in de Camp's *Lovecraft: A Biography* or in book-length studies of Lovecraft by such critics as Timo Airaksinen and Maurice Lévy. Peter Cannon's study gives the tale a couple of paragraphs, concluding merely that elements of the tale "tantalize, without adding up to a coherent whole. . . . The narrator . . . comes across as a pure Gothic stereotype. His presence in a western, even a supernatural one, borders on absurdity" (22). S. T. Joshi's Starmont Reader's Guide on Lovecraft (1982) does not discuss the tale, though Joshi does address it in his later books, including his biography of Lovecraft. Donald R. Burleson is perhaps the most generous in his treatment of the story; his page-long examination of it suggests that "Lovecraft was thinking in terms of globally significant phenomena" and that "the pattern of motifs and images in Lovecraft's work is one scarcely to be explained in simple terms; his was a complex mind" (33).

Joshi's bibliography of Lovecraft lists no critical articles about the tale. T. E. D. Klein touches briefly upon the tale in his introduction ("A Dreamer's Tales") to the corrected Arkham House edition of *Dagon* (D xxxiii), but only to comment that its narrator is a typical Lovecraft narrator—well-travelled, well-educated, and able to quote lines from Prescott and Poe despite now working as a common labourer in a mine.

Darrell Schweitzer has adjudged it be "much worse" than the contemporaneous minor story "Old Bugs." He summarises the plot as follows:

> The protagonist is even more reticent than most HPL narrators, and never does say exactly what happens. A blast in a gold mine reveals a vast abyss, from which eldritch throbbing sounds emanate. The hero and a Mexican laborer investigate, and something shocking happens to Romero. Then the scene shifts to a bunkhouse, where the narrator is awakened and Romero is dead. All witnesses insist they never left the room, but mysterious glowing Hindu ring is gone . . . (9)

Schweitzer doesn't venture an opinion as to why the tale is supposedly so bad. S. T. Joshi merely believes that the tale is "not an entire success" (*Subtler Magick* 59), an opinion with which I concur. Nevertheless, I believe all Lovecraft's tales deserve critical examination; hence while "Transition" can be regarded as an apprentice effort, there is much of interest to be found in this story if we look hard enough.

We may assume that the tale was conceived and written quickly, for the manuscript bears a single day's date—September 16, 1919. The tale was published for the first time in *Marginalia* (Arkham House, 1944), edited by August Derleth and Donald Wandrei. The editors called it an example of Lovecraft's "middle work . . . which was written not long before 'The Picture in the House,'" commenting that "the advance from it to this latter story is remarkable" (vi).

S. T. Joshi has written of Lovecraft's disavowal of the tale. "Lovecraft recognised that 'The Transition of Juan Romero' was a false start, and he refused to allow it to be published, even in the amateur press. He disavowed it relatively early in life and it fails to appear on most lists of his stories; he does not seem to have shown it to anyone until 1932, when R. H. Barlow badgered him into sending him the manuscript so that he could prepare a typescript of it" (*H. P. Lovecraft: A Life* 168).

This is borne out by Lovecraft's correspondence with Robert H. Barlow regarding the tale. In a letter of March 12, 1932, Lovecraft wrote: "there is a repudiated story of mine [so far below my standard that I wouldn't have it in print under any circumstances] called 'The Transition of Juan Romero' which is also innocent of type, & which you could have for nothing if you'd be willing to type me a private copy for my files. Possibly, though, a frankly poor story wouldn't make a good collector's item" (*OFF* 25). On March 21 Lovecraft sent Barlow the manuscript, with the comment: "Don't feel obliged to copy 'Juan Romero' unless you want to keep a copy. I want only one, and this scrawl is plenty so far as I'm concerned" (*OFF* 26). Ten days later, Lovecraft authorised Barlow to keep the manuscript: "To be sure—keep the ms. of 'Juan Romero' if you wish. I fear that it is a rather poor tale, & doubt if it would be worth working over" (*OFF* 27). On April 14, Lovecraft was still unconcerned about "Juan Romero"'s return: "No hurry at all about 'Juan Romero.' I hadn't looked at it for ten years when I dug it out,

& probably shan't want to see it again in less than that time." He goes on to answer a query about the Spanish use of the inverted question mark (*OFF* 28). By May 19, he had received the copy Barlow had made of it: "Thanks indeed for 'Romero'—the copy of which is better than I'd have made. I read it over for the first time in over a decade, and have to admit that it's a pretty poor attempt at a story. I don't blame editors for rejecting it" (*OFF* 31). The last statement at least suggests that Lovecraft *may* have shown it a few editors before withdrawing it on his accord.

In a letter of March 19, 1934, Lovecraft refers again to "Juan Romero" as a failed tale, noting to Barlow that he has expunged from it from his list of acknowledged writings, along with other tales he considered failures such as "The Street," *The Dream-Quest of Unknown Kadath*, and *The Case of Charles Dexter Ward*, which were now "relegated to oblivion" (*OFF* 120).

But at least Lovecraft did not destroy the tale, as he had done with many of his other early fictional efforts. While not on a par with his most accomplished later tales, "Juan Romero"'s motifs foreshadow themes that are central to Lovecraft's later fiction, and thus "Transition" is not wholly without interest.

The narrator of the tale remains nameless; but he implies he is an immigrant to the United States, for he says: "my name and origin need not be related to posterity; in fact, I fancy it is better that they should not be, for when a man suddenly migrates to the States or the Colonies, he leaves his past behind him" (*D* 337). We learn of him that his present name "is very common and carries no meaning"; it is a name he has "accepted" (or more likely, adopted) presumably for the purposes of remaining anonymous. But we do learn some facts about him. We deduce that he is English, for he refers to his use of "Oxonian Spanish" when speaking to Romero. ("Oxonian" is a term for someone affiliated with Oxford University in England.) He has served in India and admits: "I was more at home amongst the white-bearded native teachers than amongst my brother officers. I had delved not a little into odd Eastern lore when overtaken by the calamities which brought my new life in America's vast West." He does not specify the nature of these calamities, and we must be satisfied with a subtle implication that perhaps it has something to do with the Hindu ring that he wears. (Lovecraft spells it in the old style of "Hindoo.") R. Boerem comments that the narrator of "Transition" "left his life as a British officer apparently because of some scandal" (266).

Lovecraft sets up this nameless narrator, then, as someone who has already seen or researched some mysteries. We also learn that he is telling this tale "in these last years of my life," and that despite having no desire to speak of what he calls the "Transition" of Juan Romero, all that impels him to recall the story is "a sense of duty to science."

The setting of the tale is unusual in Lovecraft's oeuvre, as compared with that of many of his later tales, which are set in the vicinity of the Eastern States—New England and so on. It is his only tale set in the Southwest apart from the revisions "The Curse of Yig" and 'The Mound." Norton Mine is said to be located in the "drear expanses of the Cactus Mountains." This appears to be a fictitious location, although there is a real Cactus Mountain in Fremont County, Colorado, in America's West, and one in Wallowa County, Oregon, on America's West Coast. Perhaps we could feasibly visualise the Norton Mine being located in either Oregon or Colorado as the most likely real-world location. Joshi speculates that the Norton Mine is "somewhere in the Southwest, one imagines, although Lovecraft is not specific as to the actual location" (*H. P. Lovecraft: A Life* 167).

The mines have been started due to the discovery some years previous by an "aged prospector" of "a cavern of gold, lying deep below a mountain lake" (*D* 337). Since then, due to large-scale blasting, "additional grottoes had been found, and the yield of yellow metal was exceedingly great"; a minor character, Mr. Arthur, the mine superintendent, speculates on the probable extent of what Lovecraft calls, in a delicious phrase typical of his Latinate vocabulary, "auriferous cavities" (*D* 337).

There is a "Jewel Lake" in the vicinity of the mines and their adjacent caverns in the tale. There is a real Jewel Lake in Jackson County, Colorado, but no Jewel Lake in Oregon; a hint that Lovecraft may have visualised Colorado as the setting of "Transition," although the name is not so unusual that Lovecraft could simply have invented it.

The narrator becomes friendly with a Mexican peon named Juan Romero. We learn several things of Romero. Described as "ignorant and dirty" (*D* 338), he had been found as a child in a crude mountain hut, "the only survivor of an epidemic which had stalked lethally by." Two skeletons found nearby were presumably his parents. An avalanche closed a rather unusual rock fissure nearby the skeletons, and Romero was reared by a Mexican cattle-thief who had given him his name. One wonders whether Lovecraft is implying something here about Romero's mysterious origins lying in the caverns beneath the earth, but unfortunately he has not given enough information for us to do more than guess.

Romero seems of different blood from the rest of the "unkempt Mexicans" attracted to the mine. "It was not the Castilian conquistador or the American pioneer, but the ancient and noble Aztec whom imagination called to view when the silent peon would rise in the early morning and gaze in fascination at the sun as it crept above the eastern hills, meanwhile stretching out his arms to the orb as if in the performance of some rite whose nature he himself did not comprehend" (*D* 338). Is Lovecraft hinting here that Romero is actually of Aztec blood? If so, does that imply that the later horror has some connection with Aztec rites or history? This is never made clear.

There is also an example of Lovecraft's racism in the phrase where Lovecraft says that Romero "first commanded attention only because of his features; which though plainly of the Red Indian type, were yet remarkable for their light colour and refined conformation, being vastly unlike those of the average 'Greaser' or Piute of the locality" (*D* 338).

Apart from the pejorative term "greaser" that Lovecraft applies to the Mexicans (one hardly thinks Indo-Americans of today would take kindly to this terminology!), Lovecraft is subtly hinting that Romero's racial stock is more acceptable because he is a bit closer to the white man—the "lighter colour" and "refined conformation" mean he is one step up from the other natives. This is in accord with Lovecraft's racial attitudes at the time he wrote "Transition."

"Paiutes" or "Piutes" refers to two related groups of native American peoples, who hailed from the states east and south of Colorado—Oregon, Nevada, California, Utah, and Arizona. These native American tribes spoke a language known as Uto-Aztecan. It would be fascinating to learn more of Lovecraft's possible research sources for the native American references he puts into "Transition"; perhaps they derived from his delvings into his set of *Encyclopaedia Britannica*, but this is only a guess.

A new vein at the mine is dynamited and, instead of a rich vein of gold, an inconceivably deep gorge is revealed. That night, as a storm gathers, Romero hears above the gorge weird sounds coming from the earth, which he dubs *"el ritmo de la tierra*—THAT THROB DOWN IN THE GROUND!" As Burleson points out, "Lovecraft superbly describes this subterranean sound or impression as being 'like the pulsing of the engines far down in a great liner'" (33); the narrator, who also hears the throbbings, likens them to the strange chantings of Orientals whom he had heard when he was in India. Becoming obsessed with the throbbing sounds, Romero charges headlong toward the gorge, with the narrator following close behind. Lovecraft seems to be implying that these throbbings, emanating from subterrene regions, imply the existence of some immense entity dwelling beneath the surface, but the exact nature of this entity is never made clear.

Romero starts to repeat the cry "Huitzilopochtli" as the two characters plunge down a succession of abysses into the vast rift, as the narrator's ring lights the way: "I realised that the ancient ring on my finger was glowing with eerie radiance, diffusing a pallid lustre through the damp, heavy air around" (*D* 341). The narrator later shudders when he learns the association of that word, which he says he placed in the words of a great historian. (Only a footnote indicates that this is Prescott's [*History of the*] *Conquest of Mexico.*) Huitzilopochtli was a war god, legendary wizard, and sun god of the Aztecs. (This ties in with Romero's apparent gesture of homage to the sun earlier in the tale.) The god was often represented in art as a hummingbird, with a black face, and holding a snake and a mirror. There are many legends about him, but none seems especially enlightening in regard to the action of "Transition." Most likely Lovecraft was throwing his name in here as a touch of exotic strangeness, as he did later in "The Rats in the Walls" with its references to strange gods like Atys and the Magna Mater.

Lovecraft seems not to have had a copy of Prescott in his library, and he does not refer to Prescott in his letters, but he may well have read the volume—it had been published in 1843 and was for many years a standard volume on the history of Mexico. If he had read Prescott's book he might have been intrigued by the mention of Huitzilopochtli in chapter 3 of Prescott's volume, where the author states:

> At the head of all stood the terrible Huitzilopochtli, the Mexican Mars; although it is doing injustice to the heroic war-god of antiquity to identify him with this sanguinary monster. This was the patron deity of the nation. His fantastic image was loaded with costly ornaments. His temples were the most stately and august of the public edifices; and his altars reeked with the blood of human hecatombs in every city of the empire. Disastrous, indeed, must have been the influence of such a superstition on the character of the people. (38)

A note includes the information that "Huitzilopochtli is compounded of two words, signifying 'humming-bird,' and 'left,' from his image having the feathers of this bird on its left foot" (38n).

Burleson has pointed out that the motif of an unthinkably enormous and ominously inhabited space underground occurs again in Lovecraft eleven years later, in "The Mound" (ghostwritten by Lovecraft for Zealia Bishop), in which "he hints of links between his pantheon and the gods of Amerind myth; and in that tale there is also a connexion with Mexican and Aztec culture, myth and history" (33).

Amerind myths and knowledge of Aztec and other South American cultures certainly came within Lovecraft's sphere of general knowledge. A Mr. and Mrs. Eugene Smythe gave him and Sonia Greene a striking wedding gift of a Mexican clay calendar disc between 1000 and 3000 years old. In correspondence with Clark Ashton Smith, Lovecraft speculated on the possible connections between the Indian groups of Alaska and British Columbia and those of the Incas and Aztecs. He wrote to August Derleth that his "private museum" contained "2 early Mayan images, an earthen Aztec image, an Aztec bowl, & an earthen Aztec calendar-stone" (*Essential Solitude* 752). He was excited by a trip made by E. Hoffmann Price in which price saw many Aztec ruins, and he corresponded with Clark Ashton Smith and Frank Belknap long about aspects of history including the Aztecs and Incas: their art, their history, and the transmission of their culture. From such references we can safely conclude that the early interest he evinced in Amerind myth in "Juan Romero" stayed with Lovecraft as an appreciable element of his interest in world cultures.

On another note, Lovecraft's inordinate fondness for "gibbous moons" (that is to say, moons that are three-quarters full during either the waxing or waning part of the lunar cycle) led him look up the moon's phases for October 1894 to find when a gibbous moon was visible at 2 A.M. and to change the dates of the story to fit. "Here is a lesson in scientific accuracy for fiction writers," he wrote in the appended note (D 340).

The tale continues as Romero apparently perishes. The narrator, peering into the chasm, declares: "*I dare not tell you what I saw!*" (D 342). He sees "shapes, all infinitely distant began to detach themselves from the confusion" (D 342). Then there strikes a titanic lightning-bolt which knocks the narrator unconscious. The next morning he awakes, and the men of the camp perform an autopsy on the body of Romero, whose dead body has been found in his bunk. The men swear that neither the narrator nor Romero left their cabin the night before; the narrator finds that his Hindu ring is missing.

The Influence of Jonathan Hoag, Poe, and Bierce

Apart from Lovecraft's desire to top "Phil Mac's" use of a somewhat exotic setting, another important influence upon the genesis of "Transition" appears to have been a line in a poem by Jonathan Hoag, a contemporary of Lovecraft's to whom he dedicated a number of his own poems. With a friend Lovecraft cooperatively published Hoag's poems, for which Lovecraft also wrote a preface. George Wetzel has pointed out in his "The Cthulhu Mythos: A Study" that in that preface Lovecraft quoted a line from Hoag's "To the Grand Canyons of Colorado" (1919) where in black caves "vast nameless satyrs dance with noiseless feet." Wetzel (93) feels this imagery recurs in "Transition" (as well as in Chapter 5 of *At the Mountains of Madness*). Certainly the chronological placement of Hoag's poem in the same year as the composition of Lovecraft's story lends credence to the possible influence of this phrase. The title of Hoag's poem would also incline us believe that Lovecraft visualised Colorado as the setting for the Norton Mine in "Transition."

I believe the influence of Poe shows heavily in "Transition." Lovecraft had first read Poe at the age of eight. A letter in *Selected Letters II*, quoted by Joshi in *H. P. Lovecraft: A Life* (27), makes this clear: "Then I struck EDGAR ALLAN POE!! It was my downfall, and at the age of eight I saw the blue firmament of Argos and Sicily darkened by the miasmal exhalations of the tomb!" We know from the catalogue of Lovecraft's library and references in *Selected Letters* of the editions of Poe that Lovecraft owned; they included the Raven edition of *The Works of Edgar Allan Poe* in 5 volumes published in 1903 by P. F. Collier and Sons. While it doesn't follow that Lovecraft owned this set from the time of its publication, and while I have not spent the time to ascertain (if indeed it can be ascertained) when Lovecraft first read "The Tell-Tale Heart," we can confidently assert that Lovecraft had absorbed the bulk of Poe's best-known tales and poems including "The Tell-Tale Heart" well before the time he came to write "Transition."

A central motif in "Transition" is the mysterious throbbing that comes from underground and which draws Romero and the narrator on to investigate the cavern. The word "throbbing" means "to beat with increased force or rapidly, *as the heart* under influence of emotion or excitement; palpitate" (my italics). What more appropriate sensation could be utilised in a horror tale? Lovecraft may have used this motif in "Transition" as a semi-conscious device to indicate the increased excitement of a heart beating due to the anticipation or encountering of a horror and perhaps to assist in evoking the requisite sense of fearful anticipation in the reader.

Poe used the motif of "throbbing" to indicate horror in several of his works. The poem "For Annie" includes the following lines as its fourth stanza:

> The moaning and groaning,
> The sighing and sobbing
>   Are quieted now,
> With that horrible throbbing
> At heart:—ah, that horrible,
>   Horrible throbbing!

The throbbing in that poem seems to form part of the "the fever called Living that burned" in the brain of the poet (Poe 98).

Poe's poem "To F——" includes the line "Some ocean throbbing far and free," although contextually the throbbing in that poem forms part of the poet's memory of his beloved, which is a positive rather than a horrid memory (Poe 74).

What we may term "sonic horror" is also exemplified in Poe's poem "The Bells." The last stanza of this celebrated poem deals with the solemn iron bells (Poe 95). Some of the lines include a reference to throbbing:

> To the throbbing of the bells: —
> Of the bells, bells, bells—
> To the sobbing of the bells: —
> Keeping time, time, time . . .

Lovecraft's *Fungi from Yuggoth* sonnet cycle (1929–30) also contains many references to the horrible nature of throbbing or beating, usually in the form of the chiming of bells.

Lovecraft's own sonnet "The Bells" in the *Fungi from Yuggoth* sequence (*AT* 71) centres on the memories of a past life evoked by "that faint, far ringing / Of deep-toned bells on the black midnight wind." The narrator is beckoned: "back through gateways of recalling / To elder towers where the mad clappers tolled" (*AT* 72). Whether or not Lovecraft's sonnet was partly inspired by Poe's poem of the same title, there can be no doubt that the notion of bells tolling, that is, a continuous insistent sound akin to throbbing, is integral to Lovecraft's notion of the horror in the poem.

Poe's "The Tell-Tale Heart" (1843) ends with the words: "I felt that I must scream or die!—and now—again—hark! louder! louder! louder! LOUDER!—'Villains!' I shrieked, 'dissemble no more! I admit the deed!—tear up the planks!—here, here!—it is the beating of his hideous heart!" (Poe 559). The main motif in the story is the psychological pressure exerted upon the protagonist by the beating of the heart of the old man whom he has killed. (That the beating of the heart after the old man is dead is likely *imaginary* does not matter in the least.) Lovecraft must have been highly affected by this tale, with its motif of the insistent beating or throbbing of the heart, and the horror arising therefrom. The centrality of the motif of the horrible throbbing sound in "Transition" certainly seems to owe much to the similar motif in Poe's tale. Consider this passage "The Tell-Tale Heart": "And now—have I not told you that what you mistake for madness is but over-acuteness of the senses?—now, I say, there came to my ears a low, dull, quick sound, such as a watch makes when enveloped in cotton. I knew that sound well too. It was the beating of the old man's heart. It increased my fury, as the beating of a drum stimulates the soldier into courage" (Poe 557).

The key word in Poe's tale is "beating" rather than "throbbing," and yet these words are closely connected in sense. I would suggest that the motif of a horrible beating or throbbing as Lovecraft read it in Poe influenced "Transition." It may even have influenced other instances of "sonic horror" in his work. Consider the way Azathoth is usually described:

> [O]utside the ordered universe [is] that amorphous blight of nether-most confusion which blasphemes and bubbles at the center of all in-finity—the boundless daemon sultan Azathoth, whose name no lips dare speak aloud, and who gnaws hungrily in inconceivable, unlighted chambers beyond time and space amidst the muffled, maddening beating of vile drums and the thin monotonous whine of accursed flutes. (*The Dream-Quest of Unknown Kadath*; MM 308)

Clearly, for Lovecraft, certain sounds were associated with horror. In the description of Azathoth we have "maddening beating of vile *drums*." This sound is closely akin to the notion of "throbbing." Indeed, notice again the Poe passage from "The Tell-Tale Heart" quoted above and Poe's comparison of the beating of a heart to "the beating of a *drum*." Note also the "muffled" nature of the heartbeat sound in Poe's tale: it makes a sound "such as a watch makes when enveloped in cotton." This may form an analogue to the "*muffled, maddening*" nature of the vile drums in the Azathoth descriptions.

I don't believe it is drawing too long a bow to suggest that Love-craft absorbed the references to "beating" and "throbbing" (and per-haps to the idea of the noxious sound of certain instruments in Poe's work) and utilised them as suggestive of horror in "Transition" and perhaps other works. Most likely Lovecraft already had a psy-chological aversion to certain types of sound, so that his encountering Poe's use of "beating" and "throbbing" the motif struck a chord with Lovecraft.

Another Poe influence is discernible in the tale. The narrator says that to his mind "rushed fragments of a passage in Joseph Glanvill which Poe has quoted with tremendous effect:—'the vastness, profundity, and unsearchableness of His works, *which have a depth in them greater than the well of Democritus'*" (*D* 340). This is, of course, the motto of Poe's "A Descent into the Maelstrom" (Poe 432). It is evidence of the very profound effect that various works of Poe's had on Lovecraft, and his citation of this passage from Glanvill (author of *Sadducismus Triumphatus*, a work on witchcraft) by way of Poe inextricably links the horrible abysses of "Transition" with the terrible watery abyss of Poe's "Descent." (Lovecraft also cites Glanvill in "The Festival," in which the narrator notices Glanvill's book in the house on green Lane in Kingsport, Massachusetts.)

Lovecraft likely had a purpose in citing the Glanvill quotation that went beyond simply a tip of the hat to Poe. The mention of Democritus in the Glanvill quotation is telling, for Democritus was one of the pre-Socratic philosophers who co-founded atomism, reasoning that space is a "void" of infinite size in which float innumerable particles—the atoms—too miniscule to be perceivable by the senses, but which have formed the heavens (earth and the planets). Atoms could not destroyed, only changed from one form to another over time. Democritus' philosophy is crucial to mechanistic materialism, the philosophy to which Lovecraft adhered. Since a well (or a cavern) dug deep in the earth is also a "void" of great depth, Glanvill used "the well of Democritus" figuratively to represent the infinite void of our physical universe. (I am indebted to the entry on Glanvill in Anthony Pearsall's *The Lovecraft Lexicon* for bringing this point to my attention.)

By referring to Democritus in "Transition," Lovecraft is offering us a clue to his own philosophy—a completely non-supernatural one—and this elevates the basis of the horror in "Transition" from an instance of supernatural occurrence to a manifestation of the strangeness of the cosmos itself. On this point, "Transition" is very much in keeping with Lovecraft's interest in "cosmic outsideness."

But let us return to the sonic motifs in *Fungi from Yuggoth*. The sonnet "Mirage" also includes the notion of tolling bells: "evening chimes for which I listen still." And of course, in "St. Toad's," the phrase "St. Toad's cracked chimes" is repeated thrice; another instance of insistent repetitive sound drawing the narrator on to some unspecified doom. Very similar in function—that is, the notion of a sort of "unearthly music"—are the harbour-whistles of "Harbour Whistles": "The harbour whistles chant all through the night; / Throats from some strange ports and beaches far and white." While the motif of chanting or whistling in this particular sonnet (*AT* 77) is perhaps a step removed from the tolling of chimes that occurs in other fungi, and which corresponds in effect to the throbbing in "Transition," it is another instance of Lovecraft's fascination with the effects of repetitive sound.

In "The Elder Pharos" (*AT* 75), the imagery of the insistent sound of drums is recapitulated: "the last Elder One lives on alone, / Talking to Chaos *with the beat of drums*" (my italics). The theme of throbbing sound in "Transition," then, can be seen as an early instance of a theme of sonic horror that runs like a thread through various works of Lovecraft's.

The horror of sound and repeated cries also figure largely in "The Nameless City" (1921) and *At the Mountains of Madness* (1931), but this may form the subject for another essay.

Chris Perridas of the *H. P. Lovecraft and His Legacy* blog has suggested that "Transition" is reminiscent in places of various phrases to be found in several tales by Ambrose Bierce. Lovecraft did read Bierce at Loveman's prompting sometime in 1919. I am not entirely convinced by all the similarities of phrase that Perridas adduces between phrases in "Transition" and in tales of Bierce's such as "The Moonlit Road," "The Eyes of the Panther," "The Night-Doings at 'Deadman's,'" and "The Damned Thing." Some of them, however, are suggestive, and interested readers should check the detailed textual comparison made by Perridas by consulting http://chrisperridas. blogspot.com/search/label/The%20Transition

Inconceivable Depths

"Transition" ends with these thoughts of the narrator:

> My opinion of my whole experience varies from time to time. In broad daylight, and at most seasons I am apt to think the greater

part of it a mere dream; but sometimes in the autumn, about two in the morning when the winds and animals howl dismally, there comes from *inconceivable depths below* [my italics] a damnable suggestion of rhythmical throbbing . . . and I feel that the transition of Juan Romero was a terrible one indeed. (*D* 343)

The phrase "inconceivable depths below" adumbrates a similar and more memorable phrase used in Lovecraft's later story "The Rats in the Walls." Who can forget the following resonant sentence from that tale? "These creatures, in numbers apparently inexhaustible, were engaged in one stupendous migration from inconceivable heights *to some depth conceivably, or inconceivably, below*" (*DH* 36; my italics). The word "inconceivable," we may recall, also occurs in the description of Azathoth from the *Dream-Quest* as quoted above—Azathoth "gnaws hungrily in inconceivable, unlighted chambers." "Inconceivable" is a partial semiotic analogue of "nameless" or "unnamable"; another example of Lovecraft's use of non-explicitness in his horror fiction to increase the *frisson* provided to the reader.

The Charge of Excessive Vagueness

Joshi has criticised "Transition" because it "suffers from excessive vagueness" (*H. P. Lovecraft: A Life* 167), and Burleson has also called it a tale of "vague horror" (32). While the story is certainly not satisfactory in all its aspects, I take issue with Joshi on this point to some extent. Hints and portents, the technique of keeping the actual horror offstage, form an integral part of Lovecraft's technique in later stories.

Let us cite just a few examples. Recall "The Unnamable" (1923), whose very point is that some horrors must remain nameless because they cannot be described. Again, consider the vague yet portentous references Danforth utters at the end of *At the Mountains of Madness*: "He has on rare occasions whispered disjointed and irresponsible things about 'The black pit', 'the carven rim', 'the proto-shoggoths', 'the windowless solids with five dimensions', 'the nameless cylinder', 'the elder Pharos', 'Yog-Sothoth', 'the primal white jelly', 'the colour out of space', 'the wings', 'the eyes in darkness', 'the moon-ladder', 'the original, the eternal, the undying'" (*MM* 106). We know from other tales at least something about the nature of the colour out of space, and about Yog-Sothoth, and about the Elder Pharos (for which see the *Fungi* sonnet of that title); but Danforth's other mutterings point to strange and perhaps inexplicable places, things, and experiences. There are many such instances of deliberate "vaguery" in Lovecraft's work. Take, for instance, the concluding two lines of the sonnet "The Pigeon-Flyers": "The others laughed—till struck too mute to speak / By what they glimpsed in one bird's evil beak" (*AT* 68). Well, what *was* it that was in that bird's evil beak? We are not meant to *know*, but to *imagine*. And yet such a passage has not been subject to criticism for "excessive vaguery." The same may be said of the figure of the High Priest Not to Be Described in *The Dream-Quest of Unknown Kadath*. This figure, which wears a yellow silken mask over its face, is of unknown identity and its face is likewise unknown. This figure recurs in the "The Elder Pharos," where it is said, of a mysterious blue ray which shoots out from the plateau of Leng, that "Many, in man's first youth, sought out that glow, / But what they found, *no one will ever know*" (*AT* 75; my italics).

These instances of vaguery could be interpreted as meaning that Lovecraft himself did not know what the mystery was; but I suggest he deliberately utilised this artistic technique to impart more horror than could be achieved by describing the mystery outright. That great weird tale "The Night Ocean" by R. H. Barlow and Lovecraft (Autumn? 1936) could also be criticised for "excessive vagueness"; but few would disagree that in the authors' very refusal to delineate the actual nature of the horror lies the story's imaginative power. I believe that "The Transition of Juan Romero" is the more effective for leaving the horror ill-defined, whereas an artificial horror brought on stage may have lessened its power of suggestion.

Similarly, let us consider that passage from "The Thing on the Doorstep" (1933) where Edward Derby sputters out his wild tale of the events in the Chesuncook woods to his friend Daniel Upton: "Dan, for God's sake! The pit of the shoggoths! Down the six thousand steps . . . the abomination of abominations . . ." (*DH* 287). Once again we are given vagueries by Lovecraft—but *highly suggestive* vagueries. The effect of a phrase such as "the abomination of abominations" here is to allow readers to form a picture of the horror in their own mind. This is the same technique that Lovecraft has utilised in "Transition."

I suggest that in refusing to delineate the actual nature of the horror glimpsed by the narrator in "Transition," Lovecraft was beginning to work out in practice his theoretical position that horrors too specifically defined on the page are ineffectual. Of course, the scientific precision with which he describes, for instance, the dead Old One in *At the Mountains of Madness* or the dead Wilbur Whateley in "The Dunwich Horror" or the statuette of Cthulhu in "The Call of Cthulhu" could be seen as undermining this argument; but this scientific precision formed a different aspect of Lovecraft's abilities as fiction writer. It seems there were circumstances where Lovecraft felt indefiniteness was the best policy, and other circumstances where a very careful delineation of a horror or alien being lent the narrative a sense of authenticity not otherwise obtainable.

In regard to the plot of "Transition," it is true that Lovecraft left things unclear or unresolved. What, for instance, is the exact function or relevance of the Hindu ring worn by the narrator, by which Juan Romero becomes so fascinated, and which goes missing at the end of the tale? Are we to assume that Romero's death and transition have something to do with its disappearance? Or are we to assume that the dark hints about the narrator's having delved into mysteries into India mean the ring is imbued with some special power? If so, has this power aided or hindered in the events of the tale? We know that Romero is fascinated by the "hoary hieroglyphs" on the ring (presumably these are characters in Sanskrit) and that the ring "glistens queerly in every flash of lightning" (*D* 338, 340), but that is all. Why is it that the ring has the power to light the narrator's way as he chases Romero into the mines? Lovecraft has certainly not made any of this clear. Let us frankly admit therefore, that in some essentials the story is weakened considerably and that charge of excessive vagueness can be justifiably levelled in regard to plot points such as this.

The Abyss Too Deep to Sound

The motif of the "abyss too deep to sound" also recurs in Lovecraft's work as a constant motif. Consider the last two lines of the sonnet "The Well": "And yet we put the bricks back—for we found / The hole too deep for any line to sound" (*AT* 68). "The Transition of Juan Romero" can be seen as an effective early example of Love-

craft's utilisation of the idea of horrors buried, submerged, or lurking in the hidden recesses of our planet. We see this theme continu-
ing to fascinate Lovecraft as late as "The Haunter of the Dark"
(1935), where the character Robert Blake is made the author of stories that include "The Burrowers Beneath."

Compare the theme of the sonnet "The Dweller" with "Transition"; it is essentially about a nameless city unearthed by diggers
who then encounter an unseen but horrifying force or creature. Its
final two lines, "We cleared a path—but raced in mad retreat /
When from below we heard those clumping feet" (AT 76), encap-
sulate essentially the same emotions of horror that occur in "Transition," although in the story there are no "clumping feet." Lovecraft
then, in "Transition" was groping toward a motif that would find
more elaborate expression in many of his later tales.

For Lovecraft, the suggestion that the earth is riddled with unknown and horrific creatures or presences is a constant source of
horror; this is one of the most pervasive themes in his fiction. Many
of his tales, like "Transition," imply that the ground we walk on is
merely a thin crust over unimaginable horrors.

One need only consider the cavern of "The Beast in the Cave"
(1905) with its degenerated found human within; the degenerate
Martense family of "The Lurking Fear" (1922), with their subterranean mound-burrows that honeycomb the underneath of Tempest
Mountain; or "The Rats in the Walls" (1923), with its descent into
subterrene spaces, revealing successively frightful horrors, to see this
demonstrated in Lovecraft's fiction. Other examples include the ti-
tan creature buried in the cellar in "The Shunned House" (1924); the
descent into the pyramid and the encounter with the hybrid monsters of "Under the Pyramids" (1924); Pickman's painting "Subway
Accident" in "Pickman's Model" (1926), and other revelations in this
story concerning what may lurk beneath modern cities such as Boston, and the narrator's consequent fear of subways and other underground places; The Case of Charles Dexter Ward (1927), with its
hideous creatures locked up in the deep pits of Ward's catacomb;
and of course, the many instances of horror living in the deep places
of the sea, such as in "Dagon" (1917), "The Temple" (1920), "The
Call of Cthulhu" (1926), "The Shadow over Innsmouth" (1931), etc.
Let us recall also that phrase from the Necronomicon cited in "The

Festival": "Great holes secretly are digged where earth's pores ought
to suffice, and things have learnt to walk that ought to crawl" (*D*
216). Clark Ashton Smith echoed this quotation in an extended
quotation from the *Necronomicon* in his tale 'The Nameless Off-
spring" (1932): "Many and multiform are the dim horrors of earth,
infesting her ways from the prime" (3). I suspect that both Lovecraft and Smith partly derived this concept from the alliterative
opening of Poe's "Berenice": "Misery is manifold. The wretchedness
of earth is multiform" (Poe 225).

The parallelism of plot between "Transition" and 'The Statement
of Randolph Carter" may seem too obvious to mention. In both stories, two men venture into an underground location (in "Statement"
it is a crypt) and encounter a force or creature (or creatures) of such
hideousness or horror that the first explorer dies. Harley Warren in
"Statement' perishes; so does Romero in "Transition"; though Warren dies underground and Romero's body is found next morning in
his bunk. "Statement" was written some two months later than
"Transition," and I would be tempted to venture the opinion that
"Transition" was in some senses a tryout for "Statement," save for
the obvious and well-recorded fact that "Statement" derived almost
wholly from a nightmare of Lovecraft's (*SL* 1.94).

It is interesting to speculate, however, since the two stories are
so chronologically close in composition, whether the dream that
caused Lovecraft to write "Statement" was in some way derived
from the imagery of "Transition." That the theme of subterrene horror was "surfacing" in his work at this time is clear, and there may
be at the very least a psychological connection between the two
tales.

The Transition

What is the actual nature of the "transition" of Romero per the story's
title? Clearly, at one level, it is the simple transition from life to
death. Yet the tale obliquely suggests that there is more involved in
Romero's transition than this—that he has, perhaps, passed beyond
the human plane as a result of his encounter with force or forces unknown. In this sense, Lovecraft's tale implies that in encountering
some force or being that cannot be adequately described in human
language, the narrator has been privy to some terrible *gnosis*. Again,

this is a perennial theme of his work—the idea that in unearthing (willingly or unwillingly) information on the existence of beings on an order unguessed at by puny humankind, the individual narrators and characters of his stories gain an unwanted and hideous knowledge of the insignificance of humankind in the cosmos at large. "Transition" adumbrates this theme to a marked degree.

Also, what are we to make of the claim made by the men in the camp that neither Romero nor the narrator left their cabin the night they entered the vast rift? Were the men somehow hypnotized or mistaken? If not, did Romero and the narrator enter the rift in some non-corporeal state? And if that is the case, why is it that Romero's body has died after encountering the unknown forces that inhabit the cavernous void? Again, we can only speculate on the explanations for these things, and one has to admit that Lovecraft did not do a very good job of tying together these loose threads of the plot. Likewise, he has incorporated references to both the widely disparate Aztec and Hindu cultures, but there seems no clear reason why these might be connected through the events of the story. On these points, Lovecraft has let the reader down; and it was probably in recognising these facts that he refused to allow the story to be published in his lifetime.

Deus ex Machina

At the climax of the story, when the narrator looks into the final cavern which has swallowed up "the unfortunate Romero," there is a terrible bolt of lightning that strikes the mountain: "Some power from heaven, coming to my aid, obliterated both sights and sounds in such a crash as may be heard when two universes collide in space. Chaos supervened, and I knew the peace of oblivion" (*D* 342). Some "power from heaven," indeed! Not only does this attribution of nature to deity sit badly philosophically with Lovecraft's avowed mechanistic materialism, but this tendency to utilise *deux ex machina* involving lightning-bolts that "supervene" and bring "merciful oblivion" to the narrator of various tales is one of Lovecraft's least effective literary devices. Lovecraft was fond of merciful oblivion: recall the opening of "The Call of Cthulhu," "The most merciful thing in the world . . ." (*DH* 125), and that phrase from "The Outsider" (1921) regarding the figure in the mirror, "it was . . . the awful baring of that which the merciful earth should always hide" (*DH* 51). As to lightning and convenient thunderbolts, Lovecraft used this awkward and unconvincing device again in "The Picture in the House" (1920), where the tale ends with the following: "I did not shriek or move, but merely shut my eyes. A moment later came the titanic thunderbolt of thunderbolts; blasting that accursed house of unutterable secrets and bringing the oblivion which alone saved my mind" (*DH* 124), an ending that has always seemed to me laughably convenient. Lovecraft verges on it in "The Lurking Fear" (1922), whose plot is rife with storms: the tale opens: "There was thunder in the air the night I went to the deserted mansion atop Tempest Mountain to find the lurking fear" (*D* 179). The last episodes of that tale take place amidst "faint glows of lightning" (*D* 198) and "insane lightning over malignant ivied walls" (*D* 199). There is a far more mature use of a lightning storm at the conclusion of "The Haunter of the Dark" (1935), where the storm is integrated more convincingly as part of the plot. "Transition," with its crash which obliterates the narrator's consciousness, is a fumbling first attempt to use this rather ineffective device.

Conclusion

"The Transition of Juan Romero" is neither a very good story nor a very bad one. It has its points of interest, but it remains a relatively insignificant tale in Lovecraft's corpus because of the unresolved nature of various of its plot elements. One can at least see in it in the partly formed outlines of motifs and themes that Lovecraft would use in his later fiction when he had more command of his craft.

Works Cited

Boerem, R. "Lovecraft and the Tradition of the Gentleman Narrator." In *An Epicure in the Terrible: A Centennial Anthology of Essays in Honor of H. P. Lovecraft*, ed. David E. Schultz and S.T. Joshi. Rutherford, NJ: Fairleigh Dickinson University Press, 1991.

Burleson, Donald. *H. P. Lovecraft: A Critical Study*. Westport, CT: Greenwood Press, 1983.

Cannon, Peter. *H. P. Lovecraft*. Twayne's United States Authors Series. Boston: Twayne/G. K. Hall, 1989.

Joshi, S. T. *H. P. Lovecraft: A Life*. West Warwick, RI: Necronomicon Press, 1996.

———. *Lovecraft's Library: A Catalogue*. Rev. ed. New York: Hippocampus Press, 2002.

———. *A Subtler Magick: The Writings and Philosophy of H. P. Lovecraft*. San Bernadino, CA: Borgo Press, 1996.

Joshi, S. T., and David E. Schultz. *An H. P. Lovecraft Encyclopedia*. Westport, CT: Greenwood Press, 2001.

Lovecraft, H. P. *Essential Solitude: The Letters of H. P. Lovecraft and August Derleth*. Ed. David E. Schultz and S. T. Joshi. New York: Hippocampus Press, 2008.

———. *Lord of a Visible World: An Autobiography in Letters*. Ed. S. T. Joshi and David E. Schultz. Athens: Ohio University Press, 2000.

———. *Marginalia*. Sauk City, WI: Arkham House, 1944.

———. *O Fortunate Floridian: H. P. Lovecraft's Letters to R. H. Barlow*. Ed. S. T. Joshi and David E. Schultz. Tampa, FL: University of Tampa Press, 2007. [Abbreviated in the text as *OFF*.]

Pearsall, Anthony. *The Lovecraft Lexicon: A Reader's Guide to Persons, Places and Things in the Tales of H. P. Lovecraft*. Tempe, AZ: New Falcon Publications, 2005.

Poe, Edgar Allan. *Poetry and Tales*. New York: Library of America, 1984.

Prescott, William H. *History of the Conquest of Mexico and History of the Conquest of Peru*. New York: Modern Library, n.d.

Schweitzer, Darrell. *The Dream-Quest of H. P. Lovecraft*. San Bernadino, CA: Borgo Press, 1978.

Smith, Clark Ashton. *The Abominations of Yondo*. Sauk City, WI: Arkham House, 1960.

Wetzel, George. "The Cthulhu Mythos: A Study." In *H. P. Lovecraft: Four Decades of Criticism*, ed. S. T. Joshi. Athens: Ohio University Press, 1980.

Acknowledgments: I would like to extend my thanks to S. T. Joshi and David E. Schultz for assistance lent in the course of preparing this essay for publication.

"The Shadow out of Time" and Time-Defiance

Will Murray

Writing to August Derleth on November 21, 1930, Howard Phillps Lovecraft wrote: "Time, space, and natural law hold for me suggestions of intolerable bondage, and I can form no picture of emotional satisfaction which does not involve their defeat—especially the defeat of time, so that one may merge oneself with the whole historic stream and be wholly emancipated from the transient and the ephemeral" (*Essential Solitude* 1.288). The theme of "time-defiance," to invoke a term Lovecraft used elsewhere, is central to his work. It was to him one of the most compelling themes to which the cosmic writer could turn his pen. It threads through such of his weird tales as "The Dreams in the Witch House," *The Case of Charles Dexter Ward,* and "The Silver Key." It had its greatest expression in Lovecraft's last major story, "The Shadow out of Time," arguably his masterpiece. "The Call of Cthulhu" might well be the seminal Cthulhu Mythos story, and his more traditional horrors, such as "The Outsider" or "The Rats in the Walls," of greater universal appeal. But to me, and many Lovecraft aficionados, "The Shadow out of Time" is the absolute high-water mark of H. P. Lovecraft as a writer of cosmic horror.

It is astonishing, then, to look back upon the extended genesis of this Lovecraftian masterpiece and see its strange origins, its uncertain history, and its several brushes with destruction. Even—frightening thought—the revelation that Lovecraft actually gave the original story germ, gratis, to another writer, for his own use!

The same month that Lovecraft wrote of his fascination with time-defiance to Derleth, he was engaged in a lively correspondence with Clark Ashton Smith about weird fiction plots. Smith triggered an amazing chain of associations that would later culminate in "The Shadow out of Time" in a letter to Lovecraft dated October 30, 1930:

> By the way, your "Whisperer" suggested an idea which you might develop to more advantage than I could. Why not write a tale about some extraplanetary being who has undergone (either at the hands of his own kind, or of some human plastic surgeon) a facial transformation which enables him to pass as a human. His body, of course, would be 'teratologically fabulous' beneath his clothing; and there would be all sorts of disquieting suggestions about his personality. I think you could work this up to perfection if the idea appeals to you. (*Letters to H. P. Lovecraft* 17)

Lovecraft dutifully recorded Smith's suggestion—which in altered form would become central to "The Shadow out of Time"—in his commonplace book. But strangely enough, this wasn't the inspiration for the story, but an idea that was later subsumed into it.

The true inspiration began forming when Lovecraft wrote back on November 7:

> "The Canal" [by Everil Worrell] certainly has atmosphere. The final dynamiting—like my dynamiting of the house in Tempest Mountain in "The Lurking Fear"—is probably less subtly handled than it ought to be, yet is in a certain sense necessary as a means of explaining why the whole world hasn't 'gone vampire'. Whenever a fantastic tale introduces a horror which, if unchecked, it is necessary to explain why these results have not occurred—necessary, in short, to check the full action of the thing—unless the tale is laid in the *future*. There is really no way of escaping this dilemma. We must either explain the present survival of the existing order, or choose a remotely future period at which the existing order is assumed to be destroyed. The only adumbration of a middle course open to us is to have the original horror so subtle as to produce only imperceptible effects for a very long period, or to have a partial checking in which the action of is vastly diminished or delayed. In "Dagon" I shewed a horror that *may appear*, but that has not yet made any effort to do so. In "Cthulhu" I had a coming horror checked by the same convulsion of Nature which produced it. (Earthquake—sinking of R'lyeh). In "The Colour out of Space" I had a *partial* checking. Just enough of the Outside influence remains in the well to provide a *slow, creeping blight*. And in "Dun-

wich" I had full artificial destruction, as in "The Canal." When one does have full artificial destruction, the important thing is not to make the process too bold, crude, or incongruous with the atmosphere or action of the narrative as a whole. (*SL* 3.213)

Lovecraft's musing about a future setting seems to have ignited a kindred spark in Smith, who wrote him back outlining a novel time-travel mechanism. In response, Lovecraft replied with the first crystallization of "The Shadow out of Time" he would share with another human being. The letter was dated November 11, 1930.

Your idea for a time-voyaging machine is ideal—for in spite of Wells, no really satisfactory thing of the sort has ever been written. The weakness of most tales with this theme is that they do not provide for the recording, in history, of those inexplicable events in the past which were caused by the backward time-voyagings of the persons of the present & future. It must be remembered that if a man of 1930 travels back to B.C. 400, the strange phenomenon of his appearance actually occurred in B.C. 400, & must have excited notice wherever it took place. Of course, the way to get around this is to have the voyager conceal himself when he reaches the past, conscious of what an abnormality he must seem. Or rather, he ought simply to conceal his *identity*—hiding the evidences of his 'futurity' & mingling with the ancient as best he can on their own plane. It would be excellent to have him know to some extent of his past appearance before making the voyage. Let him, for example, encounter some private document of the past in which a record of the advent of a mysterious stranger—unmistakably himself—is made. This might be the provocation for his voyage—that is, the conscious provocation. One baffling thing that could be introduced is to have a modern man discover, among documents exhumed from some prehistoric buried city, a mouldering papyrus of parchment *written in English, & in his own handwriting*, which tells a strange tale & awakes—amidst a general haze of amazement, horror, & half-incredulity—a faint, far-off sense of familiarity which becomes more & more beckoning & challenging as the strings of semi-memory continue to vibrate. Re-reading awakes still more memories, till finally a definite course of action seems inevitable—& so on & so on. This idea has lain dormant in my commonplace-book for ages; & if you can find a use for it, you're certainly welcome to it. I might never develop it in years." (*SL* 3.216–17)

Here is the climax of "The Shadow out of Time," one of the most potent in Lovecraft's entire oeuvre, and he simply gives it away!

Smith was very much taken by Lovecraft's suggestion: "Your suggestions about a time-voyaging story are great!" he wrote back on November 16.

> Thanks for offering me the idea—it could certainly be worked up to advantage. The notion of finding an ancient record, in English, in one's own hand, is tremendous! The *mechanism* of time-travel in this case, might be a secret vault or adytum in the ruins which the archaeologist is exploring—a place designed by some ancient priesthood for the purpose of transportation in time. The hero stumbles upon the adytum *after* finding the records in his own script, and is whirled backward through the ages. (*Letters to H. P. Lovecraft* 20)

It was not until the following August that Smith availed himself of the concept:

> I've started three new tales, but haven't gone very far with any of them yet. One, "The Master of Destruction," will bring in my time-vault idea, and will take the hero into the lost world of which the asteroids are the problematic fragments. Archaeology on the asteroids will prove somewhat mischancy! The hero starts out by finding a beautiful mummy, wearing an amulet which contains a scroll in his own handwriting! (*Letters to H. P. Lovecraft* 29)

"The Master of the Asteroid" saw print in the October 1932 *Wonder Stories*. It is perhaps fortunate that Smith created a traditional science fiction story from Lovecraft's germ. Had he turned the idea into a purely weird tale, he might have deprived us of the very best of H. P. Lovecraft.

The specific germinal idea Lovecraft mentions as recorded in his commonplace book is a minor mystery. While there is an entry to this effect, it appears *after* the notation of Smith's idea of an alien in disguise: "In an ancient buried city a man finds a mouldering prehistoric document in English and in his own handwriting, telling an incredible tale. Voyage from present into past implied. Possible actualization of this" (entry 182). All these ideas will find their way into "The Shadow out of Time," but which is the formative spring-board Lovecraft cites is difficult to judge.

And there are earlier seed notions, such as the 1920 entry that reads: "To find something horrible in a (perhaps familiar) book, & not to be able to find it again" (entry 86). Another notation, "Man journeys into the past—or imaginative realm—leaving bodily shell behind" (entry 20), also smacks of this story. A fourth entry (88), which seems tangentially associated with the core idea, concerned a philosopher and his cat. After his death, instructions are found that ask that a pen be harnessed to the cat's forepaw. When this is done, the cat begins writing in the penmanship of the deceased.

More than two years would pass after the Lovecraft-Smith exchange that would ultimately give rise to "The Shadow out of Time." Then another, seemingly unrelated, element of the slowly coalescing story emerged. On March 2, 1932, while writing "The Dreams in the Witch House," Lovecraft told Smith:

> I have this sort of time idea of very simple nature floating around in the back of my head, but I don't know when I shall ever get around to using it. The notion is that of a race in primal Lomar perhaps even before the founding of Olathoe & in the heyday of Hyperborean Commoriom—who gained a knowledge of all arts & sciences by sending thought-streams ahead to drain the minds of men in future ages—angling in time as it were. Now & then they get hold of a really competent man of learning & annex all his thoughts. Usually they only keep their victims tranced for a short time, but once in a while, when they need some special piece of continuous information, one of their number sacrifices himself for the race & actually changes bodies with the first thoroughly satisfactory victim he finds. The victim's brain then goes back to 100,000 B. C.—into the hypnotist's body to live in Lomar for the rest of his life, while the hypnotist from dead aeons animates the modern clay of his victim. Complications can be imagined. I have no idea how—or from what angle—I shall elaborate the thing. (*SL* 4.25–26)

It was not immediately apparent to Lovecraft, but here was both the rationale and explanation for his nascent time-travel concept.

Sometime after this, a third idea—an image really—came to Lovecraft in a dream. He related it to Smith on October 22, 1933, never imagining that here was another major component of "The Shadow out of Time" taking shape.

> About a year ago, I dreamt I awaked on a slab of unknown substance in a great vaulted hall, dimly and obscurely lit, and full of similar slabs bearing sheeted objects whose proportions were obviously *not human*. From every detail I gathered the horrible notion *that I could be nowhere on this planet*. I also felt that my own body was like that of those other sheeted shapes. But I waked up in very truth at this juncture, so that no *story* was even begun! (*SL* 4.290)

Lovecraft was often inspired by dreams, and here was another fluke. Had Lovecraft not woke up before his subconscious mind had begun weaving a chain in incidents out of that arresting scene, he might have been compelled to write a story reflecting his unfinished dream. But he did not, and another "Shadow out of Time" building block was left to gestate larva-like in his brain.

By an interesting synchronicity, the very next month brought another creative trigger. As S. T. Joshi points out in his monumental biography, *H. P. Lovecraft: A Life*, Lovecraft saw in November the fantasy film *Berkeley Square*, which concerned Peter Standish, a twentieth-century man who projects his mind back into the body of his eighteenth-century ancestor. An aficionado of that era, Lovecraft was compelled to see the film four times.

Over the course of the year 1934 Lovecraft was evidently seized by other ideas that might have been inspired by these disconnected images. Two added to his commonplace book at this time were important:

> Begin story with presence of narrator—inexplicable to himself—in utterly alien & terrifying scenes. (dream?) (entry 211)

> Man with lost memory in strange, imperfectly comprehended environment. Fears to regain memory—a *glimpse*. . . . (entry 215)

Ultimately, the fertile ideas percolating in his mind impelled Lovecraft to write the story. Its original title is unknown—it may always have been "The Shadow out of Time"—but Lovecraft's first attempt to write the story proved such a failure that he destroyed the manuscript upon completing it. As he told E. Hoffmann Price on

November 18, 1934—four years after first offering the core idea concept to Smith:

> Just now I am experimenting with an old plot idea of mine which I may have described to you—that of a man who, in excavating ruins palpably of incredible antiquity, comes upon (as an unmistakable part of them) *a specimen of his own handwriting in English*. The explanation is that these ruins belong to a pre-human race of organic entities, infinitely above man in mental powers, who in their day ranged the whole gamut of time through mental transference. To learn of a future age, they have one of their number project his mind ahead and displace the consciousness of somebody in the chosen period. Then the voyaging mind in the body of its victim, would absorb all the information possible—and finally fly back through time to its original body, while the displaced mind had occupied the body of the pre-human voyager, hence had had a brief life and consciousness in the immemorial past. And of course it could then *leave* a record which, in its proper body millions of years later, it could discover during the excavation of blasphemously ancient megalithic ruins. Well—I developed that story *mistily and allusively* in 16 pages, but it was no go. Thin and unconvincing, with the climactic revelation wholly unjustified by the hash of visions preceding it. So I've torn the whole damn thing up and am rewriting it in my usual latter style—with gradual hints and slowly built-up stages of unfolding. Am now on page 27, and fear it will run to 40 before I'm through. Naturally, I know what the majority will say—if I decide to type it and show it around. "Verbose—long-winded—slow—nothing happens—novelette length for a short-story idea—etc., etc., etc." But the fact remains that it represents the best I can do with the given idea. The shorter treatment was wholly inadequate—not even scratching the surface of the many bizarre implications involved in the central assumption. And so it goes. Possibly I'll never succeed in what I'm slowly fumbling for, but only experiment will decide. (*SL* 5.70–71)

The next day, Lovecraft told Duane Rimel: "Am about 3/4 through the second writing of a tale called 'The Shadow out of Time', which may come to 50 pages—I'm beginning p. 32 now" (ms, John Hay Library). A month later, the story was stalled, as Lovecraft made clear to Price on December 30:

> This new thing—a second version—fails to satisfy me, and I don't
> know whether to finish it as it is or destroy once more and start
> afresh. Pressure of other duties has for the moment made any original
> writing impossible. The incomplete effusion is about 3/4 done. It will
> probably mark my last attempt in the vein of recent years. (SL 5.86)

For weeks, "The Shadow out of Time" teetered on the precipice of
oblivion. Lovecraft busied himself with the writing of voluminous
letters. Eventually, his attention returned to the difficult story. "Am
snatching moments & getting near the end of 'The Shadow out of
Time,'" he told Price in a February 4, 1935 letter (ms., John Hay Library). On March 13, he reported the following to J. Vernon Shea:
"I've finished 'The Shadow out of Time' (second version) Feby. 22,
but am too doubtful of its merits to attempt the appalling task of
typing its 65-odd pages" (ms., John Hay Library).

Oddly, Lovecraft's letters disagree on the story's true date of
completion. While he told Shea that it was finished on February 22,
he told Emil Petaja that it was the 24th (SL 5.120), and in a March
14 letter to E. Hoffmann Price, he claimed to have "finished 'The
Shadow out of Time' last week" (SL 5.124)—a full two weeks after
the other dates. The actual completion date, as verified by the recently discovered autograph manuscript, is February 22. A letter to
August Derleth shows how precarious the story's future was then—
and how terrible a judge of his own work was H. P. Lovecraft at
that point in his career.

> As for "The Shadow out of Time"—which I'm just finishing up
> now—I'm hanged if I know whether it's worth preserving or not.
> This is the *second* version I have completed, & I may tear it up as I
> did the first . . . although it is not quite as unsatisfying to me as that
> was. At any rate, I simply can't waste energy *typing* it until I decide
> whether it's worth preserving or not. If I send it as it is, the chances
> are that you can't make out more than half of it . . . so what the
> hell? If I do decide to let you try your hand at making out the hi-
> eroglyphs, you mustn't feel under any obligation to go through the
> whole thing. Probably the waste basket is the real ultimate destina-
> tion. Most readers will complain of the *length* of the thing—but I
> don't yet know how the given material can be presented more suc-
> cinctly. The destroyed version was short—but it didn't convey
> what I wished to convey. The conditions & implications brought up

by the central concept left all sorts of obvious questions unanswered, while the experience in Australia remained wholly unconvincing for lack of atmospheric preparation & emotional modulation. Whether the present version is any better, remains to be seen. It is possible that I ought to tear everything up & abandon the whole idea for an altogether fresh start. And then again, it is possible that I have wholly lost the knack of fictional formulation, & ought to cease altogether from attempting stories. . . . this is the only thing since "The Thing on the Doorstep" which I have not destroyed. (*Essential Solitude* 2.679–80)

Fortunately for his readers, Lovecraft relented, and added the following postscript: "P. S. Well—after all, I'm sending the damn thing . . . although a final reading makes me fear more than ever that the waste-basket is the one logical destination. Don't try to wade through if it seems too utterly repellent—either chirographically or literarily. I am utterly sick of it—the very sight of it turns my stomach!" And there matters stood for several months.

In August, writing to Duane Rimel, Lovecraft complained: "Derleth didn't finish 'The Shadow out of Time', so I recalled it to shew Barlow . . . & now *he* hasn't finished it. The bad handwriting is perhaps partly responsible for their inattention" (ms., John Hay Library). But unknown to Lovecraft, Barlow was surreptitiously preparing a typescript of the story. Later that month, Lovecraft told Price, "Barlow has typed my latest thing—'The Shadow out of Time'—& it comes to 88 pages" (ms., John Hay Library).

Barlow may have been the unsung rescuer of the story. Years later, his 1944 memoir, "The Wind That is in the Grass," he recalled:

Only one manuscript remains in my possession . . . the notebook in which he pencilled "The Shadow out of Time." He had destroyed one draught of this story and threatened to destroy the second, so when he showed it to me in the summer of 1935, I had it typed and returned him the typescript. At that time he was making his second visit to me in Florida, so I sounded him out by drawing parallels with T. E. Lawrence. He agreed that under certain circumstances manuscripts could justifiably be taken away from their authors, and this was certainly the case with the "Shadow," for I had it copied, and later on Donald Wandrei submitted it for publication, both without consulting Lovecraft. (*O Fortunate Floridian* xxxiii)

Even with a typed manuscript suitable for submission, Love-craft's dissatisfaction with the story inclined him against submitting it to *Weird Tales*. Fortunately—perhaps only because of Barlow's effort to prepare a typescript—he decided against destroying "The Shadow out of Time." And so it went the rounds of his correspondents.

Lovecraft's letters are silent on initial reaction to the story except for an occasional passing reference like the one in a September 28, 1935 letter to Duane Rimel:

> Price, I think, is a little premature in saying that my newer tales all concentrate on weird aspects of human character. He gets that idea from "The Thing on the Doorstep", which he liked especially, but this story is not by any means typical of my whole output. It is only one of many experiments—each different from the other. "The Shadow out of Time," for example, is nothing at all like this—being a straight *phenomenon* story close to the borders of science-fiction. *Nothing* is really "typical" of my efforts at this stage. I'm simply casting about for better ways to crystallize and capture certain strong impressions (involving the elements of *time, the unknown, cause and effect, fear, scenic and architectural beauty*, and other seemingly ill-assorted things) which persist in clamouring for expression. Perhaps the case is hopeless—that is, I may be experimenting in the wrong medium altogether. It may be that poetry instead of fiction is the only effective vehicle to put such expression across. (*SL* 5.199)

This period of inertia and doubt was ultimately dispelled by several events in November 1935. Both "The Shadow out of Time" and *At the Mountains of Madness* were swiftly accepted by *Astounding Stories* at that time, and Lovecraft was greatly encouraged. This changed when they appeared in print. *At the Mountains of Madness* was truncated horribly. "The Shadow out of Time" did not suffer greatly, according to Lovecraft—which is fortunate, since it is the only major Lovecraft story whose manuscript did not resurface in time to be fully restored for the current reedited Arkham House editions. Still, the experience put the brakes on further fiction writing, although Lovecraft continued to keep open the possibility that he would write more fiction.

Only four months before he died, Lovecraft wrote to Wilfred Blanch Talman on November 10, 1936:

I have for the last several weeks been trying to clear my programme for another of my seasons of fictional experimentation (like the season of 1934–35, when I wrote half a dozen things and destroyed all save "The Shadow out of Time" ... which was itself the 3rd complete version of the story), and if I do succeed in getting going it is quite possible that I might arrive at the novel-synopsis stage—or the novel-writing stage. Who can say? (*SL* 5.346–47)

This version does not jibe with previous accounts of writing "The Shadow out of Time," but that is unimportant. Whether there were two or three drafts, it matters only that the story did survive its protracted, painful, and precarious birth. And while we may regret that the story's original 16-page version does not survive for comparison, there is no question but that "The Shadow out of Time" was Lovecraft's last great story, if not his greatest story.

I thought so when I first read it over twenty years ago, and a recent rereading affirms this feeling. Although knowing the ending does make the early pages seem draggy and obvious, once Nathaniel Wingate Peaslee arrives in Australia and begins exploring those portentous ruins, the pace picks up so that, in spite of my foreknowledge of its shattering climax, I experienced anew its powerful urgency. And I realized, perhaps for the first time, what truly moves me about the story: its theme. What Lovecraft called "time-defiance."

The concept was elaborated by Lovecraft in an August 31, 1934 missive to E. Hoffmann Price: "What I know of detailed human activities is very slight—and what I care about them slighter still, except so far as the element of historic pageantry is concerned. Nothing but the element of *nature-defiance*—especially *time-defiance*—sets off the spring that starts my creative imagination running" (*SL* 5.25). As Lovecraft wrote to Barlow on August 8, 1933:

> *Time* is really one of the most baffling and fascinating things in human experience. What is it that has created a 1933 H. P. L. differing from the 1903 H. P. L.—and can the 1903 H. P. L. be *really* annihilated when all his moods and memories can be recalled by the 1933 edition? I give it up—but there is a whole wealth of fantastic story material in the reflections arising from these things. I think that of all the concepts inciting me to expression, the mystery of *time* is perhaps the most potent and persistent. My "Silver Key" is an example of how I react to it. (*SL* 4.233–34)

Lovecraft's other major work written at this time in his waning career, *At the Mountains of Madness*, also focused on this theme. He reiterated his approach in a letter to E. Hoffmann Price dated March 16, 1936:

> As for Mts. of Madness—the idea of *time*—its vastness, mystery, menace, hellish cruelty, essential horror, & dim, profound connexion with the most basic & persistent factors in all the cosmos—fascinates me more hauntingly than any other conception in the field of consciousness. Absolutely nothing has the power to hold my interest more than *the idea of persistence in time* as typified by survivals from antiquity, either relatively recent (my own youth—the 18th century—the age of imperial Rome) or immeasurably, immemorially & blasphemously vast . . . the youth of organic life . . . the youth of the planet or of the solar system . . . the youth of Time itself . . . The *only thing I really want to do* is portray *time* somehow—to capture, if only fragmentarily & for an elusive moment, some spark, of its horrible & mysterious essence . . . or to suggest in some dimly convincing way its momentary circumvention or defeat. I realise that fiction is not the best medium for this. It ought to be expressed in *poetry*—but when one isn't a poet, what the hell is one to do? (Ms., John Hay Library)

I suspect I was first struck by the cosmic immensity of time around 1964 when—of all things—reading a *Superman* comic book. In it was a reproduction of the first issue's cover, from 1938. How fabulously old that seemed to my youthful mind! How impossibly rare that comic book seemed to me then. Today, more years yawn between 1964 and the present than separated that young boy from the hoary year of 1938. But I still remember the thrill of dwelling on this seemingly unattainable artifact from many years before I was born.

Lovecraft had a similar experience, I discovered. He related it to J. Vernon Shea on February 4, 1934, while struggling with "The Shadow out of Time":

> My first acute realisation of *time* was when I saw newspapers bearing the heavily-inked date-line TUESDAY, JANUARY 1, 1895. *1895!!* To me the symbol *1894* had represented an eternity—the eternity of *the present* as distinguished from, such things as 1066 or

1492 or 1642 or 1776—& the idea of personally outliving that eternity was absorbingly impressive to me, even though I fully realised,
in an abstract way, that I would do so ... that I had been born in
1890 & would probably (in view of the average death-ages of near
kinsfolk) live till about 1960. I shall never forget the sensation of
moving through time (if forward, why not backward?) which that '95
date-line gave me. (*SL* 4.357)

Another, similar experience was told to Derleth on September 9,
1931:

In 1896, when I was six years old, I was taken to visit in the Western Rhode Island region whence my maternal stock came; and there
met an ancient gentlewoman—a Mrs. Wood, daughter to a rebel
officer in the late unfortunate uprising against His Majesty's lawful
authority—who was celebrating with proper pride her hundredth
birthday. Mrs. Wood was born in the year 1796, and could walk and
talk when Genl. Washington breath'd his last. And now, in 1896, I
was conversing with her—with one who had talked to people in
periwigs and three-cornered hats, and had studied from school-
books with the long s! Young as I was, the idea gave me a tremendous feeling of cosmic victory over Time—a sense that I was
actually working my way back into that 18th century which had
produced the Georgian doorways on the hill and the brown-leather
books in the trunk room. (*Essential Solitude* 1.381)

Although these themes are so deeply imbedded in "The Shadow
out of Time," they elude a reader unfamiliar with Lovecraft's *Selected Letters*, as they eluded me when I first read "The Shadow out
of Time" as a teenager. Today these meditations on time resonate
for me in a way I don't think I was consciously aware during my
earlier readings of the story.

The *Superman* anecdote might explain why I later became interested in the pulp magazine era of the 1930s—its writers and characters. My interest in Lovecraft is an offshoot of that, too. It is
virtually identical to the impulse that fixated Lovecraft on the
eighteenth century, with which he had no first-hand contact. The
same igniting spark, but a different flame, I imagine.

But the notion of the time-track a human being occupies in his
allotted span—the very concept of years before and after one's exis-

tence—these fascinate me, too. Moving through time—backward more than forward, since we are always moving forward in time—is a powerful concept. I never walked this planet while Lovecraft lived, and the conceit that I could defy time and walk Lovecraft's Providence remains a compelling one to me—perhaps because of its very impossibility.

"The Shadow out of Time" is about just such an impossibility. But Lovecraft makes it resonate for a reader such as myself precisely because Lovecraft and I share the same longings and yearnings to escape the limitations of our natural spans, and to know eras that are forever denied us because we were born too late or died too soon.

H. P. Lovecraft died too soon, to be sure. If "The Shadow out of Time" is any indication, he died at the pinnacle of his creative powers, with many great unrealized stories orbiting his uncanny imagination—much as "The Shadow out of Time" did for four long years. Still, I can't help wondering what the 1930 Lovecraft did with "The Shadow out of Time" and how that would differ from the story we know today. It would be wonderful to read that destroyed draft. But one would have to achieve the Lovecraftian ideal of defying time to do so.

"The Shadow out of Time" first saw print in the June 1936 issue of *Astounding Stories*. Howard V. Brown painted the cover, depicting the conical beings Lovecraft called the Great Race. Lovecraft's work rarely rated the cover, but this one was notable for another reason: After Lovecraft's death, sketches of the Great Race were discovered among his notes. They bore an uncanny resemblance to the cover Brown painted, using only the author's textual descriptions for a guide. For that, and many other reasons, that issue of *Astounding Stories* has to be the ultimate Lovecraft pulp magazine collectible, for it is his greatest tale in the perfect showcase for his work.

Works Cited

Joshi, S. T. *H. P. Lovecraft: A Life*. West Warwick, RI: Necronomicon Press, 1996.

Lovecraft, H. P. *Essential Solitude: The Letters of H. P. Lovecraft and August Derleth*. Ed. David E. Schultz and S. T. Joshi. New York: Hippocampus Press, 2008. 2 vols.

————. O *Fortunate Floridian: H. P. Lovecraft's Letters to R. H. Barlow*. Ed. S. T. Joshi and David E. Schultz. Tampa: University of Tampa Press, 2007.

Smith, Clark Ashton. *Letters to H. P. Lovecraft*. Ed. Steve Behrends. West Warwick, RI: Necronomicon Press, 1987.

Briefly Noted

A remarkable bibliographical discovery by Richard Bleiler, a scholar and librarian in Connecticut. He has located the appearance of Lovecraft's poem "To Mr. Lockhart, on His Poetry" in a South Dakota newspaper. Previously, only a clipping of this item, from an unidentified newspaper, had been seen. Mr. Bleiler has identified the publication as the *Aberdeen Daily American* (11 March 1917): 5. Aberdeen is a town of some significance about 90 miles west of Milbank, where Andrew Francis Lockhart, the subject of the poem, lived. It is still conceivable that the poem also appeared in a Milbank newspaper. The poem appeared in the *Tryout* (March 1917), and it is just possible that the appearance in the Aberdeen newspaper actually predates the *Tryout* appearance and therefore constitutes the first publication of the poem.

Poems Not in *The Ancient Track*

H. P. Lovecraft

Edited by S. T. Joshi

The Ancient Track: Complete Poetical Works (2001) represented, at the time, the most comprehensive edition of Lovecraft's poetry ever compiled. But the volume knowingly had at least one omission: "An American to the British Flag," a poem whose existence was known but whose text was then unavailable. This text has now been found by Sean McLachlan, conducting research among British amateur journals in the British Library. In the course of my own work on Lovecraft bibliography and Lovecraft's letters, I have found several more poems or poem fragments, and the results are printed below. Pending the discovery of yet more items, we can conclude that these poems, taken along with *The Ancient Track*, constitute the entirety of Lovecraft's poetic output. The poems are presented chronologically; I have appended brief notes with them, in the manner of the notes in *The Ancient Track*.—S. T. J.

To the Recipient of This Volume

Congenial Cole, I pray thee condescend
To take this off'ring of a distant friend.
Within these year-worn pages canst thou find
A feast of culture for the eager mind.
Here shine the precepts of a statelier age,
To mould the line, and smooth th' unpolished page.
With study'd grace the sentence to adorn,

And rise to images sublimely drawn.
E'en now the Muse's choicest gifts are thine:
How, then, will glow thy labour'd, polish'd line!
Son of the plains! May thy Pierian flights
Sustain thee upward to Parnassus' heights!

FP: *To the Recipient of This Volume* (Madison, WI: Strange Co., 1988). Dated 7 December 1915. The poem was written on the flyleaf of a book sent to Edward H. Cole. The book's title is unknown.

As London wits at Will's or Button's knew
The letter'd leisure of a favour'd few;
So our small band, more scatter'd and less able,
May meet in mind, if not about the table!

LUDOVICUS THEOBALDUS, JUN.

FP: Letter to the Kleicomolo (8 August 1916); in *Letters to Rheinhart Kleiner* (New York: Hippocampus Press, 2005), p. 37. Will's and Button's were London coffeehouses that, in the early eighteenth century, were frequented by the leading literary figures of the day.

The cluster'd spires and roofs that gaily gleam
Across the verdant plain and glist'ning stream.
[. . .]
The bending corn that in profusion grows
Where rural virtue earns its calm repose.
[. . .]
The twining thicket and the shady grove
Where supple Fauns in artless pleasure move.

FP: Letter to Rheinhart Kleiner, 8 November 1917; in *Letters to Rheinhart Kleiner* (New York: Hippocampus Press, 2005), pp. 119–20. HPL is presenting Kleiner with examples of the kind of eighteenth-century poetry he likes to write; the first relates to "a pleasing prospect of a distant town"; the second "some idyllic vistas of tilled land & cottages"; the third "a tangled brake or cluster of trees."

An American to the British Flag

In zealous rage our fathers swore
To fly the ancient flag no more;
    To trail it in the dust:
They curs'd the holy cross of red,
For which th' embattled free had bled,
    And deem'd their hatred just.

Another lag in pomp they rais'd,
And whilst the world stood by amaz'd,
    A nation had its birth.
Forgetful of the blood that gave
Their pow'r to prosper, free and brave,
    They welcom'd all the earth.

The Land that English prowess made,
A horde of mongrel breed display'd;
    The scourings of mankind.
The pauper and the weakling swarm'd
O'er realms our English fathers form'd:
    O nation proudly blind!

Our dear ancestral glories wane
From teeming town, from grove and plain,
    And well-remember'd leas.
'Mid changing scenes we sadly plod
As strangers on our native sod,
    And live in memories.

O Flag of Old! At last we hail
Once more thy ripples in the gale,
    And watch thy wistful face.
Thy folds remain, tho' aliens rise
To taint each story'd scene we prize,
    Thou symbol of our race.

FP: *Little Budget of Knowledge and Nonsense* 1, No. 9 (December 1917):
110. One of several of HPL's poems celebrating England and especially
the uniting of England and the United States against Germany in
World War I.

Suspicious Souls with Pride are wont to tell
How quick they can a Rodent's Presence smell;
Yet if the scamp'ring Train be swift and small,
'Tis easie not to glimpse the Rogues at all.
In PRINTER's Day, when Act was quick as Thought,
How few the Mice that cou'd survive uncaught!
Our languid Age displays a lesser Skill,
And the brown Nibblers vex our Cheese at will!
But here and there, where western Rivers pour,
Young Heads preserve their Sires' forgotten Lore;
Catch the old Scent, and trap for future Time
The brood that burrows deep in doubtful Rhyme.

FP: Unpublished. Found in a letter to Helm C. Spink, 13 August 1930 (ms., JHL). The poem is one of a sequence of verses relating to the pets of Mrs. Miniter, this one dealing with a cat named Printer (see "Veteropinguis Redivivus," *AT* 177–79).

Dirge of the Doomed

Dulce et decorum est pro basilica mori

Still dream the placid ancient ways
    That once your footsteps knew,
Tho' with uncertain, number'd days
    The courthouse greets our view.

Behold a chart of all the change
    Men hereabouts would fix—
New pinnacles and belfries strange . . .
    But no 256!

A sadden'd twilight drap'd the shore
    Not so many bygone evens
When in the dark of Adams' store
    I met your partner Stevens.

(I'd come for milk, be sure to grant—
  And not for bootleg gin;
I was a-dining with my aunt*,
  And helping cart things in!)

We talk'd, we mourn'd, yet overhead
  Still lower'd the pall of doom;
For Adam's last fond hope is dead—
  Across the street, no room!

Eheu! *Sic transit*—as they cry
  On many a tardy 'bus;
'Tis sad to see a mem'ry die—
  A shrine be shatter'd thus!

But hope pervades the pious dream,
  For just below the hill
Safe nestling by the perfumed stream
  Our Jacques is with us still!

*Mrs. Gamwell, who lives at the Handicraft Club in the old Beckwith mansion at College & Benefit.

FP: Wilfred B. Talman, "The Normal Lovecraft," *The Normal Lovecraft* (Saddle River, NJ: Gerry de la Ree, 1973), p. 9. The epigraph is a parody of *Dulce et decorum est pro patria mori* (Horace, *Odes* 2.3.13): "It is sweet and fitting to die for one's country." HPL's version translates to: "It is sweet and fitting to die for one's shop." The reference is to Jacque's (named for one Adam Jacques), a restaurant that HPL favoured because of its generous portions, cheap price, and the fact that it catered to truck drivers and sailors. The poem probably dates to April 1935, when HPL learned it had closed. (HPL referred to it in correspondence as *Jake's* because the owner pronounced it so himself.)

(Wet) Dream Song

Homer had the pox,
Sappho had the itch,
But I'm just a vox-
Popular sonofabitch.

Mustard without cress,
Cakes without ale,
Satisfy me less
Than a cat without a tail.

I who loved the light
Of extinguished moons,
Chanted all night
My cacophonous tunes.

For hours and hours
On the arid Atlantic,
The clamour of flowers
Drove me quite frantic.

What should one do
When one's on the blink?
Have an oyster stew,—
Or another drink?

FP: [Untitled note on amateur journalism], *Collected Essays, Volume 1: Amateur Journalism* (New York: Hippocampus Press, 2004). A parody of amateur poetry, in an attempt to criticise some amateurs' "yen for a sort of fourth-rate, bastard decadence, in which downright incoherence with maundering silliness is fatuously mistaken for some kind of God-help-us Symbolism." HPL claimed that he wrote the poem *currente Corona* ("with my Corona [i.e., typewriter] running"); i.e., composed as HPL was at his typewriter (although the text is a handwritten ms.). Probably written in the mid-1930s.

Black and unform'd, as pestilent a Clod
As dread Sadoqua, Averonia's God.

FP: Letter to Fritz Leiber, [25 January 1937]; in *Selected Letters 1934–1937* (Sauk City, WI: Arkham House, 1976), p. 387. A poem about Tsathoggua (Sadoqua) written in eighteenth-century verse. HPL pretends that it is a translation of a Latin line (*Niger informisque ut numen Averonum Sadoqua*) found in the imaginary *De Noctis Rebus* (c. A.D. 390) by Valerius Trevirus, in "Theobald's privately printed English translation (1711)," i.e., a translation purportedly made by Lewis Theobald (1688–1744), British editor and author whose name HPL appropriated for his pseudonym "Lewis Theobald, Jun."

Lovecraft and the Polar Myth

John M. Navroth

One of the most enduring of humanity's adventures into the discovery of the natural world has been the exploration of the North and South Poles. No satisfactory comparison, other than perhaps the bleak landscapes of the moon or Mars, can match the vast, expansive *awe* that is evoked from images of the North Pole and Antarctica. Of the very few places left on earth for humankind and science to conquer, the icy wastes at the top and bottom of terra firma have withstood many attempts to penetrate their secrets. In truth, until the latter part of the twentieth century, little was known of these strange, earthbound lands other than ways to navigate and traverse on and around them. As a result, many legends have grown up surrounding their mysteries: ancient cities and races, hollow earth theories, UFO bases, and Nazi survival are just a few of the spurious subjects that have persisted in both hemispheres of the minds of men. History and pseudohistory teems with conjecture regarding what is hidden in these white deserts of ice. One could go so far as to say that there even exists a Polar Mythos cult.

And to be sure, science in the late nineteenth and early twentieth centuries still held many theories, hypotheses, and speculation about those remaining few little-explored areas of the globe, not the least of which were the poles. It wasn't until just after the beginning of the twentieth century that the Northwest Passage was navigated successfully by Amundsen's little ship. There were many near-mythical tales to tell about these voyages. Amundsen's North Pole adventure was one of them that captured the public's attention.

Born 16 July 1872 in Norway, Roald Engelbregt Gravning Amundsen was the son of a ship owner. Oddly, he was steered away from the maritime industry, and his parents, especially his mother, wanted him to be a doctor. Amundsen's father died when he was just fourteen, and his mother died when he was twenty-one. After her death, Amundsen turned headlong back to the passion that he had been harboring in secret all along, that of following in the footsteps of his father as a seaman. He had surreptitiously been studying ships and sailing all the while, and it was not long before he had his own boat. His credit became too much of a burden, however, and, just when his creditors were to sweep down on him, a second cousin came to the rescue and paid his debts. Shortly after, he was on the voyage that led to his successful trip through the Northwest Passage. During the voyage he spent over a year with the indigenous Inuit (Lovecraft's Esquimaux) who taught him not only about living, but *surviving* in the polar wastes. He learned many things that gave him an advantage over other, larger expeditions, and which probably saved his life more than once. Amundsen's main advantage was a smaller boat and crew that sailed more easily through ice floes and shallows. His British and American counterparts tried to bull their way through with large, steel-hulled ships and heavy equipment and crews. Comparatively speaking, one might even say that Amundsen finessed his way through the Passage. Even today, huge 35,000-horsepower ice-breakers can get stopped dead in an icy grip anywhere along the treacherous Northwest Passage. The entire route is mapped *daily* by the Canadians to help prevent this and to keep commerce sailing smoothly.

Amundsen was not alone. Byrd, Scott, and Shackleton all contributed to showing the world through their adventure and heroism the real wonders of both the North Pole and Antarctica. However, romantic notions about these barren, ice- and snow-covered deserts would die hard, even to the point where some persist today.

So, one may ask by now, where does Lovecraft fit into all of this? It is not hard to imagine the impact of these heroic adventurers on the young and precocious Rhode Islander. Indeed, the subject fascinated him practically all his life. He wrote about the Antarctic as a young lad of twelve, and as early as the age of nine he read a book about a reanimated freebooter called *The Frozen Pirate* by W. Clark Russell (1887). Lovecraft was also keenly aware of Richard Byrd's historic polar explorations and referred to him on numerous occasions in his letters.

One does find it queer, however, that Lovecraft chose to delve repeatedly into the subject of *cold*. For someone near the point of being phobic about it, he turns to the topic again and again, in such stories as "Cool Air" and, of course, *At the Mountains of Madness*. As mentioned, he was fascinated with the various explorers' polar adventures of the time. Incredibly, one of his favorite foods was ice cream! It makes one wonder if he let it melt first before eating it. The answer is probably not, because in a letter to Maurice Moe on 30 July 1927 he says: "There are *twenty-eight* varieties this season, and we *sampled them all* within the course of an hour."[1] Still another reason may be cathartic. In *Primal Sources: Essays on H. P. Lovecraft*, S. T. Joshi offers Maurice Lévy's opinion that Lovecraft is "vicariously attempting to bestow the horror in his tales upon himself" (51).

It is commonly suggested that, in writing *At the Mountains of Madness*, Lovecraft was influenced by Poe's *The Narrative of Arthur Gordon Pym of Nantucket* (first book publication 1838). True, he does mention the tale outright during the course of his own story:

> Danforth was a great reader of bizarre material, and had talked a good deal of Poe. I was interested myself because of the antarctic scene of Poe's only long story - the disturbing and enigmatical Arthur Gordon Pym. On the barren shore, and on the lofty ice barrier in the background, myriads of grotesque penguins squawked and flapped their fins, while many fat seals were visible on the water, swimming or sprawling across large cakes of slowly drifting ice. (*MM* 8)

Again he mentions Pym (obliquely, as if he had really existed), as well as "Tekeli-li!," the cry of those "spectrally snowy birds of that malign region's core":

> The new sound, as I have intimated, upset much that we had decided; because it was what poor Lake's dissection had led us to attribute to those we had judged dead. It was, Danforth later told me,

---

1. Some sources assume that Lovecraft is talking about the Friendly's Ice Cream Corporation in his letters. According to the Friendly's website (http://www.friendlys.com), they did not start business until 1935 in Springfield, Massachusetts. Any mention prior to this would have obviously been referring to another brand or establishment.

precisely what he had caught in infinitely muffled form when at that spot beyond the alley corner above the glacial level; and it certainly had a shocking resemblance to the wind pipings we had both heard around the lofty mountain caves. At the risk of seeming puerile I will add another thing, too, if only because of the surprising way Danforth's impressions chimed with mine. Of course common reading is what prepared us both to make the interpretation, though Danforth has hinted at queer notions about unsuspected and forbidden sources to which Poe may have had access when writing his *Arthur Gordon Pym* a century ago. It will be remembered that in that fantastic tale there is a word of unknown but terrible and prodigious significance connected with the antarctic and screamed eternally by the gigantic spectrally snowy birds of that malign region's core. *"Tekeli-li! Tekeli-li!"* That, I may admit, is exactly what we thought we heard conveyed by that sudden sound behind the advancing white mist-that insidious musical piping over a singularly wide range. (*MM* 97)

Another inspiration that is quite evident by the numerous references to him in the story is Russian artist/explorer/mystic Nicholas Roerich. This is further illuminated by a letter from Lovecraft to James F. Morton in early 1937:

Better than the surrealists . . . is good old Nick Roerich, whose joint at Riverside Drive and 103rd Street is one of my shrines in the pest zone. There is something in his handling of perspective and atmosphere which to me suggests other dimensions and alien orders of being—or at least, the gateways leading to such. Those fantastic carven stones in lonely upland deserts—those ominous, almost sentient, lines of jagged pinnacles—and above all, those curious cubical edifices clinging to precipitous slopes and edging upward to forbidden needle-like peaks! (*SL* 5.436)

While the date of the letter is past both the writing and the publication date of the story, Lovecraft was still no doubt aware of Roerich's exploits into the Himalayan wastes well before.

Nicholas Konstantinovich Roerich (b. St. Petersburg, Russia, October 9, 1874; d. Kullu, India, December 14, 1947), son of Konstantin and Maria, grew up in a household that saw the visit of many writers, artists, and scientists of the time. At the age of nine, he was invited to go along on a local archaeological exploration. From then on, Nicholas fostered a lifelong interest in the subject. He also became very adept at illustration and thought he might have a career in art. His father objected, however, and wanted him to follow, as was expected in the day, in his footsteps as a lawyer. They reached a compromise and he enrolled concurrently in both law and art school. Upon the completion of his studies in the late 1890s, Nicholas planned to tour Europe. Just before leaving he met Helena, the daughter of the architect Shaposhnikov and niece of the composer Mussorgsky. They married shortly thereafter.

Helena was widely read and was something of an intellectual. She wrote many books and translated Helena Petrovna Blavatsky's *The Secret Doctrine* into Russian. In later years, Nicholas and Helena re-formed the Agni Yoga Society in New York.

Roerich saw the mystic's view of life in things. He viewed everything as to how it corresponded with everything else, which is the classic "as above, so below" hermetic philosophy of many poets (e.g., Baudelaire), occultists, and metaphysicians.

It was Roerich's gift that these "connections" appeared so natural to him and presented themselves in all life's manifestations. And it was this talent for synthesis, which he admired in others and encouraged in the young, that enabled him to correlate the subjective with the objective, the philosophical with the scientific, Eastern wisdom with Western knowledge, and to build bridges of understanding between such apparent contradictions. He reminded us that these contradictions were often the result of human ignorance, and that an expanding consciousness, which each individual was duty-bound to pursue, would lead to eventual recognition of the illusoriness, or relativity, of things. As Garabed Paelian affirms in his book *Nicholas Roerich:* Roerich "learned things ignored by other men; perceived relations between seemingly isolated phenomena, and unconsciously felt the presence of an unknown treasure." Perhaps it is this "unknown treasure" that in Roerich's paintings speaks to the viewer who is attuned to that underlying meaning, and further explains the transcendental feelings that some experience through his canvases.[2]

2. The Nicholas Roerich Museum webpage: http://www.roerich.org.

Beginning in the early 1920s, Roerich traveled extensively in the East, writing and painting his impressions innumerable times during that time and from then on. He cultivated a deep-seated affinity for the mountainous Himalayas and the spirituality of its indigenous peoples, and, as a result, shaped much of the rest of his life around this interest. When Roerich died in 1947, he was buried in his beloved place at the foothills of the Himalayas. Kullu/Kulu (and Lovecraftians here will want to see the similarity to "Cthulhu") was at one time known as "the end of the habitable world."

It is not hard to see why Lovecraft's inspiration was enhanced by Roerich's paintings. While many of his works postdated the writing of *At the Mountains of Madness*, there were still examples that would have captivated Lovecraft to be seen at the time during one of his New York sojourns. Additionally, in a letter to Robert H. Barlow dated 13 January 1934, Lovecraft writes, "Merritt [the fantasy author Abraham Merritt] has a wide acquaintance among mystical enthusiasts, and is a close friend of old Nicholas Roerich, the Russian painter whose weird Thibetan landscapes I have so long admired" (*SL* 4.341–42).

Not surprisingly, then, as if consequential to Lovecraft's admiration of the visionary work of Roerich, he mentions Roerich's paintings in *At the Mountains of Madness* to amplify his intended impression of the *alienness* of the Antarctic to the reader. In *H. P. Lovecraft: A Life*, S. T. Joshi states:

> And, of course, it can scarcely be denied that Lovecraft's sight of the spectacular paintings of the Himalayas by Nicholas Roerich—seen only the previous year in New York—played a factor in the genesis of the work. Roerich is mentioned a total of six times throughout the course of the novel, as if Lovecraft is going out of his way to signal the influence. (491)

There can be no mistaking that Lovecraft was markedly influenced by Roerich's work in creating the "vision" of the Mountains of Madness by facilitating the association in order to enhance the reader's imagining.

Other sources of inspiration have been suggested as everything from Edgar Rice Burrough's *At the Earth's Core* to A. Merritt's *The People of the Pit* to M. P. Shiel's *The Purple Cloud*. The rise and fall of the Old Ones as described in the story has analogies to Spengler's *The Decline of the West*. Perhaps all the supposed influences are correct, but I propose that it was not only one, but numerous imaginings, ideas, and reasons that ultimately drove Lovecraft to put pen to paper and create one of his most important tales in what was to later become widely known as the Cthulhu Mythos.

Manuscript evidence shows that Lovecraft began work on *At the Mountains of Madness* on 24 February 1931 and completed it 22 March of the same year. It is a landmark story in many ways. Perhaps most importantly it can be considered Lovecraft's literary avatar of a deliberate shift from his supernaturalism to "rational" science. The term generally used, and originally attributed to Robert M. Price, is "demythologizing." While Lovecraft pushed his pen firmly through the inkwash of science fiction both previously in his story "The Whisperer in Darkness" (1930) and afterwards in "The Shadow out of Time" (1934–35), he validated his mythological framework by legitimizing the "reality" of the gods and other denizens of ancient Earth. In effect, Cthulhu and the rest of the Old Ones were no longer supernatural beings; they were extraterrestrial life forms. Although Lovecraft returned to his classic weird tales a number of times after *At the Mountains of Madness*, it was not before he pulled out all the stops from the supernatural element of his eldritch-spawned bestiary with the outflow of his account of the Old Ones and their ilk being an element of mankind's historical record. This was not at all unlike what Robert E. Howard sought to convey in his essay "The Hyborian Age" (published in 1936 in three parts in the fanzine *The Phantagraph*). The primary difference is that Lovecraft explained his pseudohistorical world within the context of an single, pivotal story instead of a separate piece of writing to explain many others, rendering it for all intents and purposes coldly (there's that word again!) unapologetic.

Speculation exists with why Lovecraft wrote *At the Mountains of Madness* when he did. S. T. Joshi, in his landmark *H. P. Lovecraft: A Life*, mentions David E. Schultz's suggestion that it was as a result of reading a poorly written story in *Weird Tales* ("A Million Years After," by Katharine Metcalf Roof, November 1930 issue): "Rotten—cheap—puerile—yet winning prime distinction [meaning it got the cover story, ed.] *because of the subject matter* ... Why, damn it, boy, I've half a mind to write an egg story myself right now" (*SL* 3.186).

Despite the possibility of acting from a knee-jerk response, there is little doubt that Lovecraft had the idea for his Antarctic story gestating in the womb of his imagination long before he read Roof's tale, perhaps even going so far to say as early as childhood. While there are indications that Lovecraft sometimes wrote a story as a result of wanting to improve another writer's tale, he nevertheless carried the seeds of many of his own ideas until the times (some would even say the stars) were right.

At first, Lovecraft could not get *At the Mountains of Madness* published. *Weird Tales* editor Farnsworth Wright rejected it. Since it has been suggested that he purposefully separated the story into parts, there is little doubt that he fully expected the tale to be serialized in The Unique Magazine. Not surprisingly, when Wright rejected it, Lovecraft seethed. Thankfully, it finally saw print four years later by being serialized in *Astounding Stories* (February, March, April 1936).

At the Mountains of Madness, more than any other story in Lovecraft's mythological canon, most clearly describes the earthbound beginnings of the Old Ones and puts them in the context of their role with the history of man. There is even an implication that man has *evolved* from them—or at least shares a sort of kinship—as, late in the story, Dyer exclaims:

And now, when Danforth and I saw the freshly glistening and reflectively iridescent black slime which clung thickly to those headless bodies and stank obscenely with that new, unknown odor whose cause only a diseased fancy could envisage—clung to those bodies and sparkled less voluminously on a smooth part of the accursedly resculptured wall in a series of grouped dots—we understood the quality of cosmic fear to its uttermost depths. It was not fear of those four missing others—for all too well did we suspect they would do no harm again. Poor devils! After all, they were not evil things of their kind. They were the men of another age and another order of being. Nature had played a hellish jest on them—as it will on any others that human madness, callousness, or cruelty may hereafter dig up in that hideously dead or sleeping polar waste - and this was their tragic homecoming. They had not been even

savages—for what indeed had they done? That awful awakening in
the cold of an unknown epoch—perhaps an attack by the furry,
frantically barking quadrupeds, and a dazed defense against them
and the equally frantic white simians with the queer wrappings and
paraphernalia ... poor Lake, poor Gedney ... and poor Old Ones!
Scientists to the last—what had they done that we would not have
done in their place? God, what intelligence and persistence! What a
facing of the incredible, just as those carven kinsmen and forbears
had faced things only a little less incredible! Radiates, vegetables,
monstrosities, star spawn - whatever they had been, they were
men! (*MM* 95–96)

As a result, *At the Mountains of Madness* also supplies the inspiration for the modern UFO-logy pseudohistory of alien astronauts
visiting Earth, as seen in such diverse books as Erich von Däniken's
Chariots of the Gods and Jason Colavito's *The Cult of Alien Gods:
H. P. Lovecraft and Extraterrestrial Pop Culture*. The result is that
Lovecraft, whether wittingly or not, after a lifelong fascination with
the cold wastelands of Antarctica and the North Pole, finally
planted the literary flag that guaranteed him a place in the marvel-
ous and mysterious world of the Polar Myth.

Works Cited or Consulted

Colavito, Jason. *The Cult of Alien Gods: H. P. Lovecraft and Extra-
    terrestrial Pop Culture*. Amherst, NY: Prometheus Books, 2005.
Godwin, Joscelyn. *Arktos: The Polar Myth in Science, Symbolism,
    and Nazi Survival*. Kempton, IL: Adventures Unlimited Press,
    1996.
Harms, Daniel. *Encyclopedia Cthulhiana*. Oakland, CA: Chaosium,
    1998.
Joshi, S.T. *H. P. Lovecraft: A Life*. West Warwick, RI: Necronomi-
    con Press, 1996.
———. *Primal Sources: Essays on H. P. Lovecraft*. New York: Hip-
    pocampus Press, 2003.
Pearsall, Anthony. The *Lovecraft Lexicon*. Tempe, AZ: New Falcon
    Publications, 2005.
Price, Robert M., ed. *The Antarktos Cycle*. Oakland, CA: Chaosium,
    1999.

Briefly Noted

A journal curiously titled *Collapse*, issued by Urbanomic in Falmouth, England, and edited by Robin Mackay, has several items pertaining to Lovecraft in the issue titled *Collapse IV* (2008). The article of greatest relevance is Graham Harman and Keith Tilford's "On the Horror of Phenomenology: Lovecraft and Husserl/Singular Agitations and a Common Vertigo" (pp. 332–64). The title may give a good idea of the nature of the article. The issue contains other articles on M. R. James, Thomas Ligotti, and other writers, as well as more theoretical discussions. The issue is already sold out, but it can be accessed online at: http://www.urbanomic.com/CollapseIV.pdf.

Reviews

KENNETH HITE. *Tour de Lovecraft: The Tales.* Alexandria, VA: Atomic Overmind Press, 2008. xiv, 108 pp. $14.95 tpb. Reviewed by Donald R. Burleson.

It may or may not be significant that the minute I brought this book home, our cat Schroedie proceeded to slap it off the coffee table. I shall be making an attempt not to be quite so summarily dismissive as that, but I must admit that my own reaction, overall, is not altogether inconsistent with Schroedie's.

Initially I was somewhat encouraged by the fact that Hite not only supplies a lengthy bibliography of critical commentaries (sixty-five entries) but begins the book with a quick chapter surveying (or purporting to survey) Lovecraft criticism to date. I must confess to conceiving a certain annoyance, though, upon noticing that not only is my own *H. P. Lovecraft: A Critical Study* (Greenwood Press, 1983) missing from the bibliography, but Peter Cannon's *H. P. Lovecraft* (Twayne, 1989) as well; apparently some of us fly well below the radar.

Well, perhaps not entirely below. One telltale evanescent blip on the screen appears, only to vanish with equal suddenness, when Hite mentions my deconstructionist study *Lovecraft: Disturbing the Universe* (University Press of Kentucky, 1990) as being symptomatic of what he calls (and, to be fair, others have called) "the French disease," a purportedly febrile malady having at one time ravaged the otherwise healthy visage of critical studies. By extension, I have to wonder if we are to tell (say) poststructuralist critic Barbara Johnson—arguably the best literary critic writing in the English language during the final quarter of the twentieth century—that her unquestionably profound commentaries on Melville and others are "diseased." Maybe it's just as well my University Press of Kentucky tome is quarantined from admission to Hite's bibliography, where it might have spread pestilence to such timeless classics as Shreffler's *The H. P. Lovecraft Companion*. But what the infection-wary objections to including Cannon's Twayne study might be, I can't quite imagine, as it appears that this scarcely would have conduced to the same eruptions of unchecked contagion.

And, by the way, with regard to Gallic intestinal pathologies, I find it curious that Lovecraft's treatment of Ricci, Czanek, and Silva (respectively Italian, Polish, and Portuguese) in "The Terrible Old Man" supposedly represents Lovecraft's "giv[ing] ugly narrative . . . vent to his racism," while culturally smearing a whole vastly extensive school of literary criticism as "the French disease" is beyond objection. The consistency of political correctness escapes me at times, I fear. Hite also calls deconstruction "the bug." Damn, if only there were a spray or something. Watch those eggs; they'll get into your mattress.

Speaking of Lovecraft's racism (which is well known and scarcely possible to deny altogether), Hite sees the choice of the character name Joe Slater in "Beyond the Wall of Sleep" as possibly motivated by racism, due to some mixed-race folks in upstate New York named Slaughter. One supposes, here, that a writer biographically familiar with Lovecraft might have done well to consider Lovecraft's attendance at Slater Avenue School in Providence possibly to have had something to do with it. Alas, it's all too easy to see racism under every textual rock, when one is predisposed to find it.

Another of my several puzzlements about this book is the question: For what audience is it intended? Despite the inevitable cover blurbs—the book is said to bring "fresh epiphanies to longtime devotees"—I find myself feeling that there is little here to appeal to serious students of Lovecraft's fiction. This is unfortunate, too, because in spite of Hite's slangy utterances, one sometimes senses, behind the ranting façade, the presence of a capable writer not unacquainted with fine literary traditions. But one is readily put off by such things as his habit of calling things "neat" and (e.g.) referring to a Lovecraft tale as "some kinda slam-bang story."

Aside from that, one finds oneself astonished at some of the critical assessments. Of "The Dreams in the Witch House" we are told: "The story is magnificent" (a remark that, however, should be read in context), in spite of the fact that stylistically the tale is quite possibly Lovecraft's worst. (The final sentence of that story barely has any grammatical or logical coherence at all, a staggering embarrassment to Lovecraft worshippers.) And that constitutes perhaps my gravest objection to this book, a work far too brief to comment meaningfully on fifty-one stories, some of them novella-length: very little attention is paid (some, but very little) to Lovecraft's use of *language*, which is usually, if not always, quite striking.

To make the point, let me suggest a sort of thought experiment. Imagine, if you will, a parallel universe, one not terribly far removed from our own sphere of existence, in which there is one difference: in this alternative world, Howard Phillips Lovecraft was never born. Instead, another guy named Howard Phillips Lovecraft *was* born, somewhat later than the (hypothetically nonexistent) original. But this person, a lonely and strange recluse with a sense of cosmic indifferentism and adventurous expectancy, has developed not as a fiction writer in the ordinary sense of the term, but rather as a comics artist. In this brave new world, we still get Dunwich and Innsmouth and R'lyeh and Randolph Carter and the Terrible Old Man, but we get them purely as comic-book entities scarcely fleshed out at all by protracted prose writing. In other words, we get them as we might once have gotten the thrashings-about of Flash Gordon or Mighty Mouse.

My point is that in this "Lovecraft as a kind of cosmic-horror Robert Crumb" universe, Hite's *Tour de Lovecraft* could have been written almost exactly as we have it, reflecting not the subtleties of Lovecraftian prose nuance but the bare-outline contours of comic-book characters and places and plot details. As for me, I would rather see serious scrutiny of the language in Lovecraft, because *that's* what good fiction writing is all about. All the conceptual cosmicism in the world still isn't Lovecraft unless it is conveyed the way Lovecraft was wont to convey it. This book does correctly call the Gentleman from Providence a great writer, but it really doesn't tell us *why*. Certainly this greatness cannot be exhaustively, or even barely adequately, considered apart from the concerns of language and stylistics.

Hite's front cover shows a picture, in keeping with the title, of a tour bus. There may be some fun moments in store for the denizens of this tour, but my inclination is to ask the driver to stop, preferably on some lightless and ghoul-haunted lane, so that I can get off and walk.

S. T. JOSHI. *The Rise and Fall of the Cthulhu Mythos*. Poplar Bluff, MO: Mythos Books, 2008. 308 pp. $40.00 hc. Reviewed by Leigh Blackmore.

One of the most remarkable things about this new volume about the curious literary subgenre of the Cthulhu Mythos is that no one until now has ventured such a detailed critical study. Lin Carter's *Lovecraft: A Look Behind the Cthulhu Mythos* (1972) combined a rudimentary account of Lovecraft's life and work with an attempt (equally rudimentary) to examine some of the better known tales of the "Lovecraft Circle"—such writers as Robert Bloch, Frank Belknap Long, and Donald Wandrei. But Lovecraft scholarship has made enormous strides in the last thirty-plus years, much of it due to the untiring efforts of S. T. Joshi himself.

It is fitting, then, that the modern master of Lovecraft biography and criticism has now turned his attention to the phenomenon of what his introduction aptly refers to as the "so-called Cthulhu Mythos"—the dissemination of Lovecraft's concepts into popular writing and culture, a limitless stream of stories, anthologies, and novels that seem to surge forth inhumanly through the spectral moonlight in a grotesque, malignant saraband of fantastic nightmare.

Joshi divides his highly opinionated (and justifiably so) study into nine chapters. The first three deal with the "Lovecraft Mythos"—an already well-defined term in Lovecraft studies which applies to the works of the (frankly inimitable) Providence writer himself, and his invented pseudomythology of gods, books, and sites which, to a greater or lesser degree, crop up across the whole of his *oeuvre*. The next two chapters cover "Contemporaries" (that is, contemporaries of Lovecraft): Long, Bloch, Wandrei, as well as Robert E. Howard, Clark Ashton Smith, Henry Kuttner, and Fritz Lieber. There follows a chapter on "The Derleth Mythos," which critically examines Derleth's fatally flawed conception of the Lovecraft Mythos, and a chapter titled "Interregnum," which interrogates works by writers such as Colin Wilson and Ramsey Campbell that preceded Lin Carter's study. The final two chapters, "The Scholarly Revolution" and "Recrudescence," deal in short compass but with remarkable insight with the thirty-odd years of Cthulhu Mythos fiction that have appeared since the early 1970s, taking us up to 2008 with commentary on Mythos works of writers such as Richard L. Tierney, Thomas Ligotti, Joseph S. Pulver, Sr., Brian Lumley, Wilum Pugmire, Donald Tyson, and others.

In his introduction, Joshi makes no bones about his expectation that written work attempting to continue Lovecraft's legacy should be possessed of "intrinsic literary merits," making clear that his study will seek to distinguish between "the scope of Lovecraft's achievement" and "what others have written in imitation of or homage to him." Joshi notes the tendency for literary neophytes to produce work of vastly variable quality, which often amounts to no more than a "tepid rewriting of Lovecraft's own stories," stories that usually lack the cosmic perspective so central to Lovecraft's own views.

In Joshi's terminology, the "Lovecraft Mythos" is the work produced by Lovecraft himself, with the "Cthulhu Mythos" being an umbrella term for the Lovecraft-inspired work of his contemporaries and successors. Joshi here, as ever, asserts the importance of studying Lovecraft's work as a philosophical and aesthetic unity, and the Lovecraft Mythos is therefore seen as a mythic framework in which Lovecraft strove to convey serious philosophical (as well as political, cultural, and other) issues. Joshi does not refrain from criticising Lovecraft where particular stories, such as "the Dunwich Horror," apparently fail to meet Lovecraft's own criteria regarding mankind's insignificance in the cosmos at large.

Defining the key elements of the Lovecraft as fivefold (a fictional New England topography; a growing library of imaginary "forbidden" books; a diverse array of extraterrestrial "gods" or entities; a sense of cosmicism; and the usage of the scholarly narrator or protagonist), Joshi manages to make sense of the basic ingredients of Lovecraft's interconnected works, while allowing that there will always be problems of defining which particular stories are "part" of the Mythos.

In the chapters dealing with Lovecraft's own work, many perspicacious comments highlight aspects of tales that many of us have read, and read about, many times over; one of the delights of Joshi's criticism is that he continually re-evaluates the tales in the light of all current scholarly knowledge. Nor does he always assent to popular interpretations of them, making novel suggestions such as that the monster seen by the narrator of "Dagon" is "not the *object of worship*, but *one of the worshippers*." The volume is valuable for Joshi's accumulated new insights into Lovecraft's work alone, and his assessment along the way of various opinions expressed by other Lovecraft scholars ranging from, *inter alia*, Will Murray through David E. Schultz to Robert M. Price.

But of course the bulk of the study is given over to elaborations of the Mythos by other hands. While of necessity many story plots must be recounted, the joy of Joshi's retellings is his contextualisation of them, as he discusses how a given author developed his or her contributions to the Cthulhu Mythos, and the critical appraisal of the literary merits (or otherwise) of each tale. The discussions of the stories of Long, Bloch, Lieber, and Kuttner are particularly enjoyable, as Joshi interweaves his unparalleled knowledge of publishing minutiae and timelines, the derivation of terms and entities, and the relation of information from Lovecraft's letters, to the literary cross-fertilisation that went on between Lovecraft and his fellow *Weird Tales* writers.

If one cannot always agree with Joshi's assessments of individual tales by particular writers (I, for one, find Ramsey Campbell's Mythos tales such as "The Voice of the Beach" convincingly and effectively Lovecraftian), he is generally very even-handed. Even in the important chapter "The Derleth Mythos," which at first reading provides a scathing assessment of Derleth's misconstruals of Lovecraft's fictional aims, reducing Derleth's so-called "posthumous collaborations" with Lovecraft to little more than conscious or semiconscious plagiarisms of Lovecraft's work, a second reading shows that Joshi has expressed himself far less contentiously than he might have. While Derleth partisans may well dislike and be tempted to take issue with this section of the study, one can hardly argue with the bald facts of the case as set out here by Joshi, leading to the conclusion that Derleth (whatever credit one might give him for preserving Lovecraft's work in hardcover) "seriously disfigured the cosmic awe of the Lovecraft Mythos and replaced it with his own fraudulent and aesthetically unimaginative knockoff."

The book provides the odd laugh, as when the author caustically opines that Colin Wilson has now become "an intellectual buffoon"; and of Brian Lumley, that "one can only hope that this talentless hack will permanently abandon his unwitting parodies of Lovecraft's themes and conceptions." Hugh B. Cave was a "cheap pulp hack"; a story by Manly Wade Wellman "deserves nothing but oblivion," and Peter Straub's *Mr X* is "tiresome, long-winded, and staggeringly verbose." The amusing way in which Joshi reveals the shortcomings of Mythos works by authors such as Graham Masterton, Michael Shea, and Jeffrey Thomas is most entertaining, even if it is somewhat painful to read the drubbing given to Richard L. Tierney's *The House of the Toad*, which Joshi dismisses as "a dismal failure." Praise is dealt out to Mythos authors whose work deserves it—Karl Edward Wagner, Stanley Sargent, W. H. Pugmire, Fred Chappell, William Browning Spencer, and some others.

Adorned in superb jacket art by Jason C. Eckhardt that evokes the mystery and awe of Lovecraftian settings, the volume is attractively presented, though there are a few typos, for instance on the spine of the jacket where part of the title is inverted. The worst internal typo comes on p. 32, where in a quotation from Lovecraft's "The Nameless City," two errors occur within the same brief quote: "mutted" for "muttered," and "changing" for "chanting"—just the sort of textual errors against which Joshi has crusaded throughout his Lovecraftian editing career. Unfortunately, the note citations for chapter 8 are missing, and the lack of an index is particularly regrettable for a work of this kind. Perhaps these matters can be rectified with a reprint.

These proofreading faults notwithstanding, *The Rise and Fall of the Cthulhu Mythos* provides a rewarding, enjoyable, and cogent analysis of a literary phenomenon of modern literature. Notwithstanding comments in his Epilogue, Joshi makes it plain that there are two versions of the Mythos: Lovecraft himself stands unmatched at the beginning (the "Rise") and the rest of the Mythos, while not entirely unrelieved dross (the "Fall"), is considerably wanting in its evocation of themes that Lovecraft proposed in his own fiction. Joshi concludes: "It is safe to say, then, that Lovecraftian and Cthulhu Mythos themes have, amidst a plethora of unimaginative and derivative hackwork, seen a number of capable treatments in recent decades, and there is no reason to believe that the trend will not continue into the future."

This entertaining and important study ought to find a place not only on the shelves of every serious reader of Lovecraft, but in the humanities and specialist fantasy collections of university libraries.